From Africa to Jamaica

UNIVERSITY PRESS OF FLORIDA

Florida A&M University, Tallahassee
Florida Atlantic University, Boca Raton
Florida Gulf Coast University, Ft. Myers
Florida International University, Miami
Florida State University, Tallahassee
New College of Florida, Sarasota
University of Central Florida, Orlando
University of Florida, Gainesville
University of North Florida, Jacksonville
University of South Florida, Tampa
University of West Florida, Pensacola

From Africa to Jamaica

The Making of an Atlantic Slave Society, 1775–1807

AUDRA A. DIPTEE

University Press of Florida

Gainesville/Tallahassee/Tampa/Boca Raton

Pensacola/Orlando/Miami/Jacksonville/Ft. Myers/Sarasota

First cloth printing, 2010
First paperback printing, 2012

Library of Congress Cataloging-in-Publication Data
Diptee, Audra.
From Africa to Jamaica: the making of an Atlantic slave society,
1775–1807/Audra A. Diptee.
p. cm.
Includes bibliographical references and index.
ISBN 978-0-8130-3482-9 (cloth: acid-free paper)
ISBN 978-0-8130-4200-8 (pbk.)
1. Slavery—Jamaica—History 2. Slave trade—Jamaica—History—
18th century. 3. Blacks—Jamaica—History—18th century. I. Title.
HT1096.D56 2010
306.3'620972929–dc22   2010004892

The University Press of Florida is the scholarly publishing agency
for the State University System of Florida, comprising Florida A&M
University, Florida Atlantic University, Florida Gulf Coast Uni-
versity, Florida International University, Florida State University,
New College of Florida, University of Central Florida, University of
Florida, University of North Florida, University of South Florida, and
University of West Florida.

University Press of Florida
15 Northwest 15th Street
Gainesville, FL 32611–2079
http://www.upf.com

For D—My friend and hero. For saving me from myself.

Contents

Illustrations

Plates

Maps

Figures

Tables

Acknowledgments

This book traces the historical trajectory of the men, women, and children forcibly transported to Jamaica in the last thirty-two years of the British slave trade. It looks at the dynamics that shaped their lives as well as how they interpreted and sometimes even forced change on the Atlantic system that wrenched them from Africa. I find it a bitter irony that as I have reached the final stages of this work, the world has recently lost two pioneers in the study of slavery: Philip D. Curtin and John Hope Franklin. Both these men have now gone the way of other great minds who have shaped my work, namely, Eric E. Williams, C.L.R. James, and Walter Rodney. My own study would not have been possible without the advances of these and other exceptional scholars. As such, this book rests on the foundation laid by those trailblazers whose work in this field has stood the test of time.

The idea for this study was conceived in Toronto about ten years ago. It was a wonderful place to be as I explored my ideas. I was fortunate to be surrounded by peers and mentors who were passionate students of Africa and its diasporas. We were all enthusiastic to share ideas and rethink the traditional questions that shaped the scholarship. In Toronto, my very first intellectual home, I was safely cushioned with support from both the Department of History at the University of Toronto and the Harriet Tubman Institute at York University. I owe many debts to colleagues, friends, and colleagues-turned-friends at both these institutions.

I am especially grateful to Martin A. Klein, who not only taught me African history but also taught me that the best research projects have "small topics but ask big questions." Those are words I carry with me every day in my role as historian and educator, from archive to classroom. Thank you for everything, Marty, but most of all thank you for supporting me as I completed this project on my own terms. It has been many years, and I have learned much from you. To Paul E. Lovejoy, I also owe much thanks. Over the years, Paul has been incredibly supportive and generous with his comments and critiques. His scholarship has played an important role in shaping my own research. His energy, vision, and belief in the possibilities for this field are matched by few. He has been an inspiration for the generation of scholars who have sprung up behind him. To David V. Trotman, my debts are quite simply incalculable. As an undergraduate student, I fell in love with history under his tutelage. I would not be a historian today without his influence; I would not have made it this far without his advice and support. David was usually the first person on whom I would test my ideas for this project. With the biblical patience of Job, he has listened to me ramble as I worked out many of the ideas with which I was struggling. He has also been the sage who has kept me calm, put things in perspective, and helped me maneuver past the many landmines in this profession. I am forever indebted.

There are many others who have helped me advance this project over the years. Michael Wayne, Rick Halpern, Gad Heuman, and Verene Shepherd have all read earlier drafts of this study. They were generous with their comments and pushed the boundaries of the study with their questions. Wilma King has heard me present parts of this study at various conferences over the years. She has always been supportive and offered solid critiques. When the project was in its earlier stages, as I undertook research in Jamaica and the United Kingdom, many scholars were generous with their advice and recommendations about documents and research strategy. These include Emma Christopher, Robin Law, David Richardson, and Mary Turner. My peers at the University of Toronto, Tracey Thompson and Chima Korieh, were with me in the trenches and have proven to be fiercely loyal in their support over the years.

At conferences and by invitation I presented many of the themes and arguments in this study. I learned immensely from the comments I received from colleagues involved with the Harriet Tubman Seminar series at York University. I also benefited greatly from the discussion at the 2004 conference L'Enfant dans l'esclavage held in Avignon and organized by Gwyn Campbell, the Diaspora Paradigms conference held at Michigan State University in 2001, the thirtieth annual conference of the Society for Caribbean Studies conference hosted at Kew Gardens in 2006, the 2001 North American Conference on British Studies in Toronto, the Southern Historical Association meetings held at Memphis in 2004, and the 2005 annual conference of the American Historical Association hosted in Seattle.

I spent eight months undertaking research in London. While there I was fortunate enough to be part of a diverse and multidisciplinary research community at Goodenough College at Mecklenburgh Square. As fellow researchers, we would congregate at breakfast and dinner to eagerly discuss our projects and exchange ideas. This setting played an important role as I formulated my ideas. In Jamaica, my experience was quite different, but there also I was lucky to be in a supportive environment. At the University of the West Indies, Verene Shepherd and Swithin Wilmot were generous with their assistance as I began my research at the university library. My good friend and colleague Colleen Vasconcellos and I coordinated our research trips to the island. We shared an apartment and worked in the national archive and at the University of the West Indies together for four months. She was wonderfully supportive during that time, and together we have countless stories that involve research, curried goat, and good Jamaican rum. I have also lost a friend who helped while I was in Jamaica: my fiery old friend Alison Delgado has since passed away. She was generous and kind but also had no inhibitions about speaking frankly and honestly. She was fearless, tough as nails, and a survivor.

At Carleton University, I received generous advice and moral support as I came closer to the end of this project. In particular, my colleagues (and fellow islanders) James Miller, Roderick Phillips, and Steve Wilson have been very supportive and have kept me positive over the last few years. Also, David Dean and Jim Opp have been kind with their advice and support.

My research took me to many libraries, archives, and research centers. I would be remiss if I did not thank and acknowledge the people at these institutions, who often went above and beyond the call of duty to help me complete my research. In the United Kingdom, I worked at the National Archives in Kew Gardens, the Institute of Commonwealth Studies, the British Library, the Bodleian in Oxford, and the National Library of Scotland. In the Caribbean, my research led me to the Jamaican National Archives and the University of the West Indies (Mona). I also worked at the John Hope Franklin Research Center at Duke University. In Toronto, I had ready access to the Thomas Fisher Rare Books Library and Government Publications at the University of Toronto. Staffs at the National Maritime Museum in London and the National Museums Liverpool were also very helpful in handling my pleas for assistance by phone and email. In addition, I owe special thanks to Joël Rivard at the Maps, Data, and Government Information Centre (MADGIC) at Carleton University, as he was incredibly helpful as I navigated the world of digital mapping. I must also thank Stephanie Shoobert, who on short notice drew the maps included in this book. Anthony Kofi Arthiabah has also been very kind in helping me work through the computing challenges I faced as I worked with software for this project.

I was fortunate to receive much financial support for this project. My research was generously funded by the Social Science and Humanities Research Council, the London Goodenough Association of Canada, the University of Toronto, the Organization of American States, the Harvard Atlantic History Seminar, the David Nicholls Memorial Trust, the Harriet Tubman Institute, Massey College, the John Hope Franklin Center, and the Faculty of Arts and Social Science at Carleton University.

Finally, to family, friends, and loved ones who have kept me grounded and held me steady, as inadequate as it might be, I offer my thanks for years of unwavering support.

Abbreviations

CO   Colonial Office

ICS   Institute of Commonwealth Studies

JNA   Jamaican National Archives

NA   National Archives (Kew Gardens)

TSTD   *Trans-Atlantic Slave Trade Database*

UWI   University of the West Indies (Mona Campus)

The Atlantic Basin

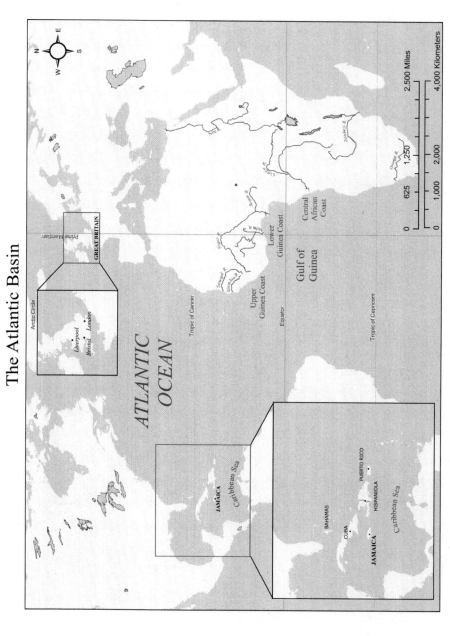

Map 1. The Atlantic Basin. Drawn by Stephanie Shoobert.

Key Slaving Regions in Africa

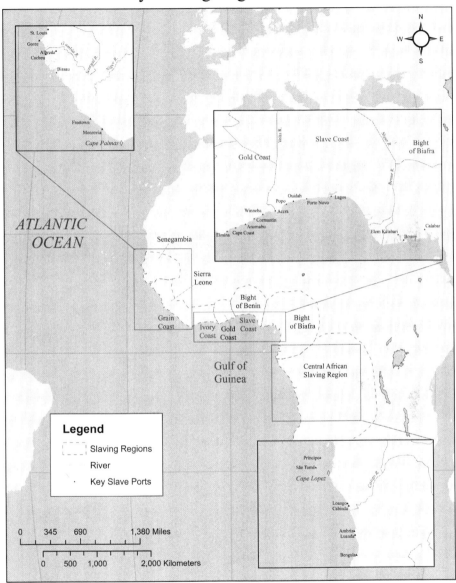

Map 2. Key slaving regions in Africa. Drawn by Stephanie Shoobert.

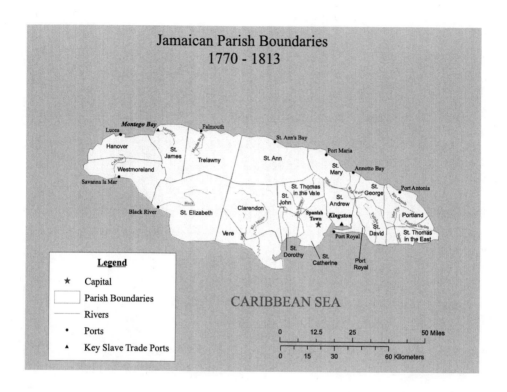

Map 3. Jamaican parish boundaries, 1770–1813. Drawn by Stephanie Shoobert.

Introduction

In the seventeenth century, there was a settlement called Jamaica Point on Sherbro Island off the coast of Sierra Leone (see map 4). It was an important, well-fortified port town. Like the island of Jamaica in the Caribbean, Jamaica Point was also intimately bound to the Atlantic slave trade. There the British established a "slave factory" from which captive men, women, and children could be readily purchased and shipped across the Atlantic. The British were sold these captives, of course, by African slave traders catering to the Atlantic demand for captive labor.[1]

The naming of Jamaica Point after one of the most important British colonies in the Caribbean is indicative of the links that connected African continent and Caribbean island. Not surprisingly, most captives sold into the Atlantic slave trade from Sherbro Island were sent to Jamaica. The use of the name Jamaica Point is also testament to the fact that trans-Atlantic influences ran not only from east to west but also from west to east. At times the complex intermingling of these shifting influences seems almost impossible to disaggregate. The very name *Jamaica*, after all, is a corruption of *Xaymaca*. It was the name given to the island by its very first settlers— the indigenous population that had been resident there for centuries prior to European arrival and African forced migration. Long after those very first Jamaicans had been displaced, killed, and alienated, the name of their homeland had made it across the Atlantic so that even they had left their mark. Although the British abolished the slave trade in 1807, and after this period captives leaving Sherbro were shipped primarily to the Spanish and French Caribbean, Jamaica Point continued to be represented on British (and French) maps of Sierra Leone at least until 1840.[2]

The link between Africa and Jamaica was, of course, the trans-Atlantic slave trade. It was the system that facilitated the killing, capture, and sale of men, women, and children who were to be shipped across the Atlantic to forcibly provide their labor. The history of this system is, first and foremost,

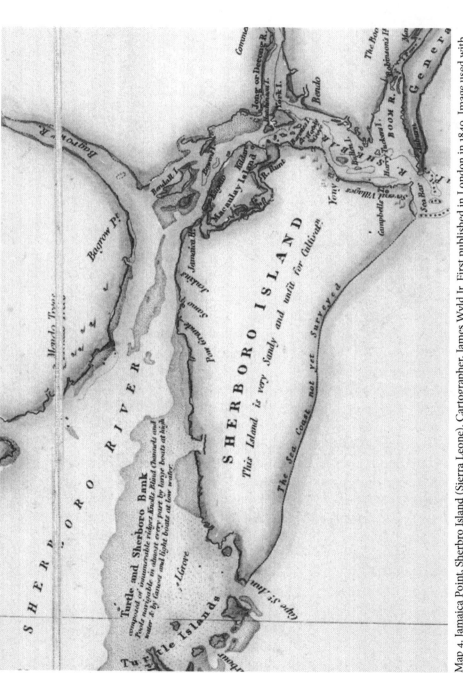

Map 4. Jamaica Point, Sherbro Island (Sierra Leone). Cartographer, James Wyld Jr. First published in London in 1840. Image used with the permission of Afriterra Library, www.afriterra.org.

then, about lives lived and lives lost. The history of these lives has been told many times, in many ways; with each retelling, efforts have been made to move one step further from "silencing the past."[3]

This study adds to a growing body of scholarship on the Atlantic slave trade. In so doing, it offers a historical narrative of captives on a forced journey from Africa to Jamaica in the late eighteenth century. It uses the American Revolution, the ramifications of which were felt throughout the Caribbean, as its starting point and ends with the abolition of the British slave trade in 1807. An analysis of the men, women, and children forcibly transported to Jamaica during this thirty-two-year period offers important insights about Atlantic slave societies in general and Jamaica in particular. As the last group of captives legally transported on British slave ships, they were among the last of the enslaved to put an African stamp on Jamaican slave society. During this period, captive Africans arrived to the island in larger numbers and were part of a process of intense Africanization.

The scholarship in this area is rich and varied. The arguments made in this study would have been impossible without the groundbreaking developments in slave trade studies of recent years. Perhaps the most influential of these developments is the 2009 publication of the *Trans-Atlantic Slave Trade Database*. The first edition of this database was published about a decade earlier, and even then it revolutionized slave trade studies as it allowed for nuanced demographic analyses that, prior to its publication, were rarely attempted. Two of the more notable exceptions to this are the pioneering demographic analyses completed by Philip Curtin and Barry Higman.[4] *From Africa to Jamaica* uses the 2009 revised edition of the database to reassess the demographic contours of the Atlantic slave trade to Jamaica. Yet as this study makes clear, the database is at best a starting point for any demographic analysis of the slave trade. The intra-American forced migration of captives and illegal slave-trading activities are but two factors that also shed light on the number of captives transported to any particular port.[5] Furthermore, any quantitative data derived from the database must be contextualized by a thorough use of qualitative source material. Only then can historians problematize the very categories used to make demographic assessments or develop insights on the key forces that shaped the patterns of forced migration among captive men, women, and children.

There have also been other important developments in the field. The resurgence of Atlantic history and its continued institutionalization in the academy has facilitated conversations between Africanists and specialists of the various African diasporas. The very first graduate program in Atlantic history, established at Johns Hopkins University in the early 1970s, was built with scholars such as Philip Curtin, Jack Greene, Ray Kea, Franklin Knight, Barbara Kopytoff, Sidney Mintz, and Richard Price. Although other universities took long to follow, since the early 1990s there has been an increasing focus on Atlantic history either through the establishment of graduate programs or by way of research seminars such as the Atlantic History seminar at Harvard University.[6] Other important milestones include the establishment of the Gilder Lehrman Center at Yale University and the Wilberforce Institute for the Study of Slavery and Emancipation at the University of Hull, as well as the Nigerian Hinterland Project (1999–2006), which would later become the Harriet Tubman Institute at York University. Such institutional developments have coincided with a burgeoning body of scholarship that has focused on the Atlantic slave trade. The contributions of scholars such as Robin Law, Paul Lovejoy, Kristen Mann, John Thornton, and others have brought an increased level of historical specificity to scholarly discussions exploring the links between Africa and the Americas.[7]

With this in mind, perhaps the boldest of the claims in *From Africa to Jamaica* is that historians have overstated the role and number of "prime" adult males transported to Jamaica in the final decades of the Atlantic slave trade. There has been, of course, an abundance of studies looking at enslaved women in recent decades and an increasing number looking at children. Historians such as Barbara Bush, Marietta Morrissey, Hilary Beckles, Bernard Moitt, and Jennifer Morgan are but a few who have worked to insert the experiences of enslaved women into the master narrative on slavery in the Americas. Studies looking at enslaved children have also been growing in number and include the work of Wilma King, Marie Jenkins Schwartz, Colleen Vasconcellos, myself, and others.[8] Despite such scholarly developments, however, the general consensus in the scholarship to date is that Caribbean planters had an unwavering preference for adult males above all other captives.[9] This study takes issue with that interpretation. In chapter 2, I suggest that, at least for the period under study, Jamaican purchasers did *not* make the buying of adult males their top priority when purchasing captives. Nor was their greatest demand necessarily for women and/or children. Ultimately, it was the health and condition of captives that had the largest influence on trading prices and patterns. British ship captains understood that Jamaican planters had the greatest demand for *healthy* African captives, and for this reason the age and sex of the enslaved they purchased was a secondary concern.

In *From Africa to Jamaica,* I also argue that although slave traders chose not to acknowledge the humanity of the men, women, and children they bought and sold, they certainly could not afford to ignore it. Unlike ivory or other trade goods that ship captains purchased in order to supplement their "cargo," the enslaved could resist, plan rebellions, needed to be fed, often got sick, and died. All of these factors had the potential to undermine the profitability of a slaving voyage. For British slave traders, the solution to all these problems was the same. They believed that a speedy voyage reduced the likelihood and potency of these deleterious influences. Of course, ship captains were not always successful in getting off the coast of Africa as speedily as they might hope, but it certainly was one of the key considerations they used to guide their purchasing decisions. This meant going to ports where their trade goods were in demand and, if circumstances were in their favor, purchasing as many captives in a reasonable physical condition as possible in as short a time as possible. If circumstances were not in their favor, ship captains had little choice but to be more flexible with their purchasing criteria as they selected captives so that they could try to leave Africa sooner rather than later. The length of stay on the African coast determined a number of costs, including food for the enslaved and crew, salaries, and ship insurance. It also increased associated risks such as the spread of disease among the enslaved, high mortality, and shipboard rebellions. In other words, few if any pragmatic-minded British traders would deliberately delay their ships on the African coast for the express purpose of purchasing the "assortment" of captives requested by buyers on the other side of the Atlantic.

Chapter 3 focuses on the experiences of captive men, women, and children during the very process of enslavement in Africa. It outlines differences in the captive experience in the three key areas of provenance—the Bight of Biafra, the Gold Coast, and West Central Africa—for the enslaved sent to Jamaica in the final decades of the British slave trade. This chapter also attempts to put a historical face on at least some of the captives before they were put on slave ships. It emphasizes that at the point of capture, the practicalities of slave raiding did not allow captors to discriminate by age and sex as they selected their victims. In addition to the capture of men and women in the prime of their lives, children and the elderly were also readily made captives. At times, those considered too young or too old were put to death at the point of capture—but this was not always the case. African traders sometimes tried to sell captives of such descriptions to ship captains. If they could find no buyer, then the enslaved again faced death. However, when ship captains were anxious to leave the African coast quickly, the elderly and those children considered "too young" were often purchased.

The captive experience during the Atlantic crossing is addressed in chapter 4. Like previous chapters, it offers a careful inclusion of the experiences of women and children. It also suggests that despite the harshness of their experience, captive Africans did not lose their sense of self. They did *not*, as recent studies on the middle passage have asserted, experience a form of "social death."[10] Scholarly discussions addressing the humanity of the enslaved have a lengthy history and have taken the form of many debates. Generations of scholars have long marched past the interpretative frameworks of Franklin Frazier and Stanley Elkins.[11] Yet the substance of their ideas echo loudly in Orlando Patterson's later advanced concept of "social death"—which, over three decades later, continues to find currency with a new generation of scholars.[12]

In fact, as chapter 5 makes clear, captive Africans were much more than the "ultimate human tool" or an extension of their owners' will. Despite the contemporary common perception, held by slave owners, that the enslaved were "bestial" and had an "innate animalism," the enslaved asserted and reasserted their humanity in their constant struggles with their legal owners. The oft-cited Thomas Thistlewood, in his effort to control his human chattel through dehumanizing punishment, was forced to deal with the enslaved as humans despite whatever may have been the prevailing conception of Africans in Jamaica. The enslaved may have been legally defined as chattel and so legally dehumanized, but in daily interactions every slave owner understood that the enslaved were human beings with independent wills. Sometimes their wills could be bent, through persuasion, threats, and/or punishment. Other times, the enslaved suffered dire consequences for independent thoughts and independent actions. At other times, there was no need to bend their will, as they behaved in ways that suited the demands of their owners. In any attempt to sketch a historical portrait of the enslaved as "wholly human," it becomes quickly apparent that like all other human beings, captive Africans were capable of both vice and virtue and, in typically human fashion, behaved in ways that seem full of contradictions.[13]

And so, not surprisingly, they had a range of responses to their enslavement in Jamaica.

Regardless of the nature of their response to slavery in Jamaica, enslaved Africans clearly arrived at the island with their own ideas and beliefs, and they used these to interpret their situation in Jamaica. In other words, as suggested by Paul E. Lovejoy and David V. Trotman, captive Africans crossed the Atlantic with certain "expectations."[14] Most Africans had been exposed to slavery, in some way, prior to their arrival in Jamaica: some were born with slave status; others were captured; others owned captives before they themselves were sold into the slave trade; and others made their living by capturing and selling captives. Those persons who fit into none of those categories certainly knew people who did. Put another way, the concept of slavery was familiar to all Africans—even those who were never enslaved until being sold into the Atlantic trade. That said, there was a large disjuncture between African notions of slavery and the reality they faced in Jamaica. The suggestion in the final chapter (chapter 5) is that the ways in which Africans responded to their enslavement in Jamaica depended in large part on their personal histories in Africa and their experience with slavery before they came to the island—before they were pulled into the Atlantic slave trade. When the evidence allows, this study looks at lives of specific individuals. Also, when possible, it uses the African names of captives as opposed to the names they were given in Jamaica. Of course, these names were recorded by English speakers long before there was any corresponding orthography in the relevant African languages. As such, the spelling used in the sources (and in this study) may not reflect the correct pronunciation.

Before addressing each of these issues, this study starts with a brief discussion of several complexities created in the crucible of the Atlantic world: it looks at African-European encounters in Africa and explores the dynamics of "race" in Africa; it reassesses the number of captives who were available for sale in Jamaica for the period under study; and it highlights the sharp differences in African responses to slavery in Jamaica by looking at the experiences of two captive Africans who were transported to the island.

1

The Atlantic Crucible

There are very few persons who would challenge the notion that British justifications for the Atlantic slave trade and slavery in the Caribbean were grounded in racist assumptions. Yet to better understand human behavior under these racist institutions, using the lens of "race" alone proves inadequate. Above all else, the history of the Atlantic slave trade is a history of human encounters. Relationships between blacks and whites under slavery may have been defined by "race" and "power," but it was also defined by perception. How Africans perceived whites and the roles they played on the African coast informed their actions and shaped their experiences. The notion that Africans had immutable conceptions of Europeans that ranged between fear and deification is a simplistic one that does not accurately reflect the historical complexities. From the point of view of those captives—some of whom spent weeks, months, or even years getting to the coast—the whites who purchased them had nothing to do with their actual capture and transport.[1] Those acts were committed by Africans.

Certainly for some of the captured Africans brought from the African hinterland, the strangeness of European phenotypical appearance coupled with the uncertainty of their eventual outcome served to aid and fuel rumors of cannibalistic whites either in reality or metaphorically.[2] But these initial fears and the horror-filled uncertainty of their capture were eventually dispelled and gave way to another reality. The enslaved gradually understood that they were captured so that they could be sold as commodified goods and as units of labor. For some this realization may have taken place on the coast, for others it was during the Atlantic crossing, and for others it was on the other side of the Atlantic. Regardless of when it took place, it was a realization that easily fit in with preexisting African notions. Slavery, after all, had a long history in Africa, and any misconceptions that Africans might have had about the humanity and intentions of Europeans would be relatively short-lived.

Of course, there were those coastal Africans who had exposure to and interactions with British men, and even women, who were on the continent for one reason or another. But the dynamics of "race" in Africa in no way resembled that which would be later encountered in the Caribbean. In fact, an analysis of European-African interactions on the African coast makes clear the dangers of formulating rigid assumptions about relations on the African coast. Resident coastal Africans, some of whom were also sold into the Atlantic slave trade, had no illusions about white vulnerability and mortality. They certainly knew that whites were trading in Africa by consent granted and not military might. They would see firsthand the lengths to which white traders had to go to bargain and negotiate for captives. They would understand how much British slave traders relied on African suppliers for food and water before every voyage across the Atlantic. And if these were not enough to persuade them about the relative powerlessness of whites on the African coast, they would see whites die in high numbers as their immune systems lost battles with the African disease environment. Whiteness was no guarantee of privilege on the African coast.

It was these kinds of encounters between Africans and Europeans, born in the crucible of the Atlantic world, that allowed for the forced transshipment of captive men, women, and children. By the late eighteenth century, the trans-Atlantic trade networks were well established, and those Africans sent to Jamaica were sent on a well-beaten path as there were millions who had preceded them in centuries past.

Consuming Captives

Between 1701 and the early months of 1808, approximately 1,090,000 African men, women, and children were put on slave ships headed to Jamaica. About 15 percent of them were dead before the ship made it to the island. It is worth noting that this number in no way represents the totality of lives lost as a result of the slave trade. At best, it can be considered a glimpse.[3] In fact, it only gives insight into the captives who lived long enough to be purchased by slave traders. This number does not tell us how many captives died at the point of capture, en route to the Atlantic coast, or while they were at the coast waiting to be sold. Nor does it tell us how many captives

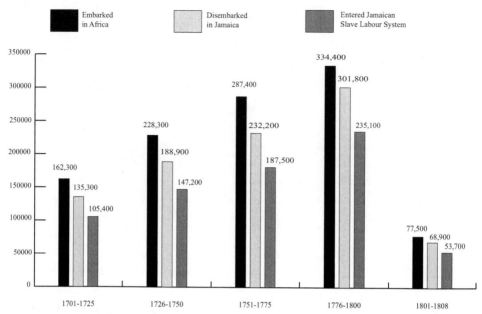

Figure 1.1. African captives purchased for sale in Jamaica, 1701–1808. *Source*: http://slavevoyages.org/tast/assessment/estimates.faces?yearFrom=1701&yearTo=1808 (accessed April 2009).

died shortly after they were sold in Jamaica because they were unable to recover from the horrendous conditions of the Atlantic crossing. Yet even without precise statistical data on mortality rates, the pattern of African arrivals to Jamaica tells a story of its own.

In the eighteenth century, there was an upward trend in the arrival of Africans in Jamaica (see figure 1.1). Jamaican planters had a voracious appetite for the labor of captive Africans. At least until the American Revolution, the island was considered the "jewel of the British Crown" and was one of the pistons in the engine that drove England's mercantilist economy. By the eve of the revolution, Jamaica had unarguably become the wealthiest colony in British America. Its rise to such economic prominence was, in part, aided by the end of the maroon wars in 1739. Until that period, Jamaican maroons had effectively managed to constrain the expansion of sugar production by systematically attacking plantations in frontier regions. In the 1740s, after colonists and maroons signed peace treaties, sugar production in Jamaica entered a new period of growth. The end of the maroon wars meant that colonists could set up new plantations in frontier regions, primarily in the western and northern parts of the island, as well as expand those plantations that were already well established. The numbers speak for themselves: in 1739, Jamaica had 419 sugar mills; by 1786, the number of mills, which had more than doubled, increased to 1,061.

Yet it was in the final decades of the British slave trade, between 1776 and 1808, that captive men, women, and children were shipped to the island in the highest numbers. During these years, 412,000 enslaved persons were put on ships headed to Jamaica.[4] Only 371,000 of them made it across the Atlantic alive. Nonetheless, dead or alive, the victims of this trade were pulled into the Atlantic system at one of its most tumultuous times—dubbed the "Age of Revolution." The American, French, and Haitian revolutions not only influenced the number of captives who were put on ships headed to Jamaica but also affected their day-to-day living once on the island.

The American Revolution of 1776, in particular, marked a turning point in Jamaican history. Jamaican planters were hard hit by the revolutionary war of the mainland colonies, and their ability to import captive Africans during this period was seriously undermined. The number of Africans brought to the island declined significantly between 1776 and 1783 (see figure 1.2). Even on the African coast, the effects of the war were being lamented. In the words of one of the governors of Cape Coast Castle (in the Gold Coast region), the situation was "deplorable," as there was "No trade of any kind." Moreover, until 1776, much of the foodstuff that the slave population needed for daily sustenance was imported from the mainland colonies. This changed when the Prohibitory Act of 1776 ended most of the trade activities between Jamaica and the mainland.

For the enslaved on the island, the situation was dire, as there were severe food shortages. There was also a series of natural disasters that exacerbated the situation. A succession of hurricanes between 1781 and 1786 not only depleted the sugar crop but also created incredible hardships for the enslaved population. A contemporary estimate put the deaths caused by starvation, disease, and natural disasters during this period at fifteen thousand.[5] Newly arrived Africans were especially vulnerable during this period. They were weakened after the physical strain of their enslavement in Africa and the horrendous conditions of the voyage across the Atlantic. In addition, any survival skills that they had developed in Africa to help them acquire food were of limited use in the unfamiliar terrain of Jamaica. Many of them starved. Furthermore, the psychological impact of hurricanes on those newly arrived from Africa can only be hinted at. Though they were

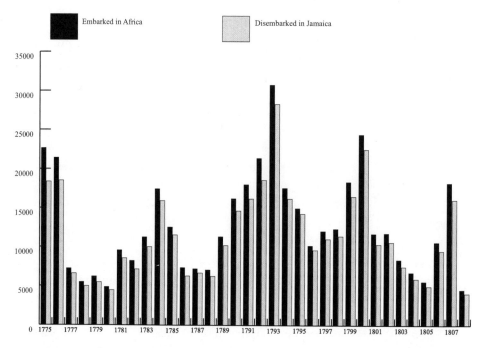

Figure 1.2. Africans forcibly transported to Jamaica, 1775–1808. *Source*: Estimates from *Trans-Atlantic Slave Trade Database*. See http://slavevoyages.org/tast/assessment/estimates.faces?yearFrom=1775&yearTo=1808&disembarkation=301 (accessed April 2009).

familiar with tropical torrents and rainstorms, in Africa they did not experience hurricanes in those storms' full ferocity—and the accompanying devastating consequences.

This period was to be followed by other political upheavals that influenced the number of captives transported to Jamaica. The Haitian Revolution (1791–1804), which was intimately linked to the French Revolution, breathed new life into the Jamaican economy and revived what seemed like a stagnating slave society. The misfortune of Saint Domingue planters proved to be the fortune of planters in Jamaica—and a life sentence for thousands of Africans who were fed into the Jamaican slave system. As Saint Domingue's plantation economy was destroyed by civil and revolutionary war, planters in Jamaica were quick to expand production in sugar, coffee, and other tropical products. Before the Haitian Revolution, Jamaica's sugar exports were less than 60 percent of that exported by Saint Domingue. By 1805, however, Jamaica had exceeded Saint Domingue's production in sugar and became the largest producer of sugar in the world. Jamaica also led in coffee production.[6]

The boom in Jamaica's economy in the 1790s meant, of course, that more captive African men, women, and children were transported to the island. Approximately 220,000 captives were put on ships heading to Jamaica during the thirteen years of the Haitian Revolution. There were wild fluctuations in the numbers from year to year, but between 1791 and 1802, they never fell below 10,000 per year and peaked at about 31,000 in 1793 (see figure 1.2). After 1804, another 39,000 captives were shipped to Jamaica before the Abolition Act of 1807 ensured that African men, women, and children could no longer be legally transported to British colonies.[7]

Although the historical record makes clear that large numbers of African men, women, and children were put on ships headed to Jamaica between 1776 and 1808, it is far more difficult to assess how many entered the Jamaican slave labor system. There is no doubt that mortality rates during the voyage across the Atlantic were high: between 1776 and 1808, only 90 percent lived long enough for their arrival to be recorded in Jamaica.[8] Yet this number does not necessarily indicate the number of men, women, and children who were available for sale on the island.

Once a ship arrived at Jamaica, the number of captives on board was reported to the custom house. These numbers were included in the *Books and Returns* as slaves imported into the island. However, there was generally a delay of several days, sometimes well over a week, between when captives were reported and when they were actually sold to Jamaican buyers. During that period of delay, it was common for there to be some mortality among the enslaved. As a result, a percentage of the African men, women, and children recorded as "imported" were dead before they could be sold. At least one contemporary report suggested that mortality among the newly arrived at this point could be as high as 5 percent.[9] Assuming that this number is accurate for the period under study, then the number of enslaved available for sale would total approximately 352,000.

For many of the captives, however, Jamaica was not their final destination, as the island was an important entrepôt from which captives were sold to other parts of the Americas. The official records show wild fluctuations in the number of captives who were sent off the island. On average, however, they suggest that between 1774 and 1808, approximately 18 percent of captives were re-exported.[10] The actual percentage was no doubt significantly higher given that these records do not account for smuggling.

Notwithstanding the problem of illegal trading, if at least 18 percent of those captives who survived were re-exported, then the number of Africans available for sale in Jamaica during the last thirty-two years of the slave trade hovered around 289,000.

The Jamaican plantocracy's heavy reliance on the slave trade to meet labor requirements has often been attributed chiefly to what has been described as its "insatiable appetite for acquiring slaves," as few captives survived long enough "to establish a naturally reproducing slave population."[11] Yet as the historians Michael Craton and Barry Higman have long argued, there was at least one other factor that determined the number of captive men, women, and children who were to be transported to Jamaica (and the Caribbean more generally): the number of captives brought to the region was not only a function of the Jamaican need "to 'top up' the numbers depleted through natural decrease" but was also linked to the increased labor requirements caused by agricultural expansion.[12] In other words, the issue of reproduction aside, the demand for enslaved African labor was also fuelled by expanding frontiers and the resulting increased agricultural production. This explains why Barbados, which had no space for further expansion by the early eighteenth century, was the only sugar colony to have a self-reproducing enslaved population in 1807. Jamaica, in contrast, had not reached its "saturation point" for enslaved laborers even when slavery was finally abolished in 1838.[13] In other words, there was a fair amount of demographic diversity throughout Jamaica during the final decades of the slave trade, and as such the notion that "sex ratios were so skewed towards males that many men never obtained partners" needs to be reassessed.[14]

In fact, the tendency to underestimate natural reproduction becomes clear when it is considered that in 1807, by Higman's estimation, African-born captives accounted for only 45 percent of the enslaved population in Jamaica. Clearly some Africans lived long enough to give birth to enslaved creoles (Jamaican-born), and these creoles were able to reproduce in growing numbers.[15] Nonetheless, if the entire slave population (including the locally born) was about 354,000 in 1808, then enslaved Africans (45 percent) amounted to approximately 160,000 in that year.[16] This, of course, is an astonishingly low number given that, between 1776 and 1808, about 289,000 African men, women, and children are estimated, by this study, to have entered the Jamaican slave labor system. This large numerical difference might be explained by a number of factors, including high rates of mortality, unaccounted-for illegal slave trading activities, and perhaps even an underestimation of the number of captives who were re-exported to other islands.[17]

Lives Lived, Lives Lost

As valuable as statistical analyses of the Atlantic slave trade may be, much is lost when discussions are grounded solely in cold hard numbers. The Atlantic slave trade is, after all, about lives lived and lives lost. Although most of the personal histories of the African men, women, and children who were made victims of this trade can no longer be recovered, for some of these captives fragmentary evidence that sheds light on their lives does exist. Such records are a reminder that Africans had a range of experiences, that they were no different from other human beings and so lived their lives with complexity and sometimes even contradiction. Their responses to slavery could be shaped by a range of human emotions: bravery or cowardice, love or hate, hope or despair, concern or callousness. Historical records that give such insights, though not without their problems, serve to complicate the historical narrative; as the following stories make clear, they act as a caution against the adoption of oversimplified assumptions about human dynamics during the era of the Atlantic slave trade.

In the early 1750s, Apongo, an adult male African, was enslaved in the Gold Coast region and forcibly transported to Jamaica. He was quite likely on one of the 225 slave ships known to have arrived in Jamaica between 1750 and 1755 and was one of the forty-eight thousand Africans who survived the Atlantic crossing. Roughly 43 percent of the African men, women, and children brought to Jamaica during that five-year period were purchased on the Gold Coast—the same area of provenance as Apongo.[18] They would have been known by whites on the island by the generic term Coromantin.

Before his enslavement, Apongo lived what can best be described as a "fortunate" life in Africa. He was part of the African elite and considered a prince in one of the tributary states of the Dahomey kingdom. The mid-eighteenth century was a time of turmoil and confusion on the coast as the emergent Asante empire, the coastal Fanti states, and the encroaching Dahomey kingdom and its client states struggled for commercial supremacy in the profitable and expanding traffic in human beings. British commercial interests among the competing European buyers were under the purview of the governor of Cape Coast Castle. The British seized the castle from the Swedes in 1655, and it was administered by a governor who was an employee of the British Company of Merchants. His primary role on the coast was to ensure that British slave-trading interests were favored during negotiations with Africans. It is not surprising, then, that the protocols of Afro-British commercial relations demanded that Apongo sometimes meet with John Cope, the British-born governor of Cape Coast Castle. Dahomey, although unable to enforce political domination in this area, still maintained trading relations and ensured that traders of Dahomey had access to the trading on the coast.[19]

Apongo's good fortune as a relatively elite African, however, eventually came to an end. Not even Apongo's high-ranking status could guarantee him safety from the vagaries of the slave trade. Although attended by a hundred well-armed men, he was taken prisoner when hunting, sold into the trans-Atlantic slave trade, and transported to Jamaica. Once on the island, he was sold to the plantation owner, Captain Forest.[20]

But Apongo and Governor John Cope met again on the other side of the Atlantic in Jamaica. After his tenure as governor at Cape Coast Castle, Cope operated a number of slave ships out of London and eventually settled in Jamaica to become a sugar planter. Cope and Apongo's relationship in Jamaica was not typical of what might be expected between whites and enslaved blacks on the island. Apparently, Apongo knew Cope well enough from his earlier life on the Gold Coast that he sometimes visited the former governor although both their circumstances were quite different in Jamaica. Upon such visits, Cope, who was no doubt sensitive to Apongo's elite status in Africa, "had a table set out, [and] a cloth & c. laid" for his guest.

Cope was reportedly amenable to purchasing Apongo's freedom but was unable to do so because Apongo's owner, Captain Forest, was not on the island. If Apongo had any such hope, it was gone after 1756, because Cope died, at the age of fifty-six, in February of that year. Not surprisingly, Apongo never abandoned the idea of regaining his freedom, and he used the leadership and military skills that he had developed in Africa to aid his cause. Apongo, also known as Wager, became the leader of the slave rebels in Westmoreland during the infamous Tacky's Rebellion of 1760. His bid for freedom cost him dearly, because he was captured and, in August, was sentenced to death by the colonial government. His sentence required that he "hang in chains" and then be "took down and burnt." He was dead before they took him down for the burning.

The account of Apongo's life stands in sharp contrast to what is known about a young African girl, renamed Clara, who was also brought to Jamaica. Clara was a "Koromantyn Negro" who was transported to the island from the Gold Coast in 1784. In total, thirty-eight known slave ships arrived to the island that year bringing approximately sixteen thousand African men, women, and children. Clara would have been on one of the fourteen known ships that brought captives from the Gold Coast to Jamaica.[21]

By Clara's account, she was born in a village near Anomabu. Her mother, father, and their nine children were enslaved to a "great man, named Anamoa." Upon Anamoa's death, Clara, two of her brothers, and several other persons with slave status were sold to pay his debts. Twenty other enslaved persons, also belonging to Anamoa, were killed at his funeral. The fates of the others are uncertain, but Clara and her two brothers became victims of the trans-Atlantic slave trade and were transported to Jamaica. At some point after their arrival to the island, Clara and her siblings were sold to the prominent planter and historian Bryan Edwards. The historical record gives no indication of the age at which Clara was transported across the Atlantic. Given that her only reference to family was to her parents and siblings and that African girls were generally married soon after they entered adolescence, however, it is reasonable to assume that she was a child or in the early stages of adolescence when she arrived on the island. Despite their unfortunate circumstances, Clara and her brothers no doubt considered themselves "fortunate" to be sold to the same individual once they were in Jamaica. The vagaries of the slave trade ensured that most Africans were separated from other family members either during sale in Africa or in the Americas.[22]

According to Edwards, when he asked Clara which "country she liked best, Jamaica or Guiney?" she replied that she preferred Jamaica. Her supposed preference for Jamaica was because "people were not killed . . . at the funeral of their masters." Of course, there is much reason to be skeptical about Clara's response and the accuracy of Edwards's account. Clara may have very well wanted to appear loyal to her master or, for fear of repercussions, may have been hesitant to tell Edwards how she really felt. In addition, given that he legally owned enslaved Africans, it was in Edwards's interest to report that the enslaved preferred life in Jamaica to that of Africa. It is interesting to note, however, that Edwards describes Clara as "a most faithful well-disposed woman." Clara seems to have offered little overt resistance to her enslavement by Edwards. It is impossible to say with any certainty why Clara was so "faithful" and "well-disposed" despite her slave status. Her disposition may have been influenced by the fact that in Africa her parents were enslaved and so she had been born into slavery long before her arrival to Jamaica. In addition, if she was particularly young when transported to the island, she may have been less capable of actively resisting the conditions of her new circumstances.[23]

Clara's story is also particularly valuable as it highlights several important facts that go against common assumptions about slavery in the Caribbean. The trans-Atlantic slave trade is often imagined as a trade of predominantly "prime" adult males. Clara was not only female but also a youth, perhaps even a child, at the moment of her sale into the Atlantic slave trade. Her story, like that of Apongo, is one of the few available that provides information about an enslaved African prior to arrival in Jamaica. As a result, we know that Clara was not enslaved by means of capture but instead had been born into a family that had slave status in Africa. In Apongo's case, there can be little doubt that his leadership skills and military training in Africa enabled him to organize aggressive campaigns against the Jamaican slave system.

The Realities of Trade

As the stories of Apongo and Clara suggest, the personal histories of enslaved Africans were influential in shaping their attitudes toward whites and their reaction and responses to slavery in Jamaica. Coastal Africans such as Apongo saw whites operate not only as slave traders but also under a range of other circumstances. Sometimes they even witnessed the unfortunate fates of some very socially and economically vulnerable British men and women who were in Africa. Though far from Apongo's homeland, John Newton, the slave trader turned abolitionist, spent two years in captive conditions on the coast of Sierra Leone. After trading for six months in Africa, Newton negotiated to stay on the coast and accepted the patronage of a white slave factor who lived just off the coast on Plantain Island. Unfortunately, Newton fell out of favor with this man and became victim to various abuses, some of which were inflicted by his African mistress. In reference to his experience during this period, many years later, Newton described his life as that of "the most abandoned of slaves."[24] Arguably, such words overstate Newton's plight when it is compared to those Africans who were captured, transported, and sold. Yet there is an irony in Newton—

Plate 1.1. *African Hospitality.* Engraved by John Raphael Smith, 1791. Based on George Morland painting, 1788/89. Companion piece to *The Slave Trade* (plate 3.1). © National Museums Liverpool.

white, British born, and trader in African slaves—being held captive and abused on the African coast.

Similarly, some Africans witnessed the sorry state of those British convicts who were sent to the African coast in the late eighteenth century— many of whom often met with unfortunate ends. One of the repercussions of the American Revolution was that it put an end to the transportation of convicts as involuntary laborers to the American colonies. Up until that point, about fifty thousand convicts had been sent. The war exacerbated an already bad situation with the British jail system: jails were overflowing with prisoners. In an attempt to alleviate the situation, convicts were being transported to West Africa. From an economic standpoint, the decision seemed to make sense. Slave ships heading to Africa certainly had the space to transport convicts, and so the opportunity could be used to generate extra revenue.[25]

Once these British convicts arrived in Africa, however, things did not go so smoothly. In 1784, the governor of Cape Coast Castle wrote a letter of complaint to his superiors from the Gold Coast of Africa. By his report, British convicts had been shipped to West Africa without any arrangements being made to provide for their maintenance. Although the governor was always in need of British men to fill posts on the Gold Coast, he was generally unwilling to employ those convicts who had been sent. Skin color was by no means a sufficient qualifier for these positions. In one letter of complaint about the staffing of posts, it was noted that the only white men available were convicts, and they were "in general a Disgrace to their color"; a request was put in for "Ten or Twelve good Sober Men fit to be Sergeants" to be sent to the Gold Coast. Hence, convicts who were transported to Africa had no means to support themselves and sometimes suffered a sorry fate. Their situation was described as that of "poor wretches" who often landed in Africa "naked and diseased." Because they had no means of support, Africans sometimes saw them dying "under the scorching heat of the sun" either "upon the rocks" or on "the sandy Beach."[26]

Nor was the plight of female British convicts who were transported to Africa anything that would impress coastal Africans in the Gold Coast region. In a letter written by Governor Richard Miles, there was a clear tone of distress when he asked his superiors to consider the fate of "Women of [their] own color" who were to be "common prostitutes among the Blacks." In Miles's opinion, such a fate was worse than death, and he advised that it would be an act of "humanity" to have their lives "forfeited" in Britain rather than to subject them to such a fate.[27] Unfortunately, there is nothing in the historical record to suggest what Africans thought of these destitute women, but it seems clear that the whiteness of their skin had little currency and gave them few privileges among coastal Africans. There is little evidence to support the notion that on the African coast, during this period, Africans had internalized European notions of beauty and so held whiteness as one of the ideals of beauty.

Prostitutes were not, however, the only white female entrepreneurs with whom coastal Africans are known to have come into contact. There is also evidence of white women participating in trade. This is clear from a letter written by slave trader James Williams from Bunce Island (in the Sierra Leone River). Williams cautioned his employer, James Rogers, that John Scasbrick, another captain in the employ of Rogers, would not turn out according to expectations. According to Williams, it was clear that Scasbrick thought "very little about his employer" because while in Africa he "carry'd on most of his trade with white women." There is nothing further in his letter that gives insight into the role of these women in Africa, though Scasbrick is known to have purchased seventy-nine Africans and transported them to Jamaica.[28] It is possible, then, that this reported "trade with white women" may have been for captive Africans.

Clearly, then, those coastal Africans whose lives had been linked to the Atlantic economy witnessed the British on the African coast in a range of roles and living under varying degrees of vulnerability. Hence, at least for some of the Africans brought to Jamaica during this period, whiteness of skin had little mystique and fear value. It was not until they were held captive on slave ships for weeks on end and eventually inserted into the Jamaican slave system that they began to perceive the reality of their circumstances in racialized terms. For coastal Africans, it was then that the link between "race" and power became clear. Prior to this, as captives awaited their fate on the coast, they had a fairly accurate understanding of slave-trade dynamics. They knew that their fate was being negotiated between slave-trading Africans and those whites on the coast; few, if any, doubted African authority on the coast.

Although the British could not begin to trade without African sanction and support and in many ways African traders had clear advantages as they were operating in their own environment, both sides understood that slave trading was a very financially precarious business. In fact, it was far more precarious than other trades. Unlike the trade in ivory, for example, the trade in human beings had many additional costs and risks. The enslaved had to be fed on a daily basis, and even if they were fed poorly, as was commonly the case, this was a large expense. The enslaved often got sick, which reduced their value on the market; even worse, they could die, which would leave no opportunity to recoup any of the financial outlay. And the enslaved, of course, could assert their humanity by fighting for their freedom. Hence, when Africans and Europeans agreed to trade, each side was carefully strategizing how best to negotiate the terms of trade in order to minimize these costs and risks. The cost of an enslaved man, woman, or child was, after all, much more than the price for which they were purchased. Added to that cost was the additional *daily* expense of keeping them alive with food, combined with the ongoing risk of sickness, death, or rebellion. All of these factors meant that traders, African and British alike, aimed to minimize the amount of time they had captives on their hands. Their goal was to buy and sell captives as quickly as possible so that they could pass on these costs and associated risks to the next buyer—with the final sale being made somewhere on the other side of the Atlantic.

For any of this to happen, British slave traders understood that they needed to maintain good relations with Africans and were furthermore expected to behave accordingly. The British were well aware that it was only under certain circumstances that Africans could be legally sent off into the Atlantic slave trade, and so British law required ship captains to respect African legalities on enslavement. They were expected to operate within the parliamentary acts for "regulating the Trade to Africa." This meant that British slave traders were prohibited from using "fraud, force or violence" or "any other indirect practice" in their efforts to fill their slave cargos.[29] Although this was sometimes breached, weighty economic considerations acted as a brake upon persistent and flagrant disregard of the law.

The British knew their position on the African coast was a tenuous one and had no illusions about how important keeping peace with African authorities was for trading ventures. Yet despite legal restrictions, there were violations. Sir George Young of the Royal Navy reported that "king Tom of Sierra Leone" was frustrated by the illegal transport of an African girl. Apparently, "the king" had sent a girl on board to act as "mistress" to the ship captain while slave-trading activities were being conducted. Her name and age are unknown, but clearly she was sent on board to provide sexual services to the ship captain. African traders sent such young females on board slave ships as a "courtesy" to the British traders during their stay on the African coast. Although these young females were seen fit to be sexually exploited, by African and British alike, this did not necessarily mean that there was any tacit agreement that these young girls were being sold into the Atlantic slave trade. In fact, in this particular case, there was a common understanding that the girl would be returned "as is usually done" before the ship left the African coast. For reasons unknown, the captain chose to violate this agreement. The king did not take this violation lightly and "begged" that an application be made to "his brother [King] George" for assistance in the girl's return.[30]

Similarly, in 1777, Captain Hughes of the slave ship *Friend* was charged for illegally selling two free men from the Gold Coast in Jamaica.[31] Of course, charges such as these had no moral basis and were concerned solely with the long-term interests of the slave trade. Hence, in the instructions to return Amissa, one of the free men sold, Thomas Rutherford, secretary of the Company of Merchants, ordered the ship captain to "restore him to his friends and country, in such a manner as will be most conducive to engage their affections, and bend them to promote the interest of the British traders."[32] No doubt the very same reasoning was used when a ship of the British navy, which was stationed at Goree, fired on a slave ship as the captain attempted to sail without paying for the slaves.[33]

And so, more often than not, British traders made efforts to shift the balance of negotiating power in their own favor while operating within the legally prescribed parameters of the slave trade. In 1780, Governor John Roberts considered the advantages to be gained by stopping slave ships from purchasing captives at Anomabu, a major port in the Gold Coast region. He noted that at Anomabu it was easier "for the Blacks to carry their slaves off to ships . . . and if they cannot agree upon the prices, they carry them back." If the trade could be organized so that all ships were to arrive at Cape Coast, however, then African traders would be at a disadvantage, as they would have to leave Anomabu during the night and "paddle their canoes for 10 miles against the current." Under such circumstances, British traders could better impose terms of trade that were in their own favor because the Africans involved "would not be very fond of carrying the Trade back to bring it a second time, but [would] dispose of it."[34]

Conclusion

The "it" that Governor John Roberts wrote of was, of course, the captive men, women, and children he hoped would be sold into the Atlantic slave trade on terms favorable to the British. As this chapter has made clear, in the final decades of the British slave trade, captive Africans not only made it onto British ships but also arrived at Jamaica in numbers that were unmatched in previous years. The expansion of the Jamaican plantation economy, for which the Haitian Revolution was a catalyst, required that more captive men, women, and children were to be caught, captured, and even killed if the increased demand for enslaved labor in Jamaica was to be met. Unfortunately, during this period, trading mechanisms on the African coast were already well established and easily facilitated the increased numbers of captives shipped to Jamaica.

The chapter that follows takes a closer look at the demographic contours of the slave trade to Jamaica. It offers an analysis of the forced migration of not only "prime" adult men but also women, children, and even the elderly. It argues that the Atlantic slave trade had a peculiar "economic character"—one that was determined by the very humanity of the "cargo" being traded.

"Provided they arrive in health"

On January 21, 1805, Simon Taylor, one of the wealthiest planters in Jamaica, wrote to his cousin Robert Taylor giving recommendations on how the latter should proceed with his slave-trading ventures as he supplied African captives to Jamaica. With reference to the slave ship *Trusty*, Simon Taylor cautioned his cousin that the success of the voyage "will depend upon what sort of Negroes she brings." He further advised that if the captain of the *Trusty* hoped to meet with good sales in Jamaica then it would be impossible for him to be "too chosie [*sic*]" when he selected Africans for purchase on the other side of the Atlantic. Simon Taylor also wrote that he and two other potential purchasers would be interested in taking "a great part of the cargo" if the *Trusty* brought the "proper assortment" of captives.[1]

It was known for merchants and planters, throughout the British Caribbean, to make requests for "slave cargoes" of a particular sex and age composition that were transported from a specific area on the African coast. But what exactly did they consider a "proper assortment"? Although current scholarship suggests that there was a widespread preference for "fit young men," there is some evidence showing that, at least in the late eighteenth century, planters and merchants were putting in requests specifically for African women and young people of both sexes.[2]

In fact, during this period, there was actually some concern about having too many adult males on the island, and there were even financial disincentives, by way of import taxes, for bringing in adults in general. Adult males were always taxed higher than adult females. There is also evidence to suggest that in Jamaica, there was some interest in purchasing captive adolescents and children. This is not to say that there was a widespread reluctance to purchase African men, but it does suggest that Jamaican preferences for captives of a particular age and sex were more complicated than has been generally assumed.

In reality, the Jamaican plantocracy's strongest preference for captives was *not* organized around age or sex: the preference was not simply for captive men; nor was it, for that matter, for captive women or captive children. The strongest preference was for African captives who were believed to be in good condition and "tolerable" health. Age and sex were secondary concerns. The priority was to buy enslaved men, women, and children who could labor for long hours under harsh conditions and who seemed likely to live long enough to make their individual purchases worthwhile. Hence, although planters and merchants routinely made requests for properly assorted "cargoes" of a particular age, sex, and even ethnic composition, there was always an understanding, sometimes implicit and other times very clearly stated, that the captives should be in a "tolerable" condition.

This, of course, served to complicate slave-trading activities on the African coast. The Atlantic slave trade—a trade in human beings—had unique and "peculiar" characteristics. Or to use the words of historian Philip Curtin, it had an "economic character different from other commodities."[3] Put another way, even if British slave traders chose not to acknowledge the humanity of the African captives they bought and sold, they certainly could not afford to ignore it. In fact, the very humanity of the enslaved dictated the terms of trade. The African men, women, and children held captive needed to be fed, could potentially plot a revolt, and could die or become very ill. All of these factors affected the profitability of a slave-trading voyage, and British slave traders believed the remedy to all these challenges was, quite simply, a speedy voyage. They aimed to keep the time spent on the African coast as brief as possible. In so doing, food costs would be kept down, opportunities for revolt and resistance would be reduced, and the financial losses caused by mortality and poor health among the captives would be lower. Minimizing the time spent buying captives in Africa was the primary factor to influence purchasing decisions on the African coast, although (as later chapters will make clear) they did so with only limited success. Nonetheless, as British slave traders saw it, a speedy voyage was the most affordable and most likely way to transport captives so that they would maintain a "tolerable" state and thereby meet Jamaican planters' unwavering demand for captives perceived as being in a reasonable physical condition. Getting a "well-assorted cargo"—regardless of how the age, sex, and ethnic combination was defined—was not the first priority.

"The more women and boys and girls the better"

Writing from Barbados in 1788 and later in 1791, slave-trading merchant Samuel Richards, while trying to solicit business, advised that "Men Boys and Women Girls are the Best size for this island." He recommended that "a small Cargo of slaves from 50 to 100 men boys and women girls" would make "a great Average" if they arrived between February and March of the following year. Enslaved young women and youths also seemed to have a market in other islands. In 1786, the Antiguan merchant James Maud advised that it was important to "avoid grown men as much as possible" and that a "well assorted" cargo that was comprised of "young Men & boys, young women & W[omen] Girls from a good Country could not fail" to sell well if they arrived at the beginning of the following year. There is also evidence of a similarly positive attitude toward the importation of African youths in a report made by the Council and Assembly of Grenada in 1788. In this report, it was noted that when enslaved Africans were "not more than from twelve to eighteen years old, they [would] often become in the course of five or six years, just as valuable as Creole Slaves."[4]

Similarly, in Jamaica, at least in the final decades of the slave trade, some Jamaican planters actually preferred to purchase enslaved African youths. In his above-mentioned letter, the planter Simon Taylor advised that in a "proper assortment" of enslaved Africans none should be "above 18 years old or below 12" and the "more women and boys and girls the better." He further reported that neither he nor two other potential purchasers wanted "grown up Negroes." In fact, Taylor repeatedly expressed his interest in "young people—chiefly boys and girls." As a general rule, he never bought enslaved persons over the age of eighteen, and his requests for captives generally ranged between the ages of ten and sixteen. In his well-known diaries, Thomas Thistlewood, the late-eighteenth-century Jamaican overseer and pen owner, documented that when purchasing captives he would choose "men boys and girls, none exceeding 16 or 18 years old, as full grown men or women seldom turn[ed] out well." This might explain why the merchants of Leyland & Company advised one ship captain that in Jamaica "the full grown *and young captives* command the best price" among the islands. In the Windward Islands, however, young captives of about "4 feet 6 or 7 inches" might "answer equally well" but only if purchased at a low enough price in Africa.[5] Jamaica offered a brisk market compared to the other islands, so that women, children, and youths could be readily sold for better prices.

Caribbean planters were not only willing to purchase African women and youths but were also becoming increasingly wary of importing large numbers of adult African males to the island. In 1780 the merchant James Rolland, for example, advised that when purchasing enslaved Africans, slave traders should "avoid grown men, as much as possible & let the majority be young women, with girls & boys in proportion." But reservations about importing adult African men were not restricted to persons resident in the West Indies. The British secretary of state at the time, Henry Dundas (an advocate for the gradual abolition of the slave trade), recommended in a House of Commons debate that restrictions be placed on the importation of the enslaved brought to the West Indies. In particular, Dundas suggested that the slave trade be limited "to females not above fifteen, and males not exceeding twenty."[6]

In the case of Jamaica, Robert Sewell, the colonial agent for the island, spoke favorably of Dundas's recommendation to restrict the slave trade to "negroes under certain ages . . . as an influx of only the young as yet novices in vice, and debaucheries, unfixed in their attachments, opinions and habits . . . [would be] friendly to population and to submission." The Jamaican planter and historian Bryan Edwards, however, was less satisfied with Dundas's recommendation to restrict the slave trade by age and argued that "a greater restriction is necessary for male negroes than that which is proposed [by Dundas]. A young man of twenty is as likely to go to rebellion as one of thirty."[7]

Edwards's resistance to the importation of enslaved adult males was no doubt grounded in fears inspired by the Saint Domingue rebellion, which started in 1791 and continued until 1804. The Haitian Revolution, as it is popularly known, lasted thirteen years and was a constant reminder to the plantocracy about its precarious situation. Jamaican planters lived in close proximity to Haiti, and the realities of the rebellion were quite apparent to them, as it was not uncommon for French planters to seek refuge on the island.[8]

The fears of the Jamaican plantocracy were not unfounded. According to one contemporary newspaper report in 1800, a Jamaican printer discovered a conspiracy that involved both Jamaican captives and some newly arrived from Saint Domingue. The impact of the ideological underpinnings of the

Haitian Revolution was clear. The enslaved—who planned to set fire to Kingston, Spanish Town, and Port Royal—had flags representing a "black and mulatto, mounting a tricolored cockade and whipping a white man." It was no doubt for reasons such as this, as Bryan Edwards saw it, that the importation of enslaved males should be restricted to "boys of, and under, the height of 4 feet 10 inches."[9]

Not only did planters perceive disadvantages to the importation of adult males, but there were even financial disincentives to slave traders for bringing adult Africans into Jamaica in the late eighteenth century. In 1774, the Jamaican House of Assembly implemented an act that imposed a heavy tax on all enslaved persons over the age of thirty. By 1798, this was revised so that there was a tax on all enslaved persons over the age of twenty-five who were imported to the island. Not surprisingly, then, in 1803 Captain Caesar Lawson of the *Enterprize* was advised by his employer that he should not "buy any above 24 years of Age" in case he had to go to Jamaica, where "any exceeding that age would be liable to a Duty of £10 per head."[10]

Further, some of the men shipped to Jamaica were transported there for the sole purpose of being re-exported to places such as Cuba. In fact, Captain Lawson was also advised by his employer that the captive Africans he was instructed to purchase at the Biafran port Bonny were to be sold on the "Spanish market." As a result, the preference was for all the captives purchased to "be males, if possible to get them"; if not, he should "buy as few females as in [his] power." Apparently, females were "a very tedious sale" among Spanish buyers. Similarly, in a letter reporting on the sale of captives brought to Jamaica, Captain James Hunt, of the ship *Rodney*, noted that the captive women sold quickly but that planters had such an "aversion" to both "old Slaves" and captives from Old Calabar that they would have had far more difficulty selling the "men on Hand" had it not been for "the Spaniards."[11]

Although planters continued to defend the importation of enslaved persons and were openly pessimistic about the possibilities of establishing an enslaved population that would grow by natural increase, they certainly understood that abolition was a strong possibility and began to prepare for the worst. Judging from the repeated requests for young captives in general and young girls in particular, it seems that the Jamaican plantocracy believed that the only way to establish a self-reproducing enslaved labor force was, in the words of Henry Dundas, by "importing only such, as, from their ages, were likely to add to the future and permanent population of the islands."[12] At least one Jamaican planter believed that this end would best be achieved by restricting the trade of enslaved women "To females who have not borne children."[13]

The preferences of Caribbean buyers aside, there were also other very practical concerns that dictated how ship captains went about determining the number of men, women, and children who should be purchased. Quite simply, because slave ships were designed with separate holding rooms for men and women, a ship could transport only a limited number of each sex. This put obvious limitations on a ship captain's options. When the slave-trader-turned-abolitionist John Newton, for example, recorded his reasons for putting "13 men, and a man boy slave" on another ship, one of his justifications was as follows: "as I propose to take no slaves under 4 feet 2 inches there is a probability of getting an *over proportion of men* for our number and perhaps *more than we could stow in the room with convenience or look after with safety* for we are but weak handed—only 20."[14]

Other ship captains also made deliberate efforts to ensure that they purchased captive women and youths. Sometimes, slave traders were known to pay more for female captives in order to "assort their Cargoes" even though the females would sell for less than men in the Americas. According to the slave trader Robert Heatley, he often exchanged "prime" male captives for "very ordinary Female slaves," albeit for very practical reasons, when purchasing captives in the Gambia River basin. In this region, one of the main staples purchased to feed captives was corn, and captive women were used to pound the corn until it was reduced into flour so that meals could be prepared for the rest of the enslaved.[15] In 1793, Thomas Miles, the agent for the "Popo Factory" in Aného (in modern-day Togo), gave very specific instructions about an intended slave purchase that was to take place farther east, at Lagos. He wrote to slave trader John Ashley requesting that Ashley "purchase all undersized Slaves of the Description given," but should "it not be in [his] power to do so Women will do *or even Men.*"[16]

Determining the age of the enslaved was, of course, a problem. In a House of Commons debate about implementing age restrictions to the slave trade, one abolitionist summed up the problem nicely when he asked, "how was their age to be ascertained? What was the *baptismal register* on the Coast of Africa to which they were to go and look into for the ages of all these children?"[17] As a result, the age of African children was always estimated. British slave traders developed their own way to approximate the age of their African captives; when they were dealing with youths and ado-

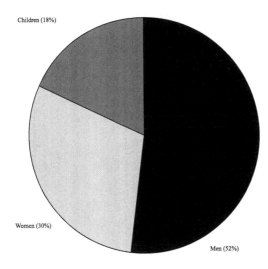

Children (18%)

Women (30%)

Men (52%)

Figure 2.1. Percentage of captive men, women, and children put on British slave ships, 1776–1800. Note that the *TSTD* does not provide statistics for adolescents. *Source*: http://slavevoyages. org/tast/database/search.fac es?yearFrom=1776&yearTo =1800&natinimp=7.

lescents, height was used to gauge their captives' age. Reports addressing slave importation in British colonies often recorded not only the number of male and female captives but also the number of enslaved individuals who were "above 4 feet 4 inches" and those who were "below 4 feet 4 inches." For the purposes of British slave traders, enslaved individuals were considered children if they were under 4 feet 4 inches. In fact, in the British Caribbean, planters generally believed that the ideal "age" of newly purchased captives should be young people who were no less than this height.[18]

Needless to say, height was not a useful gauge for determining age among adolescents or adult captives, but conceivably when slave traders were in doubt about a person's age, they used other markers of maturity. This might include physical markers such as the signs of puberty among youths, graying hair, "fallen breasts" on women, and the condition of teeth and skin. Sometimes adolescents were also recorded separately, though this seemed to be done much less regularly. When they were recorded, they were listed as "Men Boys" or "Women Girls"; otherwise, their numbers may have been included with that of adults. The challenges of determining the age of captives aside, the quantitative data make clear that in the last quarter of the eighteenth century, women (30 percent of the enslaved put on British slave ships) and children (18 percent) were transported in sizeable numbers. Combined, they accounted for almost half (48 percent) of the captives (see figure 2.1).

Although merchants and planters are known to have requested African youths and young women, they also often wrote letters of complaint if a slave ship arrived with children who were considered too young. It is difficult to determine what was considered an acceptable age when purchasing captive children, though one Jamaican merchant expressed some dissatisfaction at having to sell children who were "not more than 8 or 9 years of age."[19] Similarly, there were also complaints if a ship arrived with adults who were considered too old. Again, it is unclear what age was considered elderly, but the physical robustness of captive men and women must have been at least one factor that determined who were labeled as such.

Unfortunately, it is impossible to determine the number of captives who fell into the categories "too young" or "too old," as slave traders and merchants did not categorize them as separate groups in sale records. Regardless of their perceived age, all children below 4 feet 4 inches were listed quite simply under the category "boys" or "girls." On occasion, a separate note was made to identify infants. Similarly, elderly Africans who made it across the Atlantic were not categorized separately, as they were recorded under the category "men" or "women," so there are no statistical data for the elderly. Nonetheless, abundant anecdotal evidence makes it clear that the age of captives brought to Jamaica during the late eighteenth century was often a concern.

Writing from Kingston in 1793, the merchant Allan White reported on the sale of the 229 African men, women, and children brought to Jamaica on the slave ship *Fanny*. Of the 147 males and 87 females purchased in Sierra Leone, 3 died before their arrival at the island. White advised that the sale average might be lower than hoped, not only because there was already a large number of captives for sale on the market but also because of the age composition of the men, women, and children on board the *Fanny*. According to White, although the enslaved were "in good health and tolerable condition," the "antiquity" of some captives and "the over proportion of young people" would reduce the revenue generated. The "young people" were no doubt shorter than the acceptable height of 4 feet, 4 inches. It took approximately two weeks for the sale of these captive men, women, and children to come to a close. In the end, they were all sold, including "eight diseased people" and "two mere infants" who were given away with their mothers.[20]

There are other examples. When reporting on the sale of the men, women, and children transported on the ship *Rodney*, those affiliated with the merchant house Grove, Harris & Papps noted that "there never was a more indifferent Cargo of grown people, than the Rodneys [sic] or a worse assortment." The letter elaborated that the captives were "in general very old," and "only" eight could be described as "Men Boys" and "Women Girls." The majority of the enslaved had to be sold at reduced prices at "vendue" because they were in such an "emanciated [sic] state."[21]

A few years earlier, in 1789, the slave ship *Fly* left Sierra Leone and headed to Jamaica with 45 captives on board. Among the captives, there were 13 men, 9 women, 9 girls, 13 boys, and 1 infant. Approximately 50 percent of the captives were children. In a letter reporting on the sale of the captives, the Jamaican merchants Thomas and William Salmon reported that although "the Cargoe [sic] was healthy" and "in tolerable good order," they could not recollect ever seeing "a worse choice," as the enslaved were "either aged or very small." Approximately one-third of the adults were considered elderly and so had to be sold as "refuse" at a reduced price.[22]

Similarly, in the same year, Captain Richard Martin of the slave ship *Daniel* arrived in the Caribbean with 118 "pretty healthy" captives whom he had purchased in Old Calabar. Unfortunately for Martin, the captives on board his ship included "grown people [who] were too old & the young too small."[23] Of the 118 captives on board the *Daniel*, men accounted for approximately 33 percent, women for 39 percent, adolescents for 9 percent, and children for 19 percent. Males and females (of all ages) were transported in roughly equal proportion. Martin first tried to sell the captives at the merchant house Lytcott & Maxwell in Barbados, but they decided not to take up the "cargo." They believed that, given the age of many of the captives, it was unlikely that they would make a good sale.[24] He then left the island and headed to Jamaica, where he eventually anchored at Martha Brae. One of the captives died en route. Of the remaining 117, the merchant Francis Grant reported that their sale would not meet the expected sale average because of the age of the captives.[25]

Nor was Jamaica the only island where merchants were hesitant to take on the sale of captives who were considered too old or too young. In 1791, slave trader William Laroche also made a voyage to the Caribbean on the ship *Daniel*. He was transporting 65 men, 43 women, and 18 boys and 20 girls. Of the 146 captives purchased in Old Calabar, 20 died before the ship arrived at Saint Vincent. Laroche was unsuccessful in getting a merchant house to agree to sell the captives and so sailed to Grenada. The first merchant house he approached "did not wish to have anything to do with an

[O]ld Callabar [*sic*] Cargo." His ability to negotiate the sale of the enslaved was further undermined because only a few hours before he arrived, the slave ship *Mary* reached the island, bringing enslaved African men, women, and children from the Congo River. Laroche described the enslaved on the *Mary* as being in much better condition than those on his own ship: of those on the *Mary*, there were only a "few undersized" and "no cargo could exceed them" in "Health & youth." In contrast, when referencing the captives on his ship, he noted that "there never came to market such a sett [*sic*]. Both for age & youth." He further reported that there were a number of children under 4 feet 4 inches and that some of the elderly were "realy [*sic*] Tottering for age." After Laroche was turned down by yet another merchant house, merchant James Baillie agreed to sell the captives on board the *Daniel*. Laroche was so frustrated with his circumstances that in a letter to his employer he wrote, "I will give you my Honour I will not take on board a slave that is aged. They will not pay Freight as in the case with a number on board. Have lost Nine since my arrivell [*sic*]."[26]

In general, ship captains hoped to avoid such circumstances by being more selective about the men, women, and children they purchased. On his slaving voyages, John Newton often recorded descriptions of the captives he purchased. However, there is little in his diary to suggest a strong preference for adult males. He did complain, however, about captives who were considered "old" or women who were "long breasted." During one sale transaction, for example, Newton recorded that, for a debt owed to him, he was paid "a woman [and] a boy (4 foot 1 inch)." In the same transaction, he purchased an additional "2 boys (3 feet, 10 inches)," but he refused to buy "an old man" who was also available for sale. Newton was certainly open to buying young Africans but was hesitant to purchase children he considered too young. He sometimes refused to buy children when this was the case.[27]

No Market for Dead Captives, Little Market for the Unhealthy

Yet despite the efforts of John Newton to be selective about the captives he purchased, even he sometimes accepted captives who were younger than what he normally considered acceptable or those he described as "old."[28] This, of course, begs the obvious question: If ship captains were reluctant to purchase the "too young" and the "too old," and Jamaican planters were reluctant to buy them, why then did these captives end up on slave ships headed across the Atlantic? Slave trade specialists have long debated whether the demographic contours of the Atlantic slave trade were more strongly influenced by planter preferences in the Americas or by supply factors internal to Africa (competing markets, war, famine, and so forth). Others have suggested that the patterns of the slave trade can be explained by changes in shipping costs, trans-Atlantic war, and other factors.[29] Much of the demand and supply debate has been grounded primarily in comparative price analyses. The average price of the enslaved has been used as a gauge for assessing the demand and supply forces that shaped the demographic composition of the Atlantic slave trade. This is despite the fact that, as historian P. E. H. Hair puts it, "overall average prices have little meaning," as the price of the enslaved could be determined not only by sex, age, and ethnicity but also by health and condition.[30]

More to the point, dead captives had no value and sickly captives had little value—regardless of their age and sex. There can be little doubt about this. Even the most superficial analysis of sale records will show that there are numerous instances of sickly adult males being sold for significantly less than children who were considered to be relatively healthy. In fact, mortality rates were so much a concern that the merchants of Isaac Hobhouse & Company instructed one of the ship captains in their employ to supplement his purchase of captives with that of ivory as "in that Commodity there's no Mortality to be fear'd."[31]

It was for reasons such as this that the Atlantic slave trade involved very complex and peculiar trading dynamics. Merchants in the slave trade had little choice but to concern themselves with mortality rates, health conditions, mounting food costs, and the possibility of rebellion by African captives. Hence, it was the very humanity of the captives that made slave trading unlike other trades. The first priority of ship captains on the African coast was to minimize the profit-reducing effect of each of these factors. Slave traders' approach to this was consistently the same. The time involved in negotiating for captives of a particular description had to be weighed against the cost of staying on the coast for longer than was necessary. As a result, they aimed to spend as little time in Africa as possible. From all indications, meeting planters' age, sex, and ethnic preferences was a secondary concern. Only under ideal circumstances did slave traders give this priority—and rarely, if ever, were circumstances ideal. Furthermore, added to all of this were other more standard costs, such as wages and insurance, that were also a function of voyage length.

The goal was to purchase as many African men, women, and children in "tolerable" health as cheaply as possible and get them across the Atlantic as quickly as possible. According to one slave trader who operated in Sierra Leone, "all slaves who were offered *(if judged saleable)* were bought without discrimination." He did, however, refuse to purchase captives who were "lame, old or blind." Slave trader Robert Heatley also maintained that during his years of slave trading he "never knew of an instance . . . were [*sic*] *a good* Female Slave, or Boy, or Girl was refused by the European Trader." Similarly, in a statement jointly written by three slave traders, it was commented that on the coast of Africa it was common to "purchase every *saleable* slave that offers, of either sex."[32]

Slave traders had no illusions about the financial repercussions they would suffer if the enslaved African men, women, and children they purchased were in poor health and/or there were high mortality rates among them. Health was *the* most important factor to determine the price of any particular enslaved man, woman, or child. Merchants in Jamaica, and the Americas more generally, often stressed the importance of good health to slave traders. Jamaican merchant Alex Macleod, for example, in a letter soliciting business, promised an "excellent [sale] average" if he received the description of captives he requested. He was sure to mention, however, that he could only do this "provided they arrive[d] in health."[33]

Captain William Jenkins of the slave ship *Fame* knew firsthand the financial losses that accompanied high mortality rates and poor health among the enslaved. In July 1792, after spending just under three weeks at Old Calabar, Jenkins left Africa with 201 African men, women, and children. When he listed the captives on board, Jenkins reported that he had purchased 59 men, 128 women "all fallen Brest [*sic*] & hears [*sic*] gray," 11 girls "under six," and 3 "infants at Brest [*sic*]." In total, the journey across the Atlantic took fifty-two days. Unfortunately, mortality rates were high during the Atlantic crossing, and 65 captives died before reaching Grenada. The original intention had been to sell them in Jamaica, but the health of the remaining 136 Africans was so poor that Jenkins decided his best option was to try to sell them as soon as possible.

Several of the merchant houses refused to take on the responsibility of the sale because of the health and condition of the captives. In the end, Jenkins made arrangements with Munro MacFarlane & Company. According to MacFarlane, he agreed to take on the sale of captives in such poor health partly because it would have been "cruelty" to send them off "in the state they were in to Jamaica." In the words of Captain Jenkins, "there was Never a Worse Cargo" brought from Africa, and in order to improve the health of the captives before sale, he would give them much "Meat & Drink." Despite this, he forewarned that the average price would be low as some of the men, women, and children were "Bline [*sic*], [with] one eye, some loasing [*sic*] fingers, some toas [*sic*]." Interestingly, none of the correspondence commented on the relatively high proportion of women among the enslaved. This is despite the fact that Jenkins left Old Calabar with approximately twice as many women as he did men.[34] It was the health and condition of the enslaved that was the primary concern and was attributed to keeping the average price of those persons sold so low.

The Importance of a Short Voyage

Perhaps the greatest irony of the slave trade was that although healthy captives were most valued among purchasers, its organization did not prioritize the health and well-being of the enslaved who were being sold. Even after the Dolben's Act of 1788, which constrained the number of captives who could be carried on British slave ships, and the 1799 Act that followed, the conditions of enslavement were horrendous and captives were forced into circumstances that were conducive to poor health.[35]

Ship captains approached the problem of health and mortality by trying to keep the period of slave trading down to a minimum. This would reduce the odds of captives dying while in their charge. Also, because the conditions under which the enslaved were kept were so poor, it was understood that a quick voyage would minimize the effects of sickness and disease. The goal, then, was to buy and sell captives as quickly as possible. In so doing, they hoped to avoid high mortality rates and to sell captives before the effects of such unhealthy conditions became visibly apparent in the physical state of enslaved men, women, and children. In reality, however, a speedy voyage was a poor solution to ill health and high mortality among captives. Most of the African men, women, and children who survived the Atlantic crossing arrived in the Caribbean in questionable health. Yet because perceived good health was so important in determining the price of the enslaved, it was common practice to make captives "fit for Market" by improving their diet a few days before they were to be sold.[36]

Speedy voyages were seen as crucial to a profitable trip; as a result, not surprisingly, slave traders were generally advised by their employers to try to keep their time on the African coast as brief as possible. An example can be taken from a letter written in 1791 to slave trader Charles Molyneaux in which he was hired to purchase captives at the Congo River. In the letter of instruction, he was cautioned that the success of the voyage would "depend entirely on . . . a short passage . . . [and] quitting the Congo before the rains set in" and before the "Crew and Negroes become sickly." Similarly, the slave trader George Merrick received written instructions to go to the Biafran port Elem Kalabari and to purchase "good healthy young negroes and ivory." He was further advised not to "stay too long" on the African coast, as the "risk of sickness and mortality then becomes great."[37]

Ironically, British slave ships were required by law to have medical personnel (contemporaneously referred to as "surgeons") on board who were assigned the responsibility of attending to the health of the enslaved. However, for a variety of reasons (including death or abandonment of duties), slave vessels were sometimes without the required surgeon. Nonetheless, ship surgeons were often rewarded financially if they could meet the challenge of keeping mortality rates low and captives in a relatively healthy condition. Such instances were quite likely rare but did occur from time to time. From Bananas Island in the Sierra Leone region, surgeon William Dinely wrote his employer, James Rogers, an optimistic note stating that "nothing in [his] power shall be wanting"; Dinely also reported that his medical training enabled him to help "a Boy which quited [sic] a tape worm 18 feet in length." In Dinely's opinion, with the tapeworm, the young captive could not have been sold for £5 on the other side of the Atlantic. Without the tapeworm, Dinely reported, "he is worth 40£." From Jamaica four months later, Dinely again wrote to his employer and stated that he was entitled to his bonus because during the voyage they "only lost two" of the 150 captives transported on the ship *Fame*.[38]

Few ship surgeons, however, could report such low mortality rates. Although surgeons and ship captains shared the same employer, they were quite often at odds while on the African coast and during the Atlantic crossing. Surgeons understood that purchasing relatively healthy captives and feeding them reasonably well was the best means to keep mortality low and the enslaved in an acceptable condition. Unfortunately, this was not something easily accomplished, as ship captains generally gave priority to keeping overhead costs low, and it was the ship captain who had the final say during trade negotiations on the African coast and who controlled food rations.

The conflicting priorities of ship captains and surgeons employed in the slave trade is without question. One captain described the surgeon on board his ship as "[as] Great a villain as . . . I could have got out of the Kingdom." He further suggested that the surgeon was "a spy" for the "Belly foging lawers [sic] and Committee."[39] He seemed to be implying that the surgeon in question had abolitionist sentiments and was doing his best to undermine slave-trading activities on the African coast. Other pieces of correspondence also make clear the tension between ship captains and surgeons. Writing from Old Calabar in late August 1790, Captain William Blake of the ship *Pearl* reported that they had "Buried 13 women & girls, 56 men & Boys [and] Sixteen White people." In Blake's mind, these 69 deaths among the captives occurred because the ship surgeon, I. P. Degreaves, was unfamiliar with African "disorders." Not surprisingly, Degreaves's explanation of the high mortality was quite different. By October 10, the death count among the captives had risen to 113. According to Degreaves, he was unsurprised that so many captives had died, because many had been "bought against [his] opinion & others without [his] advice." Moreover, the high death rate was attributable to a "purchase of bad yams," which gave them the "flux." Degreaves further complained that when he asked the ship captain to purchase a goat for the "sick slaves & white people," his request was refused.[40] As the surgeon's complaints suggest, the cost of feeding captives was a concern of ship captains. Minimizing food costs meant limiting food rations and keeping the length of the voyage as short as possible.

In another letter, Captain Blake wrote a note of clear distress from Old Calabar. After waiting on the coast for several weeks, he described Old Calabar as a "disagreeable sickly place" and reported that to keep the ship on the coast much longer "would be destroying of everything," as there would be much "*expence of provisions*, burying of slaves dayly [sic]."[41]

Although British traders took food supplies to Africa, in order to feed both captives and the crew, merchants generally expected that they would be able to supplement their food supply by purchasing rice, maize, and yams in the various regional markets. Because the slave-trading process often took several months, a ship captain who had already purchased a significant number of captives would be in a predicament should there be a shortage of provisions on the African coast.[42]

The heavy food requirements of the slave trade added another layer of complexity in the slave-trading process. Both African and British traders were aware that anyone involved in the slave trade would be vulnerable without sufficient provisions. John Roberts, the governor of Cape Coast Castle in 1780, complained that the "Negroes expect Gold in payment for what provisions we want." Moreover, African slave traders often raised the sale price of captives just before ships were ready to depart the African coast. They did this knowing that ship captains were anxious to get off the coast with as many captives as possible but also wanted to minimize the daily expense of feeding a large number of captives.[43]

This would explain why, in the Gold Coast region—much to the annoyance of other British traders—Captain Currie of the slave ship *Dumfries* purchased captives above the asking price of African slave traders at Cape Coast. He justified purchasing his captives above market value because "his ship lay at a very great expence, therefore dispatch was necessary and . . . he could save his owner money if he got off soon." Currie left the coast of Africa with a total of 635 captives. He understood that the longer he stayed on the coast, the more it would cost to feed the several hundred men, women, and children already purchased. Rapidly rising food costs had to be weighed against the extra time involved in negotiating for captives of a particular description. Currie obviously decided that he needed to get off the coast as quickly as possible—so much so that he bought the captives available at above market price.[44]

Depending on circumstances, the cost of feeding captives could work in favor of either British or African slave traders. In 1787, British slave traders on the Gold Coast entered into an agreement to stop purchasing captives until the prices had been reduced by African suppliers. For six weeks no captives were sold. Eventually the Africans gave in, as they were "being at a great expense, in keeping what slaves they had by them" and were also "threatened by every appearance of a Famine for want of Rain." Yet from the perspective of British slave traders, this situation did not come without its disadvantages. Although captives were purchased at a reduced price, the shortage of food and water on the African coast meant that the voyage across the Atlantic would have to be made with limited rations. During periods of drought, there was also the added concern that the cost of any African supplies that were available would have been much higher than usual. In fact, under particularly strained circumstances, it was not unknown for slave ships to leave Africa without enough food to feed the captives.[45] Under these circumstances, mortality rates of captives were particularly high and the health of survivors particularly poor. Hence, although captives may have been purchased cheaply, the profitability of the voyage was sometimes severely undermined by the scarcity of water and food.

Speedy voyages also reduced the risk of revolts and rebellions. The majority of revolts occurred at the port of purchase or within a week of setting sail. Slave traders were well aware of this possibility and prepared for it. In addition to physical restraints, attempts were made to psychologically terrorize captives. One slave trader, for example, displayed weaponry on the main deck with the hope that it created a "formidable appearance" that would be "sufficient to intimidate" captives "from any thoughts of an insurrection."[46]

Despite such efforts, there are numerous known instances of attempted revolts and uprisings. Reporting on the slave ship *Pearl*, William Blake noted that the ship left Old Calabar with "only" 474 captives, as 283 died before they even began the journey across the Atlantic and 3 drowned in an attempted "Mutiny with the men slaves."[47] Circumstances such as this ensured that the potential for such revolts was in the forefront of slave traders' minds.

Attempted revolts, however, were rarely spontaneous and required time and planning on the part of the captives. Efforts were organized and attempts were made to collect knives and other rudimentary weapons such as stones. Children were instrumental in planning such revolts. Unlike adult males, who were chained, enslaved boys were often left free to roam the decks. As a result, young captive boys had the means to get weapons and tools necessary for revolt and could pass them to the men. Children could also undermine efforts of escape. According to one slave trader, he surprised two captive men who were trying to remove their restraints. With information given by "3 of the boys," he was able to locate "knives, stones, shot, etc, and a cold chissel [sic]" that had been hidden among the men. As it turned out, four other boys had supplied them with these items.[48]

Regardless of how revolts were planned and executed, the very risk of revolt was another reason for slave traders to do all in their power to get off the coast of Africa as quickly as possible. An attempted revolt could potentially put the success of an entire voyage at risk. It could also result in the deaths of British traders and African captives alike. No doubt, ship captains understood that insurrection could cause both financial debt and physical death, and so this was another important factor to inspire British traders to put their efforts into making a speedy voyage.

The need to trade quickly also determined where in Africa ship captains chose to purchase their captives. Although contemporary letters often refer to the price of captives as a multiple of some fixed unit, in reality African traders sold captives for an assortment of goods. Gold Coast governor John Roberts wrote to his superiors listing the goods necessary for a "proper assortment" to purchase an enslaved man and woman: over twelve different items were required for the adult male, and over nine different items were required for the adult female.[49] In fact, having the right combination of goods was key to a financially prosperous voyage because "the deficiency or want of the smallest article" would prevent slave traders from "purchasing a slave." In another letter, Roberts reported on two British ships "in Annamaboe Road" that made "their purchases but slowly on account of their cargoes not being of the best Manufacturing and assortment." In contrast, those slave traders who made it to the African coast with the desired combination of goods often wrote favorable reports about their slave-trading activities.[50] As a result, ship captains were often instructed by their employers to move along the coast in search of places where trade could be conducted quickly given their assortment of trade goods. One ship captain, for example, was advised to go to the Congo River to purchase captives. His letter of instruction, however, also made clear that if he was unable to trade quickly, he should sail along the coast until he could find better prospects for trade (for another example, see the case of the ship *Enterprize* in text box 2.1).[51]

But the African trade routes that brought captives from the hinterland to coastal areas were also quite fluid. Enslaved men, women, and children from one region in Africa were sometimes taken to coastal trading areas farther away in order to trade for a more desired assortment of goods. With respect to the Gold Coast region, the above-mentioned Governor John Roberts noted that wherever British slave traders brought a "prime assortment of goods," Africans involved in the trade were able to find their way to it. Similarly, in writing from Old Calabar, slave trader Captain Forsyth apologetically explained to his employer that the reason he was unable to get more male captives was because they were being marched "through the cuntry [*sic*] for the Camaroo[ns] where they receive a greater price for them."[52]

Text Box 2.1. Ship *Enterprize*. Merseyside Maritime Museum. Reference number DX/1732.

Letter to the Captain of the Ship *Enterprize*

Ship Enterprize

3rd Voyage 1794

Sailed from Liverpool 6 April 1794

Returned to Cork the 24th with the Spanish ship *Virgini* retaken from the French the 15th in Latt [*sic*] 42.44 North and Long 14.20 West.

Sailed from Cork 5 May 1794

Arrived in the Congo 10 August 1794

Sailed from ditto 18 October [1794]

Arrived at Kingston, Jamaica, 25 November 1794 with 360 Negros

Sailed from Jamaica 5 February, and arrived at Liverpool 29 March 1795

Liverpool 24th March 1794

Captain William Young

Sir,

You are to proceed in our Ship the Enterprize for the Coast of Angola with the utmost expeditions [*sic*, expeditiousness] and you are to run direct for the River Congo where it is our Intention you shall Barter the Cargo for prime young Negroes and Ivory, and we desire you will not purchase any exceeding twenty years of age. . . . It must be your first care to make an agreement with the leading Traders . . . to slave the Ship off with her full number in a short time and at a price proportioned to the quantity of cloths and assortment now consigned to you for sale and returns. . . . If you find any difficulty in doing so by an unexpected opposition in the Trade there, you are then at liberty to proceed to any other place where you may have a prospect of better terms, you may likewise buy a certain proportion of small Slaves of 4 feet 6 to 4 feet 9 Inches which you will get for a reduced bundle and they will stand the middle passage much better than full grown. You will consider that a long stay in the Zaire is always attended with great mortality among both Blacks and Europeans in the best Season, and that a short purchase under the present, expense of Insurance, Outfitt [*sic*], Wages, and long dated Bills, would be equally fatal to our Voyage; do not therefore fail to protect us against these events. Treat the slaves while on board with the greatest care and humanity, and require of your Surgeon and Officers the most prompt execution of their Duty on all occasions. . . .

continued

continued

We have made an agreement for the Sale of the Enterprizes Cargoe
[*sic*] of Negroes at Kingston, Jamaica, to which Islands you are to proceed with a press of Sail and on your arrival deliver them to Messrs
Taylor Ballantine & Fairlie, to be disposed of by them to our best advantage. . . . (you are not to call at any of the Islands on your way down to
Jamaica, because no great good can attend it) and you might possibly
lose many people by desertion or the Impress, therefore leave the coast
with an abundance of wood and water for the middle passage, and do
not under any circumstances think of disobeying our orders in this particular. . . .
You will be careful to write to us by every opportunity. . . . In case of your
Death, an event which we trust in God will not happen, your Chief Mate
Mr. Hymers is to succeed you in the Command and attentively follow
these and all our future orders.
We are Sir
Your Ob[edient] Serv[ant]

[Thomas Leyland]
[Thomas Molyneaux]

Captives from Where?

Such fluidity in the trading networks served to further complicate matters
for British slave traders. Where captives were purchased determined, of
course, the ethnic composition of the enslaved put on any particular slave
ship. The need to spend as little time on the African coast as possible, then,
needed to be balanced against the goal of buying captives that fell within
the known ethnic preferences of Jamaican planters. Not surprisingly, quick
trade in Africa was always given the highest priority. However, in so doing,
ship captains sometimes were then faced with challenges in Jamaica as they
tried to sell the men, women, and children they purchased.

In general, the enslaved from Old Calabar were *not* favored among Jamaican planters and required a "brisk market."[53] In contrast, captives purchased at the other Biafran ports, Elem Kalabari (New Calabar) and Bonny,
could be sold with relative ease to the Jamaican plantocracy. Correspondence from the Jamaican merchant house Grove, Harris & Papps referred

favorably to the arrival of the slave ship *Thomas,* which came "from New Calibar [*sic*] with a cargo of fine young slaves." Writing from Trelawny, the merchant Francis Grant requested an "Eboe Cargoe." According to Grant, those captives transported from Bonny were "the sort most run upon" in Jamaica, and he hoped he could have such a cargo.[54] Nor was this preference for captives from Elem Kalabari and Bonny restricted to Jamaica. Reporting on the state of the market in Dominica, the merchants Francis and Robert Smyth reported, "we have had many arrivals here from the Coast, say Old & New Callibar [*sic*] & Bonny—those from the former Part of the Coast does not answer so well, as those from new C[alabar] & Bonny—there has been averages here of the former from £28 to £30 St[g] & for the latters from 60 [*sic*] to £62:10 currency p. Head."[55]

In reality, the distinction Jamaican planters made between the enslaved bought at Old Calabar and those purchased from the ports of Bonny and Elem Kalabari was more apparent than real. Although British slave traders went to different ports in the Bight of Biafra to negotiate the sale of captives, these ports were supplied with enslaved individuals derived from the same regions. In the Biafran hinterland, African slave traders from Aro Chukwu, for example, controlled the inland markets for captives and dominated the slave trade in much of Igbo and Ibibio country. These Aro merchants accumulated captives and sold them at inland markets. After being purchased, the captives were then transported to Bonny and Old Calabar. Elem Kalabari was essentially dependent upon Bonny for captives supplied by the Aro for most of the eighteenth century. Captives were also transported down the Niger River from the western Igbo area to both Bonny and Elem Kalabari—where the Aro did not operate. In addition, Old Calabar was also connected into both the Ibibio region and the Cameroon grass fields that were neither Igbo nor Ibibio.[56] Yet despite these overlaps in supply to the three ports in the Bight of Biafra, planters had clear preferences for captives purchased at Bonny and Elem Kalabari when compared to those of Old Calabar.

Ironically, although captives from the Gold Coast were often described as "rebellious," they were in great demand in Jamaica and generally sold at a higher price than captives from other parts of Africa. According to one merchant in Jamaica, captives from Old Calabar were "not nearly in so much estimation with the generality of people . . . as from the Gold Coast." In fact, Jamaican merchants repeatedly asked for captives from this region. The high demand for enslaved persons brought from the Gold Coast meant that the enslaved could be sold with relative ease. In December 1803, the slave ship *Princess Amelia* arrived in Jamaica with a cargo of 305 slaves. Although there were already "four or five Guinea ships [t]here," the *Princess Amelia,* having "a Gold Coast Cargo and the slaves in tolerable condition," was able to sell many of the enslaved "while the other ships [could] hardly sell a negroe."[57]

Invariably, throughout this period, Jamaican planters were willing to pay more for the enslaved transported from the Gold Coast than for those from other regions. In December 1788, merchant Francis Grant reported that "Gold Coast Negroes . . . fetch higher prices with us than those of any other Country." Three years later, he would again report that "Gold Coast Cargoes command better terms" than did Ebo and Windward Coast slaves. In January 1789, another Jamaican merchant, Thomas Pappy, reported the average sale price for the cargoes of two slave ships: the enslaved transported on the ship *George,* who were brought from "Anamaboe" on the Gold Coast, sold for an average of over £45 sterling; in the same month, the "600 Eboe slaves" brought on the *Vulture* from Bonny sold in Montego Bay for an average of only £40.9.5 sterling.[58]

Although Jamaican planters and merchants tended to distinguish the enslaved by the African ports from which they were purchased, there was certainly an awareness about the diversity of ethnic groups from which the enslaved were drawn. When advertising the arrival of slave ships to the island, Jamaican merchants commonly listed the supposed ethnicity of the enslaved. When one merchant, in February 1793, announced the arrival of the slave ship *Union* from the Gold Coast, for example, he reported there were "538 choice young Coromantee, Ashantee and Fantee slaves." Similarly, when the planter Simon Taylor described the captives he hoped to purchase, he asked specifically for "150 or 200 young Ebo [from Bonny] or Whydaw negroes [from the Slave Coast]." Even for the enslaved purchased at the preferred Biafran ports (namely, Elem Kalabari and Bonny), planters had their ethnic preferences. Of the enslaved captured in the Biafran hinterland, "Eboes" were the favored group among the Jamaican plantocracy. In 1803, Taylor similarly advised that he not only wanted a young cargo but that they should be "Eboes and not Mocos."[59]

Although merchants and planters often made clear their ethnic preferences, there is little doubt that the ethnic composition of the enslaved did not always meet their expectations. Letters of complaint noting that recently arrived enslaved Africans did not match their demands are numer-

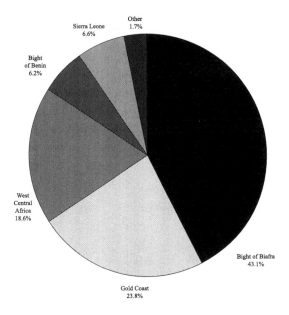

Figure 2.2. Areas of provenance for captives transported to Jamaica, 1776–1808. See note for table A.4 in the appendix. *Source*: http://slavevoyages.org/tast/database/search. faces?yearFrom=1776&yearTo=1808&mjslptimp=35100 (accessed April 2009).

ous.[60] The statistical data also support this view. Despite the fact that Gold Coast captives were the most preferred by Jamaican planters, they were not transported to the island in the largest numbers. Between 1776 and 1808, only 23.8 percent of all captives were from this region. The largest number of captives was drawn from the Bight of Biafra; this region accounted for 43.1 percent of captives. Captives taken from West Central Africa (south of Cape Lopez) were also seen favorably by planters but constituted only 18.6 percent of captives. All other areas of provenance combined accounted for 14.5 percent (see figure 2.2).

In fact, there were sometimes conflicts between merchants and slave traders over the ethnic origin of captives. For example, in 1790, the merchant Francis Grant reported on the sale of captives who were transported to Jamaica on the ship *Crescent*. The ship's captain, William Roper, had purchased the enslaved in the Sierra Leone region. Grant reported that once the *Crescent* arrived to Jamaica, he made "the mistake" of selling the ship's captives as if they had been purchased on the "Gold Coast." He suggested that he was pressured to do this because of Captain Roper's "imposition."

Similarly, the next year, another Jamaican merchant, Alex Macleod, wrote a letter of complaint about a transaction over the sale of captives. In his note, he commented that he had asked to be sent "a Gold Coast Cargo" and instead received, on the ship *Fame*, captives from the Upper Guinea region who were expected to be sold on "Gold Coast terms."[61]

The fluidity of African trade routes also led to duplicity in slave trading on the African coast. Captives transported from the Gold Coast were generally in greater demand and sold at higher prices in Jamaica and other parts of the Caribbean. British-born governors were aware that there were higher profits to be made because Gold Coast captives were perceived as being of "superior Quality . . . to that of all [other slaves]." This was so much the case that an official report produced in 1777 noted that these governors did not limit their slave-trade transactions to the buying and selling of captives from the Gold Coast region. In fact, they reportedly "bought up very many Slaves, of inferior Price and Condition, at Gaboon [*sic*], Lagos, Benin and other marts." Enslaved men, women, and children from these regions were then put in the slave castles and were sold to slave traders on British ships along with legitimate Gold Coast captives. According to the report, such transactions were to the "Certain Loss & Detriment" of "inexperienced Slave Traders," who were unable to distinguish between captives of different ethnic backgrounds.[62]

But more experienced slave traders were knowledgeable enough to protect their financial interests. A case in point would be that of Captain Dear of the slave ship *Fly*. While purchasing captives on the Gold Coast, Dear returned an enslaved woman to the governor from whom he had made the purchase. He explained that he could not "think of keeping her," because she was a "Benin slave." He further commented that if her ethnicity "was taken notice of" in the Caribbean, it would "prove to be a great detriment to [his] average [sale price]."[63]

Conclusion

Contrary to current scholarly thinking, in the late eighteenth century, Jamaican planters were willing to purchase African young women and youths. In fact, during this period, there was actually some reluctance to import adult males into the island. Financial disincentives for purchasing African adults—by means of taxes—and fear of rebellion made the Jamaican plantocracy hesitant and wary of purchasing African men to labor under slavery.

Unfortunately for Jamaican planters, their preferences for captives of a particular age, sex, and/or ethnic background had little influence on shaping the demographic contours of the slave trade. Put another way, slave traders' ability to demand Africans of a particular age, sex, and ethnic background was severely undermined when the primary concern of keeping the captives alive and subdued was being done at considerable expense. Rather than run the risk of jeopardizing the "success" of a voyage, slave traders thought it financially prudent to purchase captives quickly in order to get a full cargo—even if the enslaved did not properly match the stated preferences of Jamaican planters.

"We took man, woman, and child"

The very mechanics of slave trading meant that no segment of African society was completely spared from its horror and trauma. According to the eyewitness account of Isaac Parker, a sailor who in the 1760s was invited to go on a slave raid in the Biafran hinterland, at the moment of capture enslavers "took man, woman, and child as they could catch them in the houses." Parker (who had absconded from his employer's ship the *Latham* while on the African coast and was resident in Africa for five months and under the protection of Dick Ebro, a member of the African elite) described the enslavement process:

> we paddled up the rivers in the day-time . . . when night came we put the canoes ashore, leaving two or three Negroes in each canoe, the rest flying up to the village, taking hold of everyone we could see; and as we took them we handcuffed them, and brought them down to the canoe; after we had done so we quitted the place and went farther up the river, and so during the second time; and we got to the amount . . . of 45 Slaves at that time.[1]

Parker's account, which is drawn from his testimony at the 1790 inquiry into the slave trade, clearly illustrates the difficulties enslavers would face if they chose to discriminate by age and sex as they went after their victims.[2] Nor is Parker's description the only one that suggests this. In another account of slave trading in the Biafran region, it was noted that searches for captives were made upriver, the raids were made at night, and enslavers "seized men, women, and children promiscuously." The capture of women and children in sizeable numbers during slave raids occurred in all slaving regions, no doubt because they were more vulnerable and more likely to be overpowered by enslavers. In contrast, able-bodied men would fight to defend their community, and if all seemed lost, they were more capable of fleeing the site of capture. In fact, the effects of slave raiding were so all-

Plate 3.1. *The Slave Trade*. Engraved by John Raphael Smith, 1791. Widely circulated in Britain and France. Based on George Morland's painting *The Execrable Human Traffic*, 1788/89. Companion piece to *African Hospitality* (plate 1.1). By permission of the National Maritime Museum, London.

pervasive and indiscriminating that even pregnant women who were "big with child" were captured and sold on the coast.[3]

The mechanics of slave trading also meant that the elderly and weak were easy prey for enslavers. According to the British slave trader Captain Hall, the captives available for sale were generally "from Children up to [age] thirty," though sometimes African traders would try to sell "an Old Man, or Old Woman." He also reported that it was unusual for the old to be brought to the coast for sale, as they were generally rejected by ship captains. This is not surprising, as the elder captives were not the preference. Yet, as made clear in chapter 2, there were numerous complaints by Jamaican merchants about slave ships arriving with too many "old slaves" and, in fact, ship captains on the coast of Africa were sometimes willing to purchase elderly captives in order to leave the coast with as many captives as possible in the shortest possible time. If ship captains did refuse to purchase a captive because of "age, illness, deformity, or any other reason," it was likely that these poor captives would be put to death. If they could not be sold in either the trans-Atlantic or the local trade and were deemed as having no other purpose to their captors, there was little reason to keep them alive. These were the circumstances of one unfortunate man who was considered "too old" for purchase. He was brought on board a slaving vessel by an African trader called Lemma Lemma. When it was realized that there was no hope of selling him, "his head was laid upon one of the thwarts of the boat, and chopped off," and his body was thrown overboard.[4]

Captives who were rejected by British slave traders might also be used for ceremonial sacrifices by Africans living on the coast. According to Jerome Weuves, who acted as governor on the Gold Coast and lived in the region for several years, those captives rejected by the British were commonly "set aside for sacrifices." They were also sacrificed on the Biafran coast. Entries made in the diary of the Efik slave trader Antera Duke, who resided in Old Calabar and quite commonly sold captives to British captains, have numerous references to captives being used in ceremonial sacrifices.[5]

The impact of slave trading on African societies was pervasive and left no one exempt from its effects. Certainly, healthy adult males were in demand, but the mechanics of the slave trade meant that women, children, and the elderly were far more vulnerable to capture. Moreover, ship captains were amenable to buying such captives in order to reduce trading time (and resulting voyage costs) on the African coast. As a result, they were commonly made victims of the slave trade, though the proportion in which they were sold into the Atlantic slave trade varied from region to region and was influenced by a number of local factors.

Enslaving Men, Women, and Children

In the final decades of the British slave trade, women and children from the Bight of Biafra were transported to Jamaica (and the British Caribbean more generally) in significantly greater numbers than elsewhere. This is despite the fact that proportionally they were *not* sold in numbers remarkably different from other regions. As a demographic analysis of captives by region of departure in Africa makes clear, the percentage of women put on British slave ships varied between 27 and 33 percent, and that of children ranged between 14 and 20 percent (see table 3.1). A comparison of absolute numbers, however, highlights differences that are far more astounding. The dominance of Biafran captives (43.1 percent) in the British slave trade during this period meant that among those captives purchased for sale in Jamaica, more than twice as many women and children left this region when compared to, for example, the Gold Coast—the second most significant area of provenance for captives (23.8 percent). Interestingly, Biafran boys and girls were shipped in equal proportion, and Biafran girls outnumbered the combined number of girls from all other regions. These statistics are consistent with contemporary reports. In the words of the Bristol merchant James Jones, "More Females are had [in Bonny] and better than on any other part of the Coast: they are in general small, more than one third Females and a great many Boys and Girls."[6]

In both the Gold Coast and West Central Africa, the two other key areas of provenance for captives brought to Jamaica, men were in even larger proportion than women and children (when compared to the Bight of Biafra) and accounted for 57 percent and 56 percent of the captives exported from those regions, respectively. In absolute numbers, however, the number of men shipped from each of these regions was dwarfed by that of those shipped from Biafran ports. In both regions, boys outnumbered girls, though the large number of Biafran girls put on slave ships meant that overall girls accounted for 44 percent of all captive children. As pointed out in chapter 2, there is no way to determine what proportion of the adult captives were "prime adults," as the elderly and many adolescents were often listed under the categories "Men" and "Women."

Ultimately, these regional variations in the age and sex ratios of captives

Table 3.1. Age and Sex of Captives Embarked by Area of Provenance, 1776–1808

	Men	Women	Boys	Girls	Area total
Bight of Biafra	49%	33%	9%	9%	100%
	(86,988)	(58,585)	(15,978)	(15,978)	(177,529)
Gold Coast	57%	29%	9%	5%	100%
	(55,878)	(28,429)	(8,823)	(4,902)	(98,032)
West Central Africa	56%	29%	9%	6%	100%
	(42,903)	(22,218)	(6,895)	(4,597)	(76,613)
Other areas of	53%	27%	12%	8%	100%
provenance	(31,655)	(16,126)	(7,167)	(4,778)	(59,726)
Total from all areas	52%	30%	10%	8%	100%
	(217,424)	(125,358)	(38,863)	(30,255)	(411,900)

Source: http://slavevoyages.org/tast/database/search.faces?yearFrom=1776&yearTo=1808&natinimp=7&mjbyptim
p=60400.60600.60700; see also http://slavevoyages.org/tast/database/search.faces?yearFrom=1776&yearTo=1808&natinimp=7&mjb
yptimp=60100.60200.60300.60500.60800.60900 (accessed May 2009).

Note: According to the *TSTD*, approximately 411,900 captives were put on slave ships headed to Jamaica. These numbers do not
reflect those who died during the Atlantic crossing, and so they are not an indication of the captives who entered the Jamaican
slave labor system (see table A.2). Calculations for the absolute numbers above make the following assumptions: the Bight of Biafra
shipped 177,529 captives (43.1 percent of 411,900); the Gold Coast shipped 98,032 captives (23.8 percent of 411,900); West Central
Africa shipped 76,613 captives (18.6 percent of 411,900); all other areas of provenance accounted for 59,726 captives (14.5 percent of
411,900).

were determined by economic influences, though at least one historian has suggested that cultural influences could sometimes be more important than economic ones. As Ugo Nwokeji sees it, more women were exported from Biafran ports for three reasons. First, he maintains that there was little competition with the trans-Saharan slave trade and that female slavery in Biafra was marginal, the end result being that there were more women available for the Atlantic market. Second, he argues that the female role in agriculture was not very significant and so their labor was less valued domestically. Finally, he suggests that in Biafran warfare male captives were decapitated, which reduced the number of enslaved men who could be sold.[7] Some of his reasoning is problematic; this is particularly the case when he extends his argument to children. Nwokeji reasons that the Igbo and Ibibio custom of killing twins shortly after birth is evidence that the role of market forces has been overemphasized by historians. He maintains that economics cannot "explain why the Igbo and Ibibio killed twins, when selling two or more children would fetch more money than selling one." Yet correspondence from British slave traders makes clear that few persons were willing to purchase infants. More often than not, they were purchased reluctantly, because the conditions of the Atlantic crossing were too harsh for newborns. Furthermore, infants were rarely, if ever, sold independently of their mothers. As "sucking children," whose survival depended on being breast-fed, there was no interest in purchasing them unless they were going to be sold with their mothers or some other lactating female—and even then, few ship captains were willing to buy them. Not only were ship captains reluctant to purchase them in Africa but also, assuming they even survived the voyage, there was little market for enslaved infants on other side of the Atlantic. Quite often they were given away with their mothers.[8]

In the Gold Coast and West Central Africa, captured women and children were generally absorbed into the domestic slave trade and so left Africa in smaller numbers (compared to the Bight of Biafra). There were also specific conditions that sometimes led to an upsurge in the proportion of children being exported. In West Central Africa, for example, a period of severe drought caused an increase in the number of young boys being sold into the trans-Atlantic slave trade during this period.[9] During times of famine, selling dependents into slavery was not unusual. This was so much the case that between 1784 and 1795, the period of major drought in the eighteenth century, there was a peak in the number of captives shipped from the area. In 1784, the number of captives sold increased by 50 percent over the previous year.[10] The proportion of enslaved children also increased, accounting for approximately 31.5 percent of the captives leaving West Central Africa between 1781 and 1785. Most of the enslaved children were young boys.[11]

Women and young girls, who were no doubt also sold during times of drought, did not leave the region in the same large numbers as young males. Enslaved females were highly valued in Africa not only for their labor but also because they could more easily be socially incorporated into African societies. As a colonial census of Angola shows, as early as 1777 and 1778, girls outnumbered boys below the age of fourteen—suggesting that young boys were commonly sold into the trans-Atlantic slave trade.[12]

The link between famine and the increased enslavement of children was felt in other slave-trading regions in Africa. Although a very minor exporter of captives to Jamaica during this period, the Senegambian region experienced an extended period of drought in the 1780s that also led parents to sell their children into slavery. Parents who sold children no doubt saw this as a necessary means of survival. Not only would these parents be putting newly enslaved children into a circumstance that would guarantee them food and shelter, but the money obtained from the sale of their children would also enable the purchase of provisions for the rest of the family.[13]

Children also became victims of the slave trade through pawnship. The African institution of pawnship refers to the use of human beings as "collateral for credit." It existed in many parts of western Africa and was known to be an important mechanism of credit in European-African trade relations. Pawnship was prevalent in the Gold Coast and, from the 1750s, in Upper Guinea, Old Calabar, the Cameroons, Gabon, and Loango. It was not uncommon for ship captains to advance goods to African merchants who promised to supply captives at a later date. In exchange for merchandise, however, slave traders were obliged to leave pawns on the ship until the promised number of captives had been supplied. Children were often used as pawns in the slave-trading process. If obligations were not met, then these children could be legitimately shipped across the Atlantic as slaves. Alternatively, if child pawns were unfortunate enough to be put on the ship of an unscrupulous captain who chose to leave Africa without releasing the pawns on board his vessel, these children sometimes ended up as victims of the Atlantic slave trade. Such cases did not occur often, as British ship captains were acutely aware of the long-term importance of maintaining good trading relationships with African merchants. In fact, it was known for merchants to make particular efforts not to leave Africa with the individuals who had been pawned.[14] Nonetheless, some pawns did leave Africa as victims of the Atlantic slave trade from time to time.

In Ouidah, on the Slave Coast, children had a formal role in European-Dahomian slave trade negotiations. Traditions varied in an earlier period, but in the 1770s, when Europeans arrived at the coast, the king supplied two children to any recently arrived European who had hopes of trading. This was done before the king officially agreed to grant permission for trading in the area. Europeans were under obligation to pay for these children, at the rate demanded, if they hoped to gain permission to purchase captives. These children were used in "symbolic exchange" for customs. During this period, children were also part of normal trading activities, and some were quite likely sold by the king. In previous decades, the king had the right to sell his captives to Europeans before other African suppliers did. This custom seems to have died by the late eighteenth century—though the king may have still supplied captives for the Atlantic slave trade. As late as 1792, there is evidence that after trade was officially opened, two additional children were purchased, for the slave ship *Swallow,* from the Yovogan (the African administrator responsible for trade with Europeans). The Yovogan was quite likely selling them on behalf of the king.[15]

Regardless of the cause, there can be little doubt that many terrified children were put on ships without any relatives accompanying them. James Arnold reported that while trading in the Cameroons, they had purchased "Several boys . . . from the Age of seven to twelve, who had no relations on board." Dr. Thomas Trotter, who was employed on the slave ship *Brooke* in 1783, reported that while slaving at Anomabu on the Gold Coast, the ship's captain, Clement Noble, purchased many boys and girls who "had not father or mother, or any relation on board." In particular, Trotter made reference to "a little girl of about 8 years of age" who reported that she "had been carried off from her mother" by the men who had sold her to the ship. Whether this eight-year-old child was one of the 58 captives who died before the enslaved were sold in Jamaica is unlikely to ever be known. Nor is there any available documentary evidence that would indicate what proportion of the 638 captives purchased on this voyage were children. Trotter's claim can be given some credence, however, as Noble also reported that there were "several" children on the voyage.[16]

Efforts were often made to redeem children who were illegally sold to

British slave traders. One sailor reported an instance of a young girl who was sold to Captain James Salcraig of the ship *Lilly* while trading in Sierra Leone in 1769. The girl was brought on board by an African named Ben Johnson, who was self-titled "Grand Trading Man." Johnson brought her to the ship in his canoe and negotiated her sale on the ship and departed. Shortly after, two other African men came to the ship. They brought Ben Johnson with them, but this time he came as a captive. The two men reported that Johnson had stolen the young girl. In exchange for the girl, they offered Salcraig the now-captive Ben Johnson, their justification being that he was a "Teefee"—which meant thief. Similarly, on the Gold Coast at Anomabu in 1783, a young boy was sold to British slave traders. Fortunately for this youth, "his father, uncle, or some near relation" came to redeem him so that he was eventually freed.[17]

Like Trotter's experience on the Gold Coast, sailor William Dove also reported that while in Sierra Leone in 1769, he often saw children brought on board "separately by themselves." In his view, children were very much a part of the slave trade. As he reported it, on one particular voyage, there were as many as thirty to forty boys and girls with some "sucking at their mothers breasts" and four or five infants who were born during the Atlantic crossing.[18] The quantitative data certainly support Dove's impression, as approximately 35 percent of the captives leaving this region between 1751 and 1780 were children.[19]

Sometimes entire families were sold into the Atlantic slave trade, though they tended to be separated early on in the process. There was, after all, little incentive to keep family members together, so they were often put on different ships. James Morley, a sailor involved in the slave trade at Old Calabar, reported that one of the captives brought on his ship told him, through the aid of a translator, that "he was taken in the night . . . his wife, and children were taken with him, but they were not in the ship he was in." Similarly, a young girl who had been made captive in the Biafran region and eventually would be sold in Jamaica informed one of the sailors on the ship *Britannia* that she and her parents had been "thieved by inland traders." Her mother was on the same ship, but her father had been sold to another British trader and was on another vessel. Another sailor reported that parents and children "were divided, some in one ship and some in another." The exception, of course, was "children at the Breast," who were "always with their mothers."[20]

Given that there was little market for captive infants, they were far more likely to be put to death at some point during the enslavement process. In 1786, Captain Joseph Williams of the *Ruby* refused to purchase a mother and child, as he did not want to be "plagued with a Child on board." The next day, the mother, now clearly in a distraught state, was brought on board alone and again offered up for sale. Apparently, her child had been killed in order to make her sale possible.[21] Some infants were more fortunate. According to George Young, a captain in the Royal Navy, while in Africa he saw a "beautiful infant boy" being offered for sale to the captain of the ship *Phoenix*. The child had been offered to numerous other ships the night before, but no one was willing to buy him. The African traders made it clear that they would throw the child overboard if they could get no sale. Out of pity, Young reportedly purchased the infant for "a quarter cask of Vidonia wine" and took him to England.[22]

Sometimes an entire family could be enslaved, not through capture but through legal mechanisms. One ship surgeon reported that, while on the Gold Coast, he knew of the purchase of a man, his mother, his wife, and two daughters who had been sold on the accusation of witchcraft. Apparently, the enslaved man had been a trader and so could speak some English. He told Trotter that he had quarreled with the chief, or "Cabbo Cabbosheer," of Saltpond and in an act of revenge his entire family was accused of witchcraft and sold into slavery. One Gold Coast governor also reported that he had seen "whole families sold at once, [which included] Grandfather, father, mother and children at the Breast." It was common for the sale of an entire family to take place if they were accused of the crime of witchcraft.[23]

There were instances of young people being sold into the Atlantic slave trade as punishment for the crimes of adult relatives. This was the case of a fifteen-year-old female, from the Cameroon region, who was sold to the ship *Ruby* in 1787. She was the first captive put on board the ship and was promptly renamed Eve—as was often done for the first female captive purchased. According to this young woman, the "great men" of the village accused her father of stealing a goat that was found in his garden. By her account, the goat had been purposely put there, so that her father could be unjustly made to give up one of his daughters as a penalty for the offense. Of his three daughters, he chose Eve, who was then sold by the "great men" into the Atlantic slave trade. Her father, however, soon lost another daughter to slavery. Approximately three months after Eve was purchased, her eight-year-old sister was brought on board. The circumstances of her enslavement are unknown. Contemporary reports do suggest, however, that at times members of the same family were put on board the same ship at separate times. At other times, they were even sold at the same time to the same slave ship.[24] Captives were more likely, however, to be sold separately from their family members.

The Mechanics of Slave Trading

In key areas of provenance from which Jamaican captives were drawn, there was some variation in the slave-trading processes. Depending on region, trade negotiations could take place on land or on board British slave ships. Region would also determine the experiences of the very captives over whom negotiations were taking place.

In the Bight of Biafra, the three main slave-trading ports were Bonny, Old Calabar, and Elem Kalabari (New Calabar)—with Bonny supplying the most captives by far. Between 1776 and 1808, Bonny exported just under 56 percent of all the captives transported from the region. During the same period, Old Calabar and Elem Kalabari accounted for 17 percent and 12 percent, respectively. Jamaica, the largest single destination for captives from this region, received 46 percent of the enslaved.[25]

By the late eighteenth century, the Bight of Biafra had become a leading source of captives in the British slave trade. This region, which traditionally played a relatively minor role in supplying captives, received a new prominence after the 1730s. Its supply of captives peaked in the last quarter of the eighteenth century, but it continued to be an important supplier in the British slave trade until abolition in 1807.[26]

The Igbo (contemporaneously known as "Eboes") predominated among the ethnic groups enslaved and transported from Bonny and Old Calabar, with the Ibibio (or "Mocos," as they were known in Jamaica) making up most of the rest. Close proximity to the Niger waterway meant that captives exported from Elem Kalabari were drawn in larger proportions from the northern and Middle Belt regions. Although it is tempting to suggest that Jamaican planter preference for "Eboes from Bonny" accounts for this port's predominance in Biafran slave trading, there were, in fact, a number of internal variables that facilitated the expansion of trade in this region. In part, it can be explained by the development and expansion of Aro networks, which generated increasing numbers of captives. Bonny's ascendancy as the chief port in the region is to be partly explained by its proximity to two central water routes. As the Aros established large diaspora settlements in central Igboland, they shifted the trade away from Old Calabar to Bonny, which was centrally located, could be more easily accessed, and could better facilitate the transport of captives.[27]

Another factor that contributed to the increase of trade in Bonny was the "early growth and consolidation of royal authority," which enabled the enforcement of a sophisticated credit system that allowed for more efficient trading between Europeans and Africans. Trading ventures in Bonny took significantly less time than the other ports in Biafra as well as the Gold Coast and Angola.[28] It is not surprising, then, that for British traders, "the small space of time" in which a slave-trading venture could be "compleated [sic]" made Bonny "more resorted to than any other upon the coast."[29]

In addition, at least in the late eighteenth century, there may have been another reason why trading at Bonny was faster than at other areas. Having the appropriate assortment of trade goods was necessary for quick trading. British ships may have very well arrived with an assortment of goods best suited for trade in Bonny. This was at least the case for slave trader John Goodrich, who, after realizing that his "Cargo was badly laid for Calabar," then traveled to Bonny. After "seeing the King," Goodrich found that he "could do much better with [his] cargoe [sic] at that place." Similarly, the Bristol merchant James Jones wrote that the trade in Bonny was "most advantageous to [Britain] both as to Our Manufactures and the number [of slaves] had from thence."[30]

Like the Biafran slave trade, there was also an expansion of slave-trading activities on the Gold Coast in the second half of the eighteenth century, peaking in the final twenty-five years. Between 1751 and 1808, approximately 57 percent of all captives put on British ships in this region were purchased at the ports Cape Coast Castle and Anomabu. Although in absolute numbers Gold Coast captives purchased for sale in Jamaica could not match those of the Biafran region (see table 3.1), Jamaica was still the largest importer of men, women, and children from the region in the final decades of the slave trade. Approximately 53 percent of all the captives leaving the region on British ships were exported to the island, and it seems that few were re-exported from Jamaica to other islands.[31]

Captives sold from this region were generally Akan. In the British Caribbean, however, they were often referred to as "Coromantee"—after the coastal settlement Cormantin. Ironically, Cormantin was *not* a major port for slave ships: only 1.1 percent of captives were known to have left from this area between 1700 and 1808.[32] In reality, the notion of a "Coromantee na-tion" was an invention of the Americas that was "based on ethnolinguistic identity" and had no basis in indigenous African social organizations of the eighteenth century. In Africa, an individual's identity was tied into kinship, religious societies, and political organization. The tendency for captives to identify with other Africans on the basis of language, as in the case of the Coromantee, was a manifestation of African ideas about social interaction in the context of slavery in the Americas.[33]

As can be expected, the eighteenth-century expansion and the related peaks and troughs in slave trading in the Gold Coast were closely linked to wars and political rivalries in the Gold Coast region. By the early eigh-teenth century, the Asante had emerged as the dominant power in the re-gion. Its expansion continued well into the century, and although the origi-nal political rivalries in this region were for control of the gold trade rather than the slave trade, this was to change in later years.[34] Asante's success during these Akan wars was aided by both the "gun powder revolution" and the construction of a sophisticated road network system known as the Great Roads. The introduction of firearms, facilitated by the export of cap-tives, was crucial to Asante's dominance in the region. The Great Roads also changed the dynamics of warfare in Asante's favor. These roads allowed for the rapid movement of Asante armies in the forested inlands and so gave them an important advantage during war.[35] By the end of the eighteenth century, the Asante had only one significant rival—the Fanti.

The impact of internal African politics on the supply mechanisms of the slave trade is well reflected in the competing interests of the Asante and Fanti. Although the Asante controlled slave trading inland, the Fanti domi-nated the stretch of land along the Gold Coast. The Asante and Fanti had competing but complementary roles in supplying captives to the Atlantic market. Asante, the primary supplier of captives, was actively involved in the enslavement process. Captives taken by the Asante during the Akan wars accounted for many of the captives exported from the Gold Coast in the first half of the eighteenth century. As Asante consolidated its power, its slave-trading activities increased and reached its peak in the 1780s and 1790s. The Asante also supplied captives by demanding, from subordinated societies, that taxes be paid in human beings. These individuals were sub-sequently sold into the Atlantic slave trade.[36]

The Fanti generally acted as the middlemen who brokered with the Eu-ropeans on the coast. In that role, they restricted Asante access to the coast and consequently to Europeans aiming to purchase captives. In general, few captives were enslaved by the Fanti in the coastal areas, as they relied heavily on the Asante to provide captives from the inland forest. There were, however, some exceptions to this. Coastal wars between political factions operating in Fanteland often resulted in war captives being sold into the Atlantic slave trade. The Atlantic slave trade also led to changes in Fanti social institutions, such as criminal justice and pawning, and so provided a source of captives that could be sold.[37]

The primary mechanism for the enslavement of residents of Fanteland was through the legal machinations of the state. The Atlantic slave trade was used as a means to maintain social order and as a deterrent for criminal activity. According to Governor Richard Miles, among the Fanti, enslavement was generally a punishment for crimes of "Debt, Theft, Adultery and Witchcraft." Expressing a similar sentiment, the American slave trader Robert Norris reported that, among the Fanti, the punishment of "transportation," or sale into the Atlantic slave trade, was "represented . . . as the greatest evil that [could] befall them" and was used as a deterrent for crime.[38] The primary means by which the Fanti, and presumably other coastal Africans, became victims of the Atlantic slave trade was through legal forms of punishment.

Among those ethnic groups for which the primary reason for enslavement was punishment and not capture, men were exported in larger numbers than women and children. Men were more likely than women and children to be sold for crimes. In addition to witchcraft, men were convicted in larger numbers for the crimes of "Theft, Adultery, [and] Gambling." Because few women were "sold for any other crime than adultery," the number of men sold bore "no proportion to the women." Children, of course, would rarely be convicted of a crime, unless they were unfortunate enough to be part of a family that was accused of witchcraft. They were, however, likely to be sold into the slave trade to pay off debts.[39]

Conflict between the Asante and Fanti was always a concern for European slave traders on the Gold Coast. In 1776, David Mill, the governor of Cape Coast Castle, complained that slave-trading activities were "exceedingly dull" because of the "mutual jealousies" between the Asante and Fanti. Moreover, as Mill saw it, the British on the coast should "interfere as little as possible in their disputes." He believed not only that British involvement would ultimately "prevent the settlement of differences amongst the negroes" but also that the allotted finances on the Gold Coast would not allow for mediation efforts that involved "giving the Blacks such large presents as the Dutch."[40]

In West Central Africa, British slave-trading activities were less dominant than in the Bight of Biafra and on the Gold Coast. Nonetheless, captives were transported to Jamaica in sizeable numbers and accounted for 34 percent of all captives put on British ships in this region.[41] Unfortunately, between 1750 and 1808, records for the vast majority (63 percent) of captives purchased by the British do not specify at which ports they were purchased. Based on the data for the remaining 37 percent of the captives, it is clear that significant points of embarkation for British vessels were the Congo River, Malembo, Loango, Ambriz, and Cabinda.[42]

The British concentrated their trading ventures at the Congo River and ports north of it. After the French were removed from Cabinda in 1793, the British increased their slave-trading activities in this area. Estimates suggest that the number of captives put on British ships between 1791 and 1800 was almost seven times greater than the previous decade.[43] The British also made some efforts to trade south of the Congo. After approximately 1770, they were increasingly known to send small exploratory parties south of the river in the hope of purchasing captives. In so doing, they accessed the more southerly trade routes located between the Congo and Dande rivers.[44]

Most of the men, women, and children sold in this region were taken from the same populations that supplied Luanda, the key trading port south of the Congo, which was under Portuguese dominance. The suppliers that provided the African traders with captives north of the Congo River were the African states Jinga and Kongo, both of which were located to the south. Another, far more easterly, state (Lunda) also supplied captives north of the Congo, though its trading activities were primarily at Cabinda.[45]

Not surprisingly, political upheaval in the region served to feed the supply lines of the slave trade and so ensured that large numbers of captives were transported across the Atlantic. The introduction of European goods into the region fuelled slaving activities and contributed to the increasing levels of social chaos and political instability in the region.[46] South of the Congo River, the Kongo civil wars over succession to the throne also contributed to the supply of captives. These wars began in the second half of the seventeenth century and reached intense levels by 1780. Although periods of conflicts were sometimes followed by periods of relative peace, not until 1794 was there a period of some political calm in the region. During this period, it was largely prisoners of war who were taken during military campaigns and sold as captives. Although French slave traders benefited from tensions in Kongo the most, British slave-trading activities also reflected the vagaries of these internal conflicts.[47]

As with other regions, the problems of determining the ethnicity of captives purchased in West Central Africa is problematic. In British slave-trade records, captives from this region were often given very general "ethnic" labels. One British slave trader reported, for example, that captives transported to Loango were from "three nations": the "Congues, Majumbas, and Madungoes." More often, however, they were categorized quite simply as "Angolan" or "Kongo." Interestingly, in late eighteenth-century Jamaica, evidence from one study suggests that captives from the region were often relabeled upon their arrival at the island. This analysis of runaway advertisements shows that they were more likely to be referred to as "Kongo," with only a small minority referenced as "Angolans."[48]

Despite the use of such generalized ethnic labels, many of the enslaved came from villages or urban areas and tended to identify with the local communities in which they had resided. In many ways, the broad categories were used by traders for convenience; they were part of the "trading jargon." These labels made up a mutually comprehensible vocabulary that was common to both Africans and Europeans as they negotiated the terms under which captives were to be traded. Even slave traders of the time recognized that these labels were inaccurate and did not necessarily indicate the "ethnic origin" of captives. One French trader reported that the ethnic labels assigned to captives were often derived from either the ethnicity of the Africans who supplied them or the people whose territory the captives were transported through on their way to the coast. In other words, captives called "Kongo" purchased at Loango were not necessarily so labeled because they were of Kongo origin. They may, in fact, have been referred to as Kongo either because they were first purchased in Kongo or because they were transported through Kongo territory.[49]

The problems of identifying ethnicity continue to challenge historians. In the words of historian Joseph Miller, the "'ethnic' origins of the enslaved reaching the coast . . . might mean very little." The dynamics of slaving in the region made it possible for individuals to be "kidnapped, sold, resold and captured again." Not surprisingly, then, the occurrences of capture were in excess of the individuals made victim to the slave trade, and there was a continual movement and re-movement of individuals. As a result, as the slave trade heightened, there were more and more individuals, residing on the coast, who were born into slavery but whose parents were captured in the western hinterlands of central Africa. As Miller sees it, this forced migration of captives "in the course of repeatedly disrupted lifetimes" led to a merging of the eastern and western slaving frontiers that blurred ethnic distinctions.[50]

Nonetheless, although captives constructed their identities in relation to their local environment, there were strong social, cultural, and linguistic similarities throughout the region. Most of the enslaved men, women, and children leaving on British ships belonged to one of three "regional cultures": Kongo, Mbundu, and Ovimbundu. Captives were either from these areas or were from regions that were part of the same language family (West Bantu). In other words, it was possible for them to communicate with each other—even if only to a limited degree. Although one recent study on African ethnicities in the Americas concluded that captives sent to the Caribbean from this region were "most likely closely related Kongo group speakers," a more nuanced interpretation suggests that captives were also Kikongo speakers, from the Mayombe area, Mundongues (or Teke) from inland Congo River, and "forest peoples" from the north.[51]

The Trek to the Coast

Not surprisingly, there was a diverse range of experiences among captives, as the enslavement processes varied from region to region. In some cases, captives were the result of direct slave raids or captured in wars often not necessarily connected to the slave trade. The operation of the Aro diaspora and its networks in the Biafran region produced captives from, among other things, kidnapping, local conflicts, and witchcraft accusations. Men, women, and children who were captured in the Biafran hinterland were forced to walk to the inland trade markets where they were sold. The surgeon of the slave ship *Ruby* knew of a woman who was purchased at Bimbia Island in 1786. She had come from so far inland, in the Cameroons region, that none of the other captives on board could speak her language. During the Atlantic crossing, however, she learned enough English to explain that while on her trek, she had been sold several times by African traders and "had traveled for six moons" before arriving at the coast.[52]

Though Biafran captives did walk for part of their journey, they were also transported, for a significant part of their journey to the coast, by canoe. Once they were captured, they were taken to the inland trade markets at Bende and Uburu, which were controlled by merchants from the Aro Chukwu region. They were held at these markets and eventually sold at monthly fairs to African coastal traders from Bonny, Elem Kalabari, and Old Calabar. These coastal merchants came inland by traveling up river and commuted in groups. After purchasing their human "merchandise," they loaded their canoes with captives and returned to the coast. Each canoe held about "twenty or thirty slaves," and "the Arms of some of [the captives were] tied behind their Backs with Twigs, Canes, Grass Rope, or other Ligaments of the Country."[53]

Unlike Biafran captives, who were transported from the inland markets to their point of sale downriver by canoe, captives taken in the Gold Coast region and West Central Africa were forced to travel by foot for the entire journey to the coast. For captives from these regions, the trek to the coast would have been particularly long and difficult. While the death rate on such a march is impossible to determine, there can be no doubt that many died along the way. Even under the best of circumstances this would have been a physically trying experience. In West Central Africa and the Gold Coast, the seizure of captives during war generally took place in the dry season and made the march even more of a challenge.[54] The periods of drought in the late eighteenth century no doubt increased mortality rates even further. The long, arduous journey to the Atlantic coast ensured that those who did survive were weakened and in a poor state of health.

The physical endurance of captives was further challenged by the use of restraint devices that were developed to prevent efforts at escape. Adult male captives in the Gold Coast region were known to have a log of wood—between three and four feet in length and an estimated eighteen pounds in weight—fastened to their arm. As they walked, they carried it on either their head or their shoulders.[55] There were other forms of restraint that were probably considered more suitable for women and children. In James Arnold's observations of captives being transported from the Cameroons, he noted that some captives were forced to wear a "collar made of Roots or Twigs" that was attached to a pole about three yards long that was used to guide them. He also noticed that other captives were forced to wear another device of restraint. The use of this device individually bound the hands of captives by having them locked into a flat wooden board so that there would be little mobility in their arms.[56]

The use of devices to restrain captives was quite likely dependent on the strength and condition of the enslaved as they walked to the coast. According to Governor Weuves, however, "Inland Negroes" who were sold from ports on the Gold Coast generally walked unrestrained. Given that Weuves resided on the coast and knew little of the mechanics of inland trade, his observation can only be given credence with reference to the condition of the enslaved upon their arrival to the coast. It is possible that captives taken from inland were forced to wear devices of restraint early in their journey but would be unable to bear the burden of wearing the eighteen-pound block of wood (described above) on their arm as they got closer to the coast. Their exhaustion from the long trek would be enough to limit attempts at escape. By the time they got to the coast, captives were in a poor physical state and generally had "sores from traveling through the woods . . . and [were] much emaciated." "Gold Coast Negroes," a reference by Weuves to those captives who were enslaved in closer proximity to the coast, were considered the "most turbulent of any" leaving the region. They were more likely to wear restraints at this point in the journey. This was probably because they were less exhausted and were in closer proximity to their homeland. Both these factors increased the likelihood for attempts at escape. Similarly, Governor Miles's observation that women and children on the Gold Coast walked unrestrained may have been valid only closer to the coast, when exhaustion levels would have been high. Women and children were certainly put in restraints in other slave-trading areas.[57]

The enslaved walking from deep inland generally passed through many hands before they made it to the coast. In the Gold Coast, such transactions took place until the captives were brought to the borders of Fanti territory. They were then sold to the Fanti. The Fanti were known, among the British residing on the coast, as "slave brokers," as it was they who negotiated the sale of captives to ship captains and the governors residing on the coast.[58] Similarly, in West Central Africa, captives were generally sold and resold several times among African slavers before they were purchased by British ship captains. The trip to the Angolan coast could range between months and years. But the long walk to the coast was not specific to either of these regions. A case in point would be an incident reported by Mungo Park— one of the best-known late-eighteenth-century explorers of Africa. According to Park, he had met captives in the Senegambian region who were taken in war and had "remained three years in irons" before being sent to the coast.[59]

No doubt, the harsh trek increased the mortality rates of children and was a disincentive to transport them from deep inland to the coast. This reasoning certainly shaped the experience of one woman who was made captive in the Senegambian region: she reported that she had been "torn from her children" because they were "too young to undergo the fatigue of the journey" and had been left behind. Given that captives were sold and resold many times before arriving at the coast, children sold into the Atlantic slave trade were probably purchased from individuals or at markets en route to the coast. Such was the case of "a young slave girl" who resided in a town Mungo Park refers to as Jallacotta. According to Park, who made part of his journey to the coast with a slave caravan, a sickly male captive who was unable to proceed any farther was traded for this young enslaved girl. This young girl, who was already a victim of the domestic slave trade, was thus to become a victim of the Atlantic slave trade.[60]

For captives from the Biafran hinterland, who made part of the journey by canoe, the trip to the coast was less physically strenuous than for captives from other slave-trading areas. By canoe, the trip from inland markets to the coast took only a few days. Pregnant women, children, and even the elderly taken from the Biafran region probably had a better chance of survival during this stage of enslavement. This explains why Alexander Falconbridge could report that he knew of women captured from this area who were "so advanced in their pregnancy" that they gave birth on the journey to the coast.[61]

In slave-trading regions where captives were forced to walk for the entire journey to the coast, however, the physical strain was much more severe. Weaker slaves who were unlikely to survive the journey were sometimes abandoned, if their presence risked the "success" of the journey. This was certainly the case of the captive woman named Nealee who was enslaved deep in the interior of West Africa. After being severely stung by a swarm of bees in her weakened state, Nealee refused to march with the slave caravan any farther. She was threatened and then whipped, which induced her to continue. But her poor health required that she be carried by other captives and eventually put on a donkey in order to keep up with the caravan. In her extremely weakened condition, however, Nealee did not even have the strength to prevent herself from falling off the animal that carried her. As a result, it was decided to abandon her "where undoubtedly she soon perished."[62]

There can be no doubt, however, that the preferred option of African slavers was to sell or trade captives weakened by the strenuous march to the coast. As argued in chapter 2, the health and condition of captives was the most important factor to determine the perceived value and price of captive men, women, and children. From the standpoint of the African slavers who moved the captives to the coast, there was a direct link between the health of the enslaved and the profits to be made. Like European slave traders on the coast, African slavers used speed as their antidote to poor health. Their goal was to get the captives to the coast as quickly as possible. If captives were too weak to continue, efforts were made so that they could be traded en route to the coast. As in the case documented by Mungo Park mentioned above, a slaver was not unlikely to exchange a sickly adult for a healthy child if the latter's chances of survival on the journey to the coast were believed to be better.[63]

Captive Perspectives of Enslavement

Upon their arrival at the coast, captive men, women, and children were then prepared for sale to ship captains. In the three key areas to supply captives to Jamaica, however, there were some differences. In the Biafran region, after being brought downriver by canoe, they were taken to the houses of various traders, where they were "oiled, fed, and made up for sale" to ship captains.[64] At this point, captives were put in canoes and taken to individual ships for inspection and possible sale. On the Loango coast, ship captains came ashore and got permission to build a temporary trading house where the terms of trade could be discussed. No negotiations could take place without the permission of the Mafouk—the person appointed by the king to oversee commerce. African merchants could not trade directly with ship captains. All negotiations had to be done through brokers who had been appointed by the Mafouk. On the Gold Coast, dynamics were more complex. Ship captains could purchase either directly from the Fanti or from the various governors of the Company of Merchants. Here the British had castles and factories at each fort and would use these to "stockpile" captives. Governors sold captives at a higher price than Fanti merchants did. Because governors had the means to house a large number of captives, they generally had more captives available for sale, which meant ship captains could purchase their captives more quickly and leave the African coast sooner.[65] In so doing, ship captains reduced their overall costs and financial risk. Less time on the coast meant that food costs for captives were lower and reduced the likelihood of high mortality rates among captives.

Regardless of where British slave traders purchased captives, their goal was a speedy voyage. Despite this, there were a number of factors, many out of a ship captain's control, that could lengthen the stay on the African coast. Trade routes to the coast, for example, could be adversely affected by warfare and/or the dry or rainy season. This would make it difficult to get captives to the coast for sale. Moreover, if there were a large number of slave ships at the coast, there would be increased competition for captives, and so the time required to get a full "slave cargo" could be quite lengthy. The experience of a ship captain, his trading relationship with Africans, and the goods he had available for trade were also important in influencing trading time on the coast.[66]

Needless to say, the captive men, women, and children who were marched to the coast did not perceive their enslavement in terms of trading efficiency and cost minimization. For the enslaved, this was a matter of survival. It was a matter of inadequate food and water, of exhausting treks from the inland to the coast, of physical abuses en route, and of being wrenched from a world that was familiar and being plunged into a world unknown and to a fate uncertain. Nor did these captive men, women, and children necessarily understand their predicament in terms of market forces. Many of them had no conception that what pulled them to the coast was a demand for labor on the other side of the Atlantic. For them, other forces were at play. They understood the slave trade as a consequence of war, disorder, and famine. They were unlikely to make Europeans responsible for their enslavement given that Europeans, more often than not, played no role in the actual process of enslavement. They perceived their enslavement more often as, in the words of John Thornton, "a manifestation of local politics—the solution to problems raised by war." From the point of view of captives brought from far inland, who often walked for months to get to the coast, Europeans had limited, if any, role in their enslavement.[67]

Africans did *not* have a single and shared understanding of the slave-trading process. Elite Africans involved in slave trading certainly understood that there were market forces involved and that Europeans arrived on the African coast hoping to buy as many captives as possible. It seems reasonable to assume that many of the elite also knew that captives were being transported across the ocean for their labor. This explains why as early as 1726, King Agaja of Dahomey suggested that the English establish plantations in Africa and that "natives would sell themselves" to labor on these plantations—on the condition that they were not transported across the Atlantic. Moreover, it was not unknown, perhaps not even uncommon, for elite Africans involved in slave trading to be sold into the Atlantic slave trade. Hence, among captives, the slave trade had "multiple meanings," which would result in "multiple responses" to the experience of enslavement. Nor was there any guarantee that captives could communicate and share information among themselves—and so develop a common understanding of the process. Though the range of linguistic differences varied in areas affected by the slave trade, differences in language among captives were certain to hinder communication. Clearly, then, there were stark differences in the levels of understandings among captives. In the words of John Barnes, who was formerly a governor in Senegal, "slaves near the coast . . . know what to expect, but those from the interior are terrified by not knowing the purpose" of the trade. Captives drawn from deep inside the African hinterland commonly believed that whites purchased Africans for the purpose of cannibalism. Mungo Park reported that, upon an encounter with captives who were just about to be transported down the Gambia, he was repeatedly asked whether his "countrymen were cannibals." Apparently, when he tried to explain that Europeans purchased Africans for the purpose of cultivating crops, he was not believed.[68]

Despite such misconceptions, Africans had very clear ideas about domestic slavery. In Africa, slavery was understood to be a legitimate social institution regulated by codes. There were clear rules about who could be legally enslaved. It was considered acceptable to enslave individuals convicted of crimes or the captives of legally sanctioned wars. It was illegal, however, to enslave by means of kidnapping and banditry. Yet illegal slave trading did occur, and African communities developed ways to reduce the risk of enslavement.[69] How individual men, women, and children perceived the legality of their enslavement in Africa, however, was an important factor in shaping their responses and reaction to slavery on the other side of the Atlantic.

4

The Atlantic Crossing

After their capture and trek to the coast, the enslaved were then forcibly transported across the Atlantic to begin what British slave traders referred to as the "middle passage." From the point of view of captives, however, it is doubtful that they understood this voyage as the "middle" of their journey. For the enslaved, being put on board a slave vessel was merely part of a long process of enslavement. It was just another "leg of the traumatic journey" that moved them from their homes in Africa to their destination in Jamaica.[1]

In fact, most of the men, women, and children put on board slave vessels had left their native country, their community, and their families long before they fell into the hands of British sailors. Reporting on slave trade activities in the Gold Coast, one governor noted that captives very likely came from "a very great distance." Fanti slave brokers travelled between 100 and 150 miles to purchase them, and so he surmised that they must have been transported from much farther inland. By this governor's account, these captives spoke different languages and were of a "yellower" color than Africans who resided in the coastal area of the Gold Coast region. In fact, not even the brokers who brought them to the coast had precise knowledge about the circumstances of their enslavement, because they had passed through "so many hands."[2]

Arguably, then, for the enslaved, the "middle passage" began from the moment they were captured and began their trek to the coast—a trek that ranged between months and years. En route, they "learnt new languages, received new names, ate new foods, and forged new bonds." Their personal histories under slavery began long before they ever set sight on Europeans. For captive men, women, and children, the middle passage was not the "first stage of enslavement," nor was it the historical moment when slaves were "produced." For the enslaved, "the business of 'making' slaves" took place on African soil and most probably at a great distance from the Atlantic coast.[3]

Nonetheless, the Atlantic crossing was the portion of the journey that bridged Africa and Jamaica, and the slave ship provided an environment uniquely different from any other to which captives might have been exposed. The ship's role, after all, was multifaceted: it was a means of transport, a tool of war, and a prison. Africans entering this prison were brought on board naked, and rarely, if ever, did they have the opportunity to bring material items with them.[4] Many of them died—without ever knowing where they were going and for what purpose. For the survivors who made it across the Atlantic, the journey was a hellish experience. Many men, women, and children lived to be sold on Jamaican soil. Others arrived in such poor shape that no one was willing to buy them. After being forcibly transported from one side of the Atlantic Ocean to the other, they were left unattended to die from their ailments.

The Voyage of the *African Queen*

In early March 1792, Captain Samuel Stribling arrived at Old Calabar on the slave ship *African Queen*. His intention was to purchase just over four hundred captives and head for Jamaica as quickly as possible. Unfortunately for Stribling, nothing went as planned. The vessel stayed on the African coast for approximately eight months, and within three months, Stribling and nine members of the crew fell ill and were dead. The first mate, Hamet Forsyth, took over command. As it turned out, for all persons linked to the *African Queen*—black and white alike—the circumstances under which this slave-trading venture operated were harsh and tragic.

In early July, after taking up command, Forsyth wrote a letter reporting on events to date. Lacking the "proper assortment of Cloth" for purchasing captives, he was unable to trade for five weeks. Despite this, over the months, 290 captives had been purchased, with 160 being "on trust" and thus were yet to be delivered to the ship. Forsyth saw this as advantageous, as he was "fearfull" [*sic*] of having too many captives on board. The cost of purchasing provisions to feed the enslaved was high, and the "sickly time for the year" was causing "great Mortality dayly" [*sic*] in the region. His concerns were legitimate ones. Already, 41 captives on board the *African Queen* had died. Yet he remained hopeful that he could leave Old Calabar within six weeks.[5] He was overly optimistic. The ship stayed at Old Calabar for at least another four months, by which time Forsyth was dead, and the command of the ship passed on again, this time to John Long. It is unknown how many other captives died during this time. Of those who survived, their suitability for sale was described as "some good & some bad." When the *African Queen* finally departed in November, it left with 330 men, women, and children on board. By the time they arrived at Jamaica about nine weeks later, one-third of them were dead, and the survivors were described as the "very worst that were ever imported" into the island.[6]

The voyage between Old Calabar and Montego Bay, Jamaica, was a horrific experience for the Africans on board. Captives on the *African Queen* were purchased during a period that included the hottest time of year. Even under the best of circumstances, the heat would have been unbearable, as the enslaved were generally kept below the deck, where the temperature was much higher. The situation was made even worse by the region's high humidity.[7] Because the ship spent approximately eight months at Old Calabar, many of the men, women, and children on board were subjected to these harsh conditions for months before the *African Queen* even departed for Jamaica.

For most of the captives, if not all, this was their first experience with sea travel. In all probability, many fell victim to seasickness. For those who did not, the heat, stench, and absence of fresh air in the holds would have led to similar physical reactions, such as vomiting. To further complicate matters, the surgeon on the *African Queen* and at least thirty members of the crew died before the ship anchored on the other side of the Atlantic. The ship was heavily undermanned and had been reduced to about ten persons.[8] This had direct repercussions on the captives.

Sailors on slave ships were required to perform tasks that were not typically associated with seafaring but were necessary for a "successful" voyage across the Atlantic. Some of the more basic, yet crucial, duties included the cleaning and feeding of captives. Without enough sailors to clean away the accumulated feces, blood, and mucus, captives were locked into a space that was a fertile disease environment. They were susceptible to a range of diseases—in particular, gastrointestinal diseases, contemporaneously known as dysentery (or the "bloody flux").[9] Moreover, the poor health and eventual death of the ship's surgeon meant that while facing potentially fatal illnesses, captives had no access to professional medical attention.

The men, women, and children on board were further weakened by a poor distribution of food and water caused by the shortage of sailors. As a result, in addition to poor nutrition, they suffered from extreme dehydration brought about by insufficient water, intense heat, sweating, vomiting, and dysentery. Symptoms included weakness, delirium, cramping of the muscles, loss of appetite, sunken eyes, and apathy. For some, sodium deficiencies may have even caused convulsions or induced coma. Although it was common practice for the enslaved to be periodically brought on deck for fresh air, to exercise, and to escape the intense heat, this depended on good weather, calm seas, and available manpower.[10] Here too, captives on the *African Queen* suffered. With few sailors on board, they would rarely, if at all, be brought on deck for fresh air and exercise.

It was roughly seven weeks before the ship made its first stop at Dominica to purchase "Refreshments" for those held captive. By this time the death count among the Africans on board totalled 78 people. Counted among them were 28 men, 40 women, 8 girls, and 2 boys. Another 38 were dead before the ship arrived at the Jamaican port Montego Bay two weeks later. After about three days and only with significant difficulty, an agreement was struck with two merchants who agreed to jointly arrange for the sale of the "cargo." From the perspective of the captives, it was a hellish period. Provisions were again needed on board the ship, but sea conditions made it impossible for the ship to get to port for some days. Even after the *African Queen* had been anchored, they were made to remain on board until the day of the sale—a full twelve days after the ship arrived at Jamaica. During that time, they were fed, attended to by a doctor, and measured. There is no record of how the captives understood the events taking place, but from the point of view of the merchants, they were being prepared for sale. The hope was that a "good Feeding" and medical attention would be enough to improve the physical condition of the captives—most of whom were described as "very meagre." These efforts proved to be insufficient. Another 11 died before the scheduled sale.[11]

It took three days for the surviving men, women, and children to be sold. Each day of the sale, they were escorted to a room where they were examined by various buyers and witnessed some of the group being taken away. One captive, an adolescent male approximately sixteen years of age, was identified as a pawn. The merchants involved with the sale thought it "advisable not to sell him," and he was eventually put back on the *African Queen* for its return voyage to Bristol. Among those who were not so fortunate, the healthiest were the first to be sold. On the last day of the sale, a group of four speculators purchased 70 of the less desirable captives, at a well-bargained price, with the intention to resell. In total, the surviving 65 men, 74 women, 5 adolescents, and 58 children were sold for just under £7,800. For the owner of the vessel, James Rogers, this was far below his expectations; his initial investment was approximately £10,650. For the Africans put on board this vessel, however, their loss was much greater. The loss in lives, from Africa to Jamaica, was no less than 169—and probably significantly more. Those who lived long enough to be sold totalled 202, and some of them were dead within a month.[12]

Leaving Africa

The captive perspective notwithstanding, the Atlantic crossing was the critical link that connected the slave systems of Africa with those of the Americas. Moreover, the negotiations that took place between African and European slave traders determined the captive experience once they arrived at the coast. For captive and captor alike, the slave-trading process was a slow one. Contemporary reports make clear the frustration of British traders anxious to leave the coast and only hint at the living hell this slow-moving process created for their captives. In 1787, Richard Rogers, a ship captain at Old Calabar, reported that he was trading in "very dead times." Since the arrival of his ship in October, there had been about eight other slave ships at the port—many of which had been there for sixteen months. In just over three weeks, Rogers had purchased only 11 captives. It would take him a full year to leave Old Calabar with 449 captives, only 330 of whom survived the Atlantic crossing. Nor were such circumstances unfamiliar in other slave-trading regions. In March 1784, there were reports from Cape Coast Castle that slave-trading activities in the Gold Coast region were "extremely dull" and that there were ships at Anomabu that had been there for over six months.[13] Unfortunately for the captive men, women, and children made victim of these trading activities, British ships could stay on the African coast anywhere between several weeks to well over a year—with the upper limit being a fairly common occurrence.

When trading for captives, transactions were often small and numerous. In the case of the ship *Dobson*, at Old Calabar in 1769, the ship's captain had to participate in 328 transactions to purchase 566 men, women, and children over a six-month period. Most purchases were between 1 and 3 captives, and the largest transaction was for 6. In the end, he purchased 252 men, 133 women, 96 boys, and 85 girls. The majority of them were on the ship for months before the vessel set sail. The long wait on the coast was a deadly one. Although the ship's captain purchased 566 captives, he left Africa with only 358 on board—almost 40 percent of the survivors were children. Nonetheless, over 200 men, women, and children were dead before the ship began its voyage, and another 68 persons died during the Atlantic crossing. By the time the ship arrived in the Caribbean, there were only 290 of them alive.[14]

There were, of course, times when captives were brought to the coast and there were no slave ships present. Under such circumstances, in the Senegambian region, captives were put to labor in the fields of neighboring villages until ships arrived and negotiations were settled. According to one report, they were kept in chains, scantily fed, and harshly treated. In the Gold Coast, those captives who were "stockpiled" by British-appointed governors were made to stay in the dark, damp "slave holes" of the various castles. Once ships were on the coast, however, captives were prepared for sale. They were cleaned and oiled with the hope of creating a favorable impression with ship captains who closely inspected their body. Those captives who were deemed unfit and could not be sold to British traders were routinely put to death by their African captors. Unfortunately for ship captains, physical inspections did not ensure mental well-being. According to one surgeon involved with the slave trade, he knew of a woman who was "disposed of" the day after she was purchased, because of her "dejected State of mind." Ironically, this woman's condition may have been caused by the very trauma of enslavement—particularly if her trek to the coast was a long and drawn-out experience.[15]

Even after a ship had been "full slaved," there was no guarantee of a speedy departure from the coast. An inadequate food supply was another factor that could influence the length of stay in Africa. In 1774, for example, there were conditions of famine in the Gold Coast. Corn was scarce and expensive. As a result, several ship captains, even after purchasing the number of captives they hoped for, had no choice but to wait on the coast until they could purchase enough provisions to feed the captives throughout the voyage.[16] Conditions of famine, of course, only worsened circumstances for the enslaved.

Because captives were imprisoned on ships long before the ship's departure, and food supplies needed to last for the duration of the voyage across the Atlantic, food and water had to be distributed sparingly. On average, ships heading to the Caribbean took between seven and nine weeks to complete the Atlantic crossing. It was not unknown for voyages, however, to take longer than this. In one extreme case, the slave ship *Sally*, which left the Cameroons with 168 captives, took over six months to cross the Atlantic. Apparently, the ship had been damaged by a ground swell that caused it to hit bottom several times. As a result, throughout the voyage, the rudder no longer worked effectively and the ship was leaking. When the *Sally* arrived in Barbados, only 40 of the captives survived. The other 128 had died of starvation.[17]

Life and Death at Sea

Despite stories such as this, the late eighteenth century is a period marked by relative improvements in the transportation of enslaved Africans. In fact, although British ships carried more captives per ship than did ships of other slave-trading nations, in the final decades of the slave trade their legal carrying capacity was in constant decline because of two legislative acts. In 1788, the Dolben's Act reduced the legal capacity for transporting captives by implementing slave-per-ton ratios. In other words, the overall size of the ship (its tonnage) determined the number of captives that could be legally transported. Eleven years later, the 1799 act was passed. This act demanded that actual below-deck measurements (spatial arrangements) were used to determine how many captives could be transported.[18] In addition, during the eighteenth century, there was a general decline in mortality rates during the Atlantic crossing. Factors such as changes in ship design, financial incentives to captains and ship surgeons, and the implementation of laws that regulated health care, nutrition, and space all played a part in reducing deaths.[19]

Physical death aside, an increasing number of scholars also argue that the middle passage was one aspect of enslavement that contributed to a form of "social death" for captives. Orlando Patterson's work on slavery has led to this notion having much resonance in the scholarship. As Patterson sees it, the enslaved were socially dead, as they had "no social existence" beyond the relationship with their owner and did not belong to a community. Although he recognizes that the enslaved had "informal social relationships" among themselves, he maintains that because these relations were never legitimated and had "no social support," the enslaved were rendered "socially dead." Despite strong, well-grounded critiques of Patterson's work by Sidney Mintz and others, the idea of social death continues to influence writings on the middle passage and slavery more generally.[20]

As a concept, "social death" is not without its limitations. Although it makes clear that enslavers gave no legal recognition to the "informal" social relations of the enslaved, it does not adequately consider the ways in which captives' perception may have shaped their behavior and hence their experiences. In Africa, after all, slave trading and slavery were socially accepted institutions as long as they operated within expected legalities. In other words, African men, women, and children had their own notions about the legality of their enslavement, and their perspectives were completely independent of how Europeans legally defined slavery. More to the point, if captive Africans did not accept their enslavement as legal, it is doubtful that they perceived themselves as "socially dead" during the middle passage or at any other moment during their enslavement.

This is not an insignificant point. The ways in which African men, women, and children perceived their lives in captivity served to guide their responses and reactions to enslavement. It seems unlikely that people who understood themselves to be "socially dead" would make any effort to mount acts of resistance to their enslavement—and there is an abundance of evidence that Africans rejected their captivity. In fact, Eric Taylor's study makes clear that historians have grossly underestimated the number of shipboard insurrections that did take place. His work shows that, given the right circumstances, Africans readily planned and executed insurrections in an effort to regain their freedom. Sometimes there could be even more than one insurrection on a single voyage.[21]

Ship captains, of course, were acutely aware that captives had no reservations about mounting an insurrection if an opportunity presented itself. For this reason, they not only restrained captives and limited their movement but also used psychological terror to keep them at bay. After one failed attempt at a shipboard insurrection, for example, at least two captives involved with the uprising were killed. Their heads were then cut off while the rest of the enslaved watched. But in the mind of the ship captain, this was not enough. His goal was to terrorize the surviving captives into submission, and he was prepared to do this using either physical force or ceremony. With the latter in mind, one of the severed heads was passed on to the enslaved, who were told to kiss its lips. Those who refused were flogged and the bloody part of the head was rubbed against their faces.[22]

Captives sometimes witnessed and experienced even worse atrocities. The popularized story of the 132 captives who were thrown overboard alive by the captain of the *Zong*, as they were being transported to Jamaica in 1781, is an obvious example. The reason for such cruelty, according to statements made in court, was survival. The eleven-week voyage across the Atlantic left the *Zong* with inadequate food and water on board, and so a calculated decision was made to throw some captives overboard in a bid to save the rest. Although slave-trading merchants got no insurance coverage for captives who died a "natural death" during the voyage, they could get compensated if a ship captain "jettisoned" some of the men, women, and children in order to save the others. From the point of view of the ship's owners, this was cost-effective. From the point of view of captives, the very act was incomprehensible. What possible conclusions could Africans draw about Europeans who bartered for them on the African coast, transported them under the worst of conditions for weeks, and then randomly selected one-third of them to be thrown overboard?[23] Those who died no doubt went into the water horrified and confused. Those who survived must have been overwhelmed with despair and desperately trying to make sense of the insensible.

Yet despite such incidences, even at this stage it is unclear whether captives understood their enslavement from a purely racialized point of view. Their own experiences made it apparent that the first few legs of the enslavement process were controlled by other Africans. Not only did they make their trek to the coast under the watchful eyes of African captors, but they had no illusions about the crucial roles other Africans played in making the slave trade possible. They saw Africans involved in a number of ancillary industries linked to the slave trade. There was, after all, food and water that needed to be supplied to slave ships. There were also African porters and canoe men who benefited from the slave trade. Even on slave vessels, there were sometimes Africans who were employed as sailors, cooks, or translators, as well as in other positions. In fact, there are several records of free Africans on board slaving vessels exposing the planned insurrections of captives.[24]

Although the evidence for captives developing a "black consciousness" during the Atlantic crossing is a point for debate, there is no doubt that they all bonded over the shared experience of victimhood. Captives were not merely confined, poorly fed, and surrounded by death but were in a harsh and unfamiliar environment with many questions and few answers about their future. The sharing of this physically and emotionally horrific experience explains why, once captives arrived in Jamaica, they often established fictive relationships with others who made the Atlantic crossing on the same ship.[25]

But how captives were treated on board slave vessels varied by sex and age. Adult males were kept under particularly harsh circumstances. They were kept in shackles, at both the wrists and ankles, and were separated from the women and children. Women and girls were generally left unrestrained in a separate space, but their conditions were also quite harsh and horrendous. For reasons that are unclear, young boys were kept separately from all others. Of course, conditions did vary between ships depending on their relative size, space constraints, and the inclination of ship captains. John Riland, who travelled as a passenger on a slave ship headed to Jamaica, reported that of the 240 captives purchased, 25 African girls slept below his cot and that of the captain. The boys, 29 in number, slept below the cots of the ship's surgeon and first mate.[26]

Sometimes, young boys were even left to wander about the decks. Yet despite their relative freedom, the experience of enslavement had already begun to leave its mark on their young minds. According to Thomas Trotter, a surgeon employed in the slave trade, on one voyage across the Atlantic, he observed young boys playing a game called "slave taking." During the game, the boys mimicked all the actions involved in a slave raid. Another ship surgeon noted that it was not unusual for young boys to "insult the [chained] men," as the boys knew that the men were immobile and could not pursue them. Sometimes these juvenile taunts had serious ramifications. On one particular occasion, there was a young boy who was free to roam the ship and so entertained himself by "tormenting one of the men." Unfortunately, he was not quick enough to escape the grasp of the adult male he had been teasing. The boy was caught and then pinched hard enough so that he cried out painfully. His cry alerted the captain to the encounter; the captain's response was to tie and flog the adult male guilty of inflicting the pinch. At other times, however, the mobility of young boys also benefited other captives. In fact, they were known to carry messages between men and women who, because they were kept apart, had little if any opportunity to communicate throughout the voyage.[27]

Sexual exploitation was a reality for not only women but also children of both sexes. Although there is much evidence of women and girls being exploited, the historical record is quite silent on the exploitation of young boys. That said, acts of sodomy were certainly part of maritime culture. B. R. Burg's study makes clear that crew members in the British navy, for example, were known to have sex with young boys employed on ships. It seems reasonable to assume that individual sailors on slave ships were also capable of such actions if they had the inclination and the opportunity to participate in sexual activities with enslaved African boys.[28]

For those captives who did not overtly resist the sexual advances of the ship captain and other members of the crew, performing sexual favors could result in being given special privileges. However, this was no guarantee of good treatment. One young girl was known as the "favorite mistress" of Captain Joseph Williams. Her favored status meant that she could stay in Williams's cabin and had relative freedom on the ship. She was still a child, however, and found ways to play when Williams did not insist on her company. One of her playmates included the captain's son, who was also on the ship. One day while they played together, she accidentally tore his shirt. Her favored status, which lasted for several months, was not enough to protect her. She was beaten by Williams "unmercifully with his fist" for her transgression. The encounter was so violent that she had injuries to her head. Of course, adult females were also subjected to the sexual advances of the ship captain and others employed on the vessel. Those who resisted such advances were often punished with physical force.[29]

Despite such common themes in the middle passage experience, the specific circumstances of individual voyages are ultimately what shaped experiences and determined the rate of survival among captives. In mid-June 1793, the slave ship *Jupiter* arrived on the north coast of Jamaica, at Martha Brae, with 359 captives on board. The voyage from Bonny took thirty-seven days. It was a relatively short Atlantic crossing. But for some on board, the ship had been their prison for much longer. It took four months for the ship's captain, John Goodrich, to purchase his "cargo." After three months, he reported having "130 Young and Healthy negroes" on board his ship. Before even being sold to Goodrich, however, most of these captives were quite likely held captive by other Africans for months, as trading at Bonny had been slow owing to "the death of two of their kings." By the time the *Jupiter* left the coast, Goodrich had paid for 392 captives—11 of whom died before the ship departed. Although he seemed fairly optimistic about their health and condition, another 22 died during the voyage and 17 more died after the ship arrived at Jamaica. There are no details in Goodrich's letters about the conditions during the middle passage, but evidence does suggest that the time on board the ship was a physically trying one. Not only did 50 (13 percent) of the captives purchased die, but 100 (29 percent) of the survivors had to be sold as "Refuse" at a much reduced price.[30] Among the survivors were 110 men, 88 women, 29 men/boys, 32 women/girls, 33 boys, and 50 girls. There was also a male infant "at the breast" who was sold for £10. Adult males accounted for only 32 percent of those held captive.

Yet the circumstances of the *Jupiter* pale in comparison to the experience of the captives who made the journey across the Atlantic on board the ship *Pearl*. In addition to the approximately 300 captives who died before the ship even left Old Calabar in mid-January 1791, another 119 men, women, and children lost their lives during the nine-week voyage to Jamaica. The voyage was a horrendous experience. Captives were grossly underfed, and the very quality of the food they were given was called into question by the ship's surgeon. To make matters worse, the ship was in a state of disrepair. Although the ship's captain argued otherwise, it is difficult to believe that the high mortality was not partly caused by the "Leakness [sic] or Other Bad Quality" of the vessel. Damp conditions not only increased the heat and stuffiness below decks but also contributed to poor health and increased mortality. By the time the ship anchored in Kingston, there were 356 captives still alive. They were described by the Jamaican merchant Alexander Lindo as being of a "very inferior quality," with many "aged and inferior" captives. Not surprisingly, 29 captives died before they could be sold. One report suggests that the increased mortality and weakened state of the captives were caused by the spread of "the flux." The last 37 captives to be sold were in such a poor physical state that they were purchased at a much-reduced price at a vendue sale.[31]

The physical trauma of the voyage had such an effect on the well-being of captives that high mortality rates and poor health were common features of the voyage. Captives who landed in Jamaica were stricken by a range of ailments including malaria, smallpox, yellow fever, dysentery, ophthalmia (often causing blindness), measles, hookworm, and tapeworm. They were also likely to have sores, injuries, and wounds. On average, about 5 percent of the captives who survived the Atlantic crossing died before they could be sold in Jamaica. Death was so pervasive that slave ships were reportedly followed by large numbers of sharks that fed on the dead bodies thrown overboard. In fact, as one printed announcement in 1785 makes clear, the link between sharks, slave ships, and slave death was clear in the mind of Jamaican residents. Posted in the local newspapers, the announcement advised Kingston residents that "bathing in the river" was dangerous, as "a number of overgrown sharks" had followed the recently arrived slave ships to the island's shores.[32]

Yet the instinct to survive stayed with the enslaved to the very end. At least, this was the situation with the four hundred captives who were being taken to Jamaica for sale in the 1770s. En route to its destination, one night the ship entered shallow water and was grounded at Morant Keys, an area that was relatively close to the eastern end of Jamaica. The ship's crew abandoned the vessel and headed toward one of the small islands in the area. By morning, however, the captives on board had managed to free themselves from their shackles; they escaped the lower decks and began making their way to shore. Women and children were put on makeshift rafts while the men worked at guiding the rafts to land. Unfortunately, their efforts were in vain. The ship's crew, no doubt alarmed at the possibility of hundreds of their former prisoners descending upon the island, fired at them before they could make it to shore. In the end, only about thirty-four of them survived, and they were eventually sold in Kingston.[33]

Sale in Jamaica

Once the horrors of the voyage were behind them, men, women, and children on board slave ships faced a new round of challenges when vessels arrived at Jamaica. Once the ships were anchored and negotiations made between the ship captain and local merchant, advertisements were posted announcing the upcoming sale of the captive men, women, and children. The advertisements reflected the purchasing priorities of Jamaican buyers. They gave no specific information about the sex of the captives, though they gave brief descriptions of other criteria used to gauge the captives' perceived "quality." Sales notices generally gave information about the physical condition, youthfulness, and perceived ethnicity of the men, women, and children. There seems to have been a fair amount of false advertising: captives were virtually always described as "prime" or "young choice slaves" regardless of their actual condition. Ethnic labels were also readily applied. A typical sale announcement of the time advertised the arrival of "two hundred and sixty, choice Coromantee, Fantee, Ashantee, and Aikim Slaves." Similarly, another merchant company promoted the sale of "509 choice young QUAW, EBO, and CHAMBA Negroes."[34]

As was the case on the coast of Africa, the intent was to sell captives as quickly as possible, so that the financial burden of any further deaths and the cost of feeding captives would be assumed by the individuals who purchased them. But the harsh conditions of the voyage typically meant that it took up to two weeks for captives to be made ready for sale. During this time, they were cleaned, fed, and tended to by a surgeon. Moreover, even if a speedy sale was desirable, it was not always possible. On July 29, 1781, the merchant house Mures & Dunlop had to advertise the sale of "416 prime Gold-Coast SLAVES" a second time. Apparently, the sale was to have taken place two weeks earlier but had to be postponed, as there were too few purchasers "on account of . . . the scarcity of provisions."[35] Few people saw the wisdom in purchasing captives if there was no means to feed them.

From the captives' point of view, they were yet again made to undergo the experience of their own sale. This was not the first time they had been sold, nor was it likely the second time. After their initial capture in Africa, most of these captives had been sold and resold several times before making it to Jamaica. The very few men, women, and children who were fortunate enough to have been put on the same ship with family members or friends in Africa now faced, yet again, the possibility of separation.[36]

There were a number of ways in which sales were conducted. Up until 1784, captives could be legally sold by "scramble" on board ships. If the sale was to be conducted in this way, the captive men, women, and children available were all placed in one common area. Then all interested purchasers would, at the same time and upon a specific signal, rush toward the captives, laying claim to those they wanted. For the captives, this unanticipated and sudden "scramble" by the purchasers was no doubt another terrifying act in the long, horrid enslavement process. Contemporary observers often commented on the effect it had on the captives, who would "[cry] out for their friends" and try to cling to each other as they were being separated. In fact, it was after thirty captives jumped overboard in an effort to escape purchasers that sale by scramble on board ships was made illegal. It did, however, continue to take place on land.[37]

But not all sales took place by scramble. Sometimes private deals were struck with favored customers, who were allowed to select captives before the sale was open to the public. In fact, captives purchased at full price by wealthy planters were sometimes returned if they were discovered to be in less than an acceptable condition. In order to gain an advantage once the sale was open to the public, merchants were very strategic in determining the conditions under which the sale took place. They were known, for example, to hold sales in dark and crowded rooms, so that purchasers could not properly inspect the men, women, and children they hoped to buy. Those captives who were in a particularly poor physical condition, and so were not sold early on, were sometimes purchased "in bulk" by speculators who hoped to make a profit in their resale. Alternatively, they were sold as "refuse slaves" at a "vendue" auction. When there were no such purchasers, the remaining men, women, and children were sold, one or two at a time, to the less wealthy and perhaps even free people of color. Such was the case of a mulatto woman who purchased a captive "apparently dying of the flux" for "the small sum of one dollar." It will never be known whether this woman bought the captive out of pity or because she understood it as a risky but affordable opportunity to purchase a slave. Nor will it be known whether this captive lived long after the purchase. What is clear, however, is that some captives arrived on the shores of Jamaica in such a poor state that they could be sold for an insignificant sum.[38]

And as if that were not bad enough, in a cruel and ironic twist of fate, some men, women, and children were quite simply left to die. After being sold repeatedly, made to travel for months from deep in the African hinterland, and transported across the Atlantic for weeks, a captive was sometimes considered worth more dead than alive. One young boy, about ten years of age, was so weak and thin after the Atlantic crossing that it was decided he would not be put up for sale. Given his condition, the fear was that he would sell for so low a price that it would reduce the average sale price for the entire "cargo" of men, women, and children. If he was dead, however, he would not have to be included in the calculations. Ship officers often had a personal interest in keeping the average price high, as their compensation packages were sometimes linked to the profitability of the voyage. Hence, a decision was made to leave the young boy on the ship without any food and water so that he would languish to death. Although some felt pity on him and secretly gave him food and drink, he died after nine days.[39]

Once captives were purchased, they were taken to what would be their new homes. While in Jamaica, Maria Nugent, wife to the island's governor in the early nineteenth century, observed "a gang of Eboe negroes, just landed, and marching up the country" and reported that they did not seem "unhappy." In fact, she noted that "the women, in particular, seemed pleased . . . they were all dressed in new clothes, and the women had their colored petticoats around their waist like aprons."[40] Such a description seems highly suspect. It is probably more likely that for the captives, this trek through Jamaica reminded them of months earlier, when they had been forced to march toward the African coast. No doubt, they arrived at the plantations and pens (or other circumstances) exhausted and in poor health. Their insertion into Jamaican slave society was a lonely one, and they struggled to make sense of this new context. Their ability to adapt to this new environment depended on their place and station in Africa, their age and sex, and the specific situation into which they were now put.

5

African Expectations, Jamaican Realities

Although enslaved Africans brought to Jamaica were placed into a society organized primarily along racial lines, the social and cultural dynamics of the enslaved were grounded in dynamics far more complex. Jamaican slave society comprised not only Africans, who were divided by ethnicity, but also creoles, who were divided by color. To further complicate the matter, the enslaved in Jamaica also included persons born in other parts of the Americas. For example, in 1781 (notably, several years before the Haitian Revolution), there was an advertisement in the *Royal Gazette* announcing the escape of John Baptist, who was a "creole of Hispaniola" who spoke "the French Language well." In the same year, there was another advertisement placed in the hope of locating two Spanish-speaking runaways named Frank and Moriano. Other runaway advertisements make reference to Joe, who was "a Creole from Barbados"; Leven Morris, who was born in Virginia but purchased in New York; and Phurah, who was "Born in Trenton" but dressed "in the style of English servants." Despite the effects of the American Revolution and the ways in which it might have "isolated" Jamaica, intra-American migration among blacks clearly continued.[1]

The world into which enslaved Africans were inserted, then, was a socially and culturally complex one. Once African men, women, and children brought to the island were sold off by merchants, their new owners had a clear understanding of the type of efforts that were required as they attempted to turn the enslaved into productive and efficient units of labor. How the recently arrived enslaved understood their predicament, however, was another matter.

Although largely discredited in the scholarship, the reports of contemporary observers often suggest that African attitudes toward enslavement varied, depending on where in Africa they were from, and was determined by their cultural predisposition. Bryan Edwards, the eighteenth-century historian of the West Indies, maintained that Africans from the Gold Coast were more "bloody and cruel than [persons from] any nation that ever existed" and that they brought "contempt of death" and "indifference about life" to the West Indies. He further reported, however, that if "they fell into good hands" they could gradually be resocialized to accept life under slavery in Jamaica. This is in contrast to the enslaved taken from the Slave Coast—in particular, from "Whidah" or "Fida" (or Ouidah, which is the French orthography). Known in the West Indies as "Papaws," these Africans were perceived as "the most docile and best-disposed slaves." The "Eboes," in contrast, had a "timid and desponding temper." As Edwards explains it, an act of punishment that would lead the "Kormantyn" of the Gold Coast to rebel and drive the "Ebo" of the Bight of Biafra to suicide was received by the Papaws with no opposition, as they believed it to be the "chastisement of legal authority" and for that reason would "submit patiently."[2]

Historians have long seen past such contemporary stereotyping about Africans. Instead, they have looked to historical specificities in Africa to explain the behavior of captives on the other side of the Atlantic. Paul Lovejoy and David Trotman, in particular, have taken the analysis to another level. In their study, they argue that in order to see Africans as "wholly human," historians must recognize that they were first and foremost individuals with "peculiar histories" that resulted in their enslavement. In other words, *individual* Africans crossed the Atlantic with their "own attitudes, ideas, beliefs and expectations," and they used their previous experiences to interpret and make sense of their situation in Jamaica. Most Africans had been exposed to slavery in some way prior to their arrival in Jamaica. Those individuals who were transported to the island represented a cross section of Africans who played different roles in the arena of slavery. Among them were those who owned slaves, those who traded in slaves, those who were captured and enslaved, those who were born into African slavery, and those who sold themselves into slavery during times of economic hardship. Those persons who did not fall into any of these categories certainly would have known others who did. Slavery was interwoven into the social fabric of African life. As a social institution, it offended the sensibilities of few Africans. Of course, this in no way means that African men, women, and children embraced their enslavement. It does mean, however, that captives relied on their individual experiences with African slavery to interpret and make sense of Jamaican slavery.[3] The realities of Jamaican slavery and the racist ideology that was used to give it legitimacy made little sense to newly arrived Africans. But leaving aside those Africans who rejected slavery as an institution outright, as there is little evidence to suggest they did so in resounding numbers, captives took issue with Jamaican slavery on one or more levels. Their actions in Jamaica might be interpreted as reactions to what they saw as the illegitimacy of the institution of slavery *in its Jamaican form*, their own personal enslavement, or the terms under which they were expected to slave. Ultimately, their personal histories informed their thinking as they maneuvered the chasm between the reality of Jamaican slave life and their own notions about slavery, enslavement, and social obligations.

Badge of the Slave

There can be little doubt that the newly arrived were not only perceived by the Jamaican enslaved as "outsiders" but also perceived themselves as socially and culturally alien to Jamaican slave society. Most of them would have been easily distinguishable from other enslaved on the island. For many, there were physical differences that set them apart. Some Africans might be distinguished from the Jamaican born by their hairstyles, as it was reported that they "prefer[red] plaiting their hair . . . or at other times shaving their heads in stripes."[4] Language, pronunciation, and accent also set enslaved Africans apart from those born on the island. In some parts of Africa, ritual scarification, tattooing, and teeth filing were quite common. As a result, many of the men, women, and adolescents brought to the island often had filed teeth and very obvious scars (or what was often referred to, in Jamaica, as "country marks") on various parts of their bodies.

The historical scholarship on African body aesthetics is relatively undeveloped. Anthropological work has shown, however, that African tattoo and scarification patterns and meanings have changed over time. Contemporary European observers generally misunderstood African body markings to be signifiers that indicated a person's membership in a particular "tribal" or ethnic group. In fact, scarification was not a common mark shared within an ethnic group. It is perhaps best thought of as a sign of status and rank within certain ethnic groups. This was certainly the case for certain segments of the Igbo, a group that was transported in significant numbers to Jamaica. Moreover, not all ethnic groups used body markings as a signifier of status. Many ethnic groups in West Central Africa, another significant area of provenance for the enslaved in Jamaica, did not practice body scarification—nor did Muslims who had become enslaved.[5]

Nonetheless, ritual scarification was one of the more frequently commented-on differences between Africans and the locally born enslaved population. Scars varied from person to person and were sometimes quite extensive. One newly arrived, but also recently escaped, African was described as having country marks over "his right breast . . . [and] upper part of his right arm," as well as having a scar "extending from the ear to the angle of the eye" on each side of his head. Other African escapees were described as having "three cuts on each Temple," a "country mark over his naval," and "country marks on his face." Women and young adolescents also had these ritual scars. Maria, a "stout wench" with a "very yellow complexion," had country marks on "both sides of her face." Similarly, a "Congo Negro Boy" named Fortune who was estimated to be as young as thirteen was reported to have country marks. Descriptions of escaped Africans also included references to teeth filing, as with the case of Mary, "a New Negro Wench" from the "Mundingo Country," who reportedly had "full Breasts, small Eyes," and filed teeth.[6]

In Jamaica, enslaved Africans quite often showed their scarified bodies as evidence of their high social standing in Africa. Such was the case of Esther who was "born in the Ebo country." She was reportedly the daughter of a man who "possessed many slaves" and had "a plantation of corn, yams, and tobacco." According to Esther, her grandmother's village, which was "one day's journey" from the coast, was attacked while she was there on a visit. She and all the other women (and conceivably the children) were sent into "the woods" as the warring party descended on the community. Unfortunately, they were discovered. Those who resisted and the elderly, which included her grandmother, were put to death. Within three days, she was sold and put on a ship headed for Jamaica. As Esther saw it, her many "marks about the chest" were proof of her free birth. Esther's case was not unique. It was common for newly arrived Africans to display their marks as "testimonies of distinction in Africa," an indication of free birth, and "honourable parentage."[7] The fact that enslaved Africans clung tightly to their African sense of self is further evidence that they did not perceive their experience as one of "social death."[8]

There is little evidence to suggest that the ritual of scarification was passed on to enslaved children born in Jamaica. Although scarification was a symbol of status in Africa, the men and women who underwent the procedure found that these physical markings not only had little currency in Jamaican slave society but could actually be detrimental to an enslaved person's survival. There were very practical reasons for not passing this tradition on to progeny. Scarification made it far more difficult for the African born, who bore such scars, to blend into the background—even though they were on an island that was demographically dominated by enslaved blacks. The most colorful descriptions of Africans were in runaway advertisements, which often listed distinguishing physical markers of the enslaved. Scars were a form of identification, and it did not take Africans long to understand that, in this new context, anonymity was a desirable condition and often worked in favor of the enslaved—particularly for those who hoped to take their chances at escape. Ritual scarification was one of the African traditions quickly abandoned in Jamaica.[9]

Captive Africans brought to Jamaica were also subjected to another and very different type of scarring process: branding. The decision to brand the enslaved was made according to the discretion of individual owners. For this reason, when, where, and why the enslaved would be branded varied. The enslaved who were unfortunate enough to be branded, however, were generally subjected to the procedure soon after their arrival. For whites, branding the enslaved was a means to indicate the ownership of their "property." For this reason, the recently arrived were branded with the initials of their new owners. The procedure itself was brief but painful. The "marking irons," which were shaped in the desired letters, were placed over a flame of burning alcohol and when hot enough placed on the skin. With time, some of the enslaved might even have two different brand marks. "Philip, of the Mundingo country," for example, had been branded with the initials "JG" on one shoulder and "GMI" on the other. The different brand marks reflected a change in the legal ownership of Philip from John Grant the coppersmith to George McIntosh the mason. Nor was branding restricted to men. Women and children were also branded. This was certainly the case of Amba, a "lusty middle-aged" woman "of the Coromantee country" who had been branded with the letters "PH." Similarly, Romeo, a young boy "of the Mocco country" who was estimated to be about twelve years of age, had been branded with a different letter on each shoulder: the letter "W" on the left shoulder and "A" on the right, the initials of his legal owner, William Armstrong. Billey, who was "a [Coromantee] negro boy" about "4 feet 4 inches" tall, had been marked with the letters "ME" on each shoulder.[10]

Typically, brand marks were on one or both shoulders, but captives might also be branded on other parts of their body. One runaway, named

Tom Dickson, was described as having "an impediment in his speech" because he was missing his front teeth "owing to a shot in his mouth" and being marked "R x F" on his back, shoulders, and breast. Another runaway, named Jamaica, was described as "a Negro Man of the Mungola country" who had been branded on his cheeks. Branding on the cheeks, forehead, and other easily visible parts of the body was often used as a form of punishment. Branding was performed not only to demonstrate slave ownership but also as a form of body mutilation. Thomas Thistlewood, for example, had no qualms about branding the enslaved when they did not live up to his expectations. Lincoln, who was later to become one of Thistlewood's most favored among the enslaved, had been branded on each cheek, as punishment, two and a half years after he was brought to the island.[11]

Although those with legal ownership of the enslaved had practical reasons for branding (that is, proof of ownership and punishment), for the enslaved it had another meaning. Arguably, enslaved men, women, and children perceived brand marks as a signifier of their imposed social status. Branding was a procedure that many, among the African and Jamaican born alike, had to undergo. Brand marks were a clear indication of slave status—a social status that, unlike the scarification of Africa, was not determined by place of birth, ethnic background, social status, sex, or age. Brand marks were, quite simply, the badge of the slave.

As a result, alliances were formed that transcended the social and cultural diversity among the enslaved. A case in point was the escape of two enslaved young men legally owned by James Robertson of Savanna La Mar. According to Robertson, both of the escapees were about eighteen or nineteen years of age and had been branded with the letters "J.R." The similarity would end there, however, as one of the young men was a mulatto named Jack and the other was originally from North America.[12] Neither the color hierarchy of Jamaican slave society nor any differences in cultural orientation prevented this enslaved mulatto and black North American from escaping together. Their common slave status was symbolized in the common brand mark they shared.

As enslaved Africans were branded with this "badge of the slave," they had little choice but to recognize (though not necessarily accept) that another human being had legal rights to their bodies. Branding made it clear that in taking possession of African bodies, their captors owned the enslaved so completely that they were even given the right to mutilate the bodies of the enslaved if they so desired. Brand marks would serve as a reminder to captive Africans that they had been inserted and integrated into a caste system that gave no regard to their personal histories in Africa and no acknowledgment of it. Long after they had been branded, the mark served to remind them that in Jamaican slave society, their earlier life in Africa meant nothing. The act of branding symbolized an attempt to erase their personal histories.

That said, being branded made Africans no more willing to accept their Jamaican slave status. In fact, it was common for them to go through the painful process of removing their brand marks. On July 17, 1779, W. Bailey of Kingston reported that Cato, his "New Negro Man" of the "Mundingo Country," had escaped. Cato had been branded on his right shoulder with the initials "W.B." Approximately one month later, Cato's luck had run out, and he was "taken up" by J. Donaldson of Blue Mountain Valley. Upon his capture, Cato reported that he was a fisherman who "went away" only after his master, who was named Mesquita, died of the smallpox. Just as interesting as Cato's fabrication about his escape is that in just a few weeks after his capture, Donaldson was unsure of his brand mark. Donaldson described it as "an indistinct Mark" that looked like "W.P." It is noteworthy that although Africans were willing to remove their brand marks to gain anonymity, there is no evidence to suggest that they did the same for their "country marks." In a 1781 runaway advertisement reporting the escape of Partenia, an "old negro woman" originally from "Congo country," she was described as having country marks on her face, arms, and breast and an "almost obliterated" brand mark on her right shoulder.[13]

"A World of Bad Spirits"

For those African victims caught in the web of the Atlantic slave trade, the world of European slave traders and slave owners was a world of the unknown. Folk beliefs used to explain "the insatiable appetite of the Atlantic slave trade" included stories of cannibalism and witchcraft. Such ideas spanned the slave-trading regions of both West Africa and West Central Africa. Initially, accusations of cannibalism and witchcraft, which tended to be linked to slave-trading dynamics, were grounded in interethnic African animosities. The Aro, the major slave traders in the Biafran region in the late eighteenth century, for example, had agreements with diverse groups that made captives available, provided trade goods for their allies, and enabled friendly groups to attack enemies and eliminate troublemakers. These allies of the Aro Chukwu were made to believe that persons who were disobedient were sent to the Aro Oracle, who was reputed to eat slaves. In fact, the Aro Chukwu sold such persons into the Atlantic slave trade.[14]

As inland Africans came into contact with Europeans on the coast and during the Atlantic crossing, however, these notions of cannibalism and witchcraft were extended to include European slave traders and continued to circulate among the newly arrived in the Americas. This was certainly the case of a young Asante man named Sang, who reported that when he was first sold to whites, he was "much frightened," as he "thought he was to be eaten." Thomas King, who sailed to Africa several times in the late eighteenth century, testified that the enslaved were on board for some time before they believed that they had been purchased for labor and not food. According to Olaudah Equiano, when he was first brought on board a slave ship for sale, he was convinced that he had entered "into a world of bad spirits" and that he was going to be killed. During the Atlantic crossing, in which he was brought to the West Indies, the "dread" of being eaten by whites was ever-present. Even when the ship anchored, the enslaved on the vessel continued to believe that they would be eaten once they were taken on land. Equiano reported that it was not until some "old slaves," no doubt African born, were brought on board to pacify them was it understood that they were brought to labor and not to be eaten.[15]

African suspicion about European sailors' willingness to eat other human beings was not as far-fetched as it might initially seem. It certainly was within the realm of possibility. In the maritime world, under certain circumstances "survival cannibalism" was socially accepted and seen as the "custom of the sea." In cases of shipwreck, surviving crew members were known to eat the corpses of those who died, or they might opt to kill one or more of the survivors for nourishment. Stories of such tales were well known in Britain, and there were even ballads in circulation addressing the subject. In fact, it was not until 1884, after three crew members on the yacht *Mignonette* were arrested after being stranded at sea, that survival cannibalism was condemned by British law.[16]

There are even recorded instances of such events taking place on slave ships. In 1735, after purchasing slaves in West Africa, the slave ship *Mary* began to take on water near the Canary Islands. In an effort to save the vessel and reduce the water intake, the captives on board were put to man the pumps. Eight members of the crew believed the situation hopeless and escaped by getting into the ship's boat. They abandoned the captives as well as fifteen other members of the crew. The survivors were a mixed group: four men were from Britain; two from Portugal; one from Ireland; and another from Rhode Island. As they made their way across the Atlantic to Barbados, their hunger became "intolerable," and they began the gruesome activity of killing their "Companions to eat." The Portuguese were the first to be killed. By the time they arrived at Barbados in January 1736, there were only two survivors left.[17]

But one of the more popularized stories of a ship's crew actually eating an African captive occurred on the ship *Peggy* in 1765.[18] In July of that year, the ship left New York with a variety of trade goods, which were to be sold in the Azores. On board was also a captive named Wiltshire. The ship's captain, David Harrison, intended to sell Wiltshire once they arrived in the Azores. By early October, the *Peggy* had arrived at its intended destination, and within a few weeks trading activities were complete: the goods had been sold, and the ship was stocked with "wine, brandy, etc." that could be sold in New York. Apparently, there were no interested purchasers for Wiltshire in the Azores, and so he was put on the ship for the return voyage across the Atlantic. The ship sailed on October 24 but shortly thereafter was affected by bad weather. The *Peggy* was adrift for about two months, during which time the crew were put on strict rations. Eventually, when desperation hit, the ship's dog and cat were killed. In mid-January, a decision was made to "draw lots." The "custom of the sea" was that the person who drew the shortest lot was to be killed so that his body could be used for nourishment by the others. Under very suspicious circumstances, the lot had been drawn to the misfortune of the only enslaved African on board—Wiltshire. He attempted to escape but was eventually shot. His body was used as food "with the utmost economy" for ten days. Lots were then again drawn. However, the *Peggy*'s crew was rescued before they killed the next person.[19]

Although such cases were few, it took some captive Africans a fair amount of time to realize that whites were not interested in eating African flesh. Even the process of being sold in Jamaica may have reinforced their fears of being eaten. This was sometimes the case of those captives unfortunate enough to be sold by "scramble" (see chapter 4). In sales organized under these circumstances, the crowd of purchasers rushing toward newly arrived African men, women, and children left them with a notion that "they were [being] seized on by a herd of cannibals" and were to be "speedily devoured." The same fears were present in the case of a "Mundingo" called Boatswain who was brought to Jamaica on a slave ship in 1781. All of the captives on the vessel had been sold except for Boatswain and another captive, who were to be taken by the ship's captain to England. Boatswain, however, decided to make his escape as his "countrymen" advised him that he would be eaten if he again went "on the salt water."[20]

"To work as a slave for whites"

Once the "full weight" of slavery in Jamaica had been felt, however, the enslaved abandoned notions of cannibalism and witchcraft. It did not take long for newly arrived Africans to reassess their situation. Despite the differences in their background, *all* of the enslaved brought to the island had an understanding of African slavery that was in sharp contrast to the racialized slave system of Jamaica. Mark Cook, a late-eighteenth-century resident of Jamaica, claimed that he heard Africans "express much grief at leaving [their country]" and that he "never" knew of an African who did not wish to return.[21] Such sentiments are not only an indication of the longing that enslaved Africans felt for their homes and families but also reflect the disjuncture between the social and cultural realms of Africa and Jamaica. Even those persons who lived their lives under slave status in Africa before being sold into the trans-Atlantic slave trade had very specific notions about the social obligations and expectations of a master-slave relationship. Such notions, of course, were at odds with the realities of Jamaica's racialized slave system. How African men, women, and children perceived their encounter with the Jamaican slave labor system and how they chose to deal with these violations of their sensibilities covered a spectrum of reactions and responses—all of which were informed by their personal histories.

Take the case of the above-mentioned Sang, who, upon his arrival in Jamaica, was renamed Oliver. Sang was captured in the Asante region when his village was attacked at night and set on fire by the Fanti (a rival ethnic group). Many of the villagers, particularly the old, were killed with guns and cutlasses. The young people were taken, and he and two others were sold to "a Black merchant" who carried them into Fanti territory. Sang was bought and sold by six different black traders before his arrival at the coast. This was despite the fact that by Sang's own account, his father was a carpenter and free man. The experience of Quaw and Quamina, in contrast, was quite different. These two brothers (who were approximately twenty and eighteen years of age, respectively) were brought to the island from the Gold Coast. As these young men reported the story, they were born slaves to a man named Banafou and were sold into the trans-Atlantic slave trade as punishment after being accused of "misconduct." They maintained, however, that the accusations were falsely made, and in reality their master used this as an excuse so that he could sell them in order to pay his debts. As they saw it, people with slave status in Africa were commonly sold by their owners without being guilty of a crime.[22]

These kinds of differences in the enslavement experience characterized the enslavement process and shaped the outlook of individual Africans as they confronted the reality of life under slavery in Jamaica. Take the cases of two young people, Afiba and Sarri (renamed Adam), who were brought to Jamaica in the final decades of the slave trade. Afiba was a fifteen-year-old girl from the Gold Coast region who had slave status before she was sold into the Atlantic trade by her master, Quamina Yati, for "linen and other goods." In contrast, Sarri, who was described as "a Congo," was captured by one of his own "countrymen" approximately three miles from his home. For about one month, he was made to walk during the night and hide by day. He was eventually traded for "a gun, some powder and shot and a quantity of salt" and then resold "for a keg of brandy" to yet another African trader. This final captor continued trading until he had twenty other African boys as his captives. It was only then that Sarri and the others were sent down to the coast, where they were sold to Europeans and put on a slave ship. It was under these circumstances that Sarri, the son of Scindia Quante (who was described as a "chief or captain under the king" and "a great warrior" who had often captured and sold others into slavery), became a victim of the Atlantic slave trade.[23]

Despite the difference in their social standing in Africa, both of these young people had an understanding of African slavery that was very different from the Jamaican system. Their sensibilities about slavery and enslavement, which were shaped in Africa, would be offended in Jamaica and had little place on the island. Yet because Afiba and Sarri were each drawn from different social circumstances, their attitudes and reactions to a life of slave labor in Jamaica would be quite different. Sarri, who was taken by one of his own "countrymen" and whose father not only traded in captives but also was of high social rank, is likely to have perceived his own enslavement as illegal. Hence, his response to his slave status in Jamaica would have been informed by the notion that he had been unfairly and illegally enslaved in Africa. It seems unlikely that Sarri would have any moral objection to slavery in principle: his own father, after all, captured and enslaved others.

Afiba's perspective, of course, would be quite different. Her own experience in Jamaica was informed by the fact that she had lived as a slave in Africa long before her arrival in Jamaica. Her views on slavery will never be known. She may have felt that slavery was morally reprehensible. However, it is also quite plausible that any response she had to slavery in Jamaica had less to do with an outright rejection of her slave status (a status she had held for all of her life in Africa) and more to do with the disjuncture between her understanding of social obligations between masters and slaves in Africa and the reality of her experiences in Jamaican slave society. The suggestion here is not that Afiba was less resistant to Jamaican slavery because she had already held slave status in Africa; she may have very well been resistant or at the very least a reluctant member of Jamaica's enslaved community. Her reluctance and/or resistance, however, may have stemmed from the violation she felt when her African-oriented expectations of master-slave relationships were not met in Jamaica.

In fact, both of these African slaves may have been equally resistant to their enslavement in Jamaica—albeit for different reasons. In Sarri's case, it is probably more likely that he resisted and rejected his slave status altogether, as he considered his enslavement in Jamaica illegal. Afiba could make no such claim. She had long held slave status in Africa and was sold by her legal owner into the Atlantic slave trade. Furthermore, assumptions about gender roles would have also played an important role in shaping the expectations of these two. When they arrived in Jamaica, Afiba and Sarri not only had preconceived notions about slavery but also had assumptions about how gender relationships operated within the context of slavery.

Contemporary reports from the period certainly acknowledge that captives' social standing in Africa shaped their response to enslavement. According to the slave trader Hugh Crow, the "Breeche"—a high-ranking social group among the Igbo—were more likely than "their countrymen" to resist enslavement. Once members of this high-status group were put on board slave ships, they would often encourage others to "shake off their bondage"—so much so that ship captains, who made their purchase of captives at the Bight of Biafra, were generally averse to purchasing the Breeche. Crow's assessment of high-ranking Igbo supports another report that Gold

Coast Africans who were of a "free condition in their native country" were "the most desperate, to regain [their] freedom."[24]

Yet there is a danger in generalizing about captives' social standing in Africa and their responses to life under slavery in Jamaica. Abū Bakr al-Saddīq was about fifteen years old when he was captured in Bouna at the frontier of Asante territory and transported to a port on the Gold Coast. He was sold to a British ship captain, who took him to Jamaica in about 1805. Before his enslavement, Abū Bakr had benefited from being born into a Muslim family of high social standing. His family claimed descent from the Prophet Mohammed, and the males were "men of learning." As a result, Abū Bakr, who was born in Timbuktu, spent his early years in Jenne learning to read the Quran. At the age of nine, in the charge of his tutor, he began a tour south with his final destination being Bouna, where he continued with more advanced study of the Quran until his enslavement six years later.[25] Abū Bakr's autobiographical accounts were written well into his adult life and after he was freed in 1834. The tenor of his description of capture in Africa and enslavement in Jamaica is no doubt dimmed by the thirty years between his capture and the production of his written record. Yet from all indications, he was a devoutly religious man. According to Abū Bakr, Muslims had many religious obligations and rules to follow:

> The faith of our families is the faith of Islam. They circumcise the foreskin; say the five prayers; fast ... in the month of Ramadan; give alms ... ; marry four free women—a fifth is forbidden to them *except she be their slave*; they fight for the faith of God; perform the pilgrimage to Mecca ... ; eat the flesh of no beast but what they have slain for themselves; drink no wine ... [;] they do not keep the company with those whose faith is contrary to theirs ... [;] they teach their children to read, and instruct them in the different parts of knowledge.[26]

There is little doubt that the realities of life under Jamaican slavery restricted Abū Bakr's ability to practice Islam in the way he liked. This may have been particularly so after he was baptized by his second owner and renamed Edward Donellan. Yet there is nothing in the historical record to suggest that he overtly resisted his slave status in Jamaica. Abū Bakr's view on slavery was informed by his religious beliefs. In his own words, his capture resulted in his being sold "to the Christians." Although he experienced the "oppressiveness" and "bitterness of slavery" and no doubt desired his freedom, he saw his enslavement as "ordained" and part of a divine plan. In summing up his life under slavery, he concluded that "[God] does whatsoever He wills! No one can turn aside that which He has ordained. . . . Nothing can befall us unless it be written for us (in his book)!" Nor does Abū Bakr, even after thirty years of being enslaved, seem to be in moral opposition to the institution of slavery itself. The above quote makes it clear that, by Abū Bakr's understanding, slavery was sanctioned by Islam (albeit under certain circumstances).[27] Although he suggests that Muslim men could take on a fifth wife only if she was already enslaved, it is more likely that he meant an enslaved woman could be taken on as a concubine, for Muslim men generally did not marry enslaved women. This interpretive discrepancy aside, as the quote implies, they could own slaves.

Given that Africans brought to Jamaica had a diverse range of experiences prior to their arrival at the island, it is not surprising that they also responded to slavery in very different ways. In fact, unlike Abū Bakr, some of the newly arrived needed little time to decide that they would reject their Jamaican slave status. This included Africans who were on the island for so brief a period that they could speak little or no English and had no familiarity with the island. On February 21, 1781, the overseer of Kilbie's Estate, Patrick Killikelly, placed an advertisement reporting the escape of a "New Negro Man-Boy," named Quamina, who was estimated to be about eighteen years of age. According to Killikelly, the runaway was "from Guinea," had been on the island for only one month, and could speak "no English." Similarly, on April 20, 1781, Abigail Deleon reported the escape of a "black lusty, middle-aged female slave" named Amba. Deleon, who had recently purchased Amba, reported that she could speak only "indifferent English" and was of the "Coromantee Country." On May 1 of the same year, Alexander Rose placed a notice in the *Royal Gazette* advising readers that he had found a "negro man" whose "country" was unknown. The African in question could not speak any English, and so Rose was unable to get any information about his owner.[28]

Other Africans waited longer before attempting their escape. Some had even earned the trust of their owners. Such was the case of Jack, who was from "the Congo Country," described as "a Negro Boy" who was "about 15 or 16 years of age." How long Jack had been in Jamaica is unclear, but it was certainly long enough for him to learn "tolerable good English" and to be trusted enough to be sent on an errand outside of his home parish, St. Ann. His task was to pick up some "Papers of Consequence" from the provost-marshall's office in Spanish Town (located in the parish of St. Catherine). From Jack's perspective, this errand was a particularly good opportunity to make his escape. The runaway advertisement noted that Jack might attempt to "pass unmolested" with such official documents in his possession.[29] It is uncertain whether the catalyst for Jack's escape was a particular incident that pushed him over the edge or if he was a strategist who had waited patiently for an opportunity.

Some enslaved Africans were persistent runaways. Coobah, an Igbo whose birth name was reportedly Molia, was one such person. She was brought to Jamaica in 1761, when she was approximately fifteen years of age. Five years later she gave birth to a mulatto daughter named Sylvia. The identity of the child's father is unclear, but Sylvia, who lived a mere sixteen months, died in March 1768.[30] If Coobah's actions under slavery are to be interpreted, it can only be concluded that she was rebellious, openly defiant, and even reckless in her behavior. She was determined in her efforts to escape. In a four-year period (1770–74), she ran away at least fourteen times. In Coobah's case, punishment proved to be an ineffective deterrent. In one particular situation, Coobah escaped for just over a month, although from time to time there were reports about her whereabouts. During this period, Coobah was said to have been guilty of "robbing a Negro wench." It was a bold theft. Coobah pretended to want to help the woman and offered to carry the load of rice and pigeons the woman had with her. Once she was given the load, Coobah quite simply "marched away" with the woman's belongings. Eventually, Coobah was found and put in a device of restraint, known as "the bilboes," which was used to lock the victim's hands and/or feet. The very next day, she was "collared and chained" before being sent out to work. Within a few days, however, she had escaped again and stole "rice, beads, calabashes, &c" from another enslaved woman, renamed Nancy. She was caught before the day was over. In punishment, she was flogged and branded on her forehead. This did nothing to quell her fiery spirit: she made another attempt at escape five days later.[31]

There is little known about Coobah before she was transported to Jamaica, and so insights about how her early years in Africa may have shaped her behavior in Jamaica can only be speculative at best. What is clear, however, is that she went to great lengths to antagonize her owner, exhibiting little concern for her own well-being. There can be no other way to describe her choice to "shit" in the punch strainer one night when she was made to sleep in the cookroom. Coobah must have known that this was something that would be discovered the next day. Yet when she was punished by having the fecal matter put all over her face and mouth, she remained defiant. In the words of her owner, Thomas Thistlewood, her behavior made clear that "she minds it not." Despite his continued efforts to keep her in line, her rebellious spirit was never tamed. She continued to steal, escape, and antagonize whenever she chose. Instead, it seems Coobah broke Thistlewood's will. In May 1774, Thistlewood gave up. He would no longer try to tame Coobah's defiant tendencies. He decided that he would be better off without Coobah, and she was sold and transported to Savannah, Georgia.[32]

African adolescents and children, by contemporary accounts, had a less difficult time adjusting to slavery than did adults. As one slave-owning colonial official understood it, adults had greater difficulty adapting because they were "forcibly [taken] from their families and connections." But this was not seen as the case for children, who were reportedly better able to adjust to their new environment. It was argued by some that if Africans were captured and transported across the Atlantic when they were between the age of twelve and eighteen, they would be "just as valuable" as a locally born enslaved person within five or six years. African children and adolescents, after all, "acquire[d] the speech and manners" of Jamaica with much more ease than adults who arrived at an "advanced age"; adults had much more difficulty mastering Jamaican speech patterns and pronunciation.[33]

Yet despite their supposed ability to easily adapt, newly arrived African youths sometimes took their chances with escape and braved the unknown and unfamiliar. In 1779, a runaway advertisement announced the escape of a "Congo Negro Boy," named Fortune, who was approximately thirteen years of age. Unfortunately, there is nothing to indicate specifically why Fortune decided to run away. Given that he could speak only "tolerable English" and was only "slightly acquainted" with Kingston, however, it is clear that any fear he might have of the unknown could not rival his frustration with the conditions of his enslavement. Similarly, a young adolescent named Will, who was estimated to be about fourteen years of age, made his escape. He was reportedly of the "Mundingo country" and spoke English "very badly," as he had been on the island for only seven or eight months. But Africans even younger than Fortune and Will, and less familiar with the island, also opted to run away. This was the case of a young African, between ten and twelve years of age, who was originally from "the Coromantee country." His effort at escape was in vain, as he was later found in Kingston. Nonetheless, the fact that he could speak no English and so would be unable to communicate did not act as a deterrent, as he resisted a life where he would be made to labor under the Jamaican slave system. Newly arrived African girls also made their escape, though it is difficult to say in what proportion. Such was the case of "a New Negro Girl of the Congo Country" who was "taken up" by a pen overseer named William Prosser.[34]

African children's insertion into the Jamaican slave system pulled them into a larger world of child laborers in the British socioeconomic system. Children had long been used as a productive source of labor in various parts of the world, and Britain was no exception. As early as 1597, acts of Parliament made it "lawful to punish" poor children who refused to work if they were unable to support themselves. Until well into the nineteenth century, it was common to use organized labor systems such as workhouses to marshal the labor of poor children. Nor were the British above transporting poverty-stricken British children to far-flung places. There can be little doubt that British ideas about child labor influenced Jamaican colonial thinking about enslaved children on the island. Yet despite such influences, Jamaican colonists did develop a worldview that was distinctively local (or creole). British ideas imported into the island took new form in Jamaica. In this new context, British notions about child labor would operate in a racialized context. As a result, they were transformed to support the social and economic priorities of Jamaican colonials—which were "the defense of slavery and white male solidarity." In many ways, "it was this racialization of British thinking that is often referred to as the white Jamaican 'creole' worldview."[35]

Planter attitudes toward child labor aside, an African child or adolescent did not arrive to Jamaica as a tabula rasa culturally. Unless they were transported to the island as infants or in the very early years of their life, these young people likewise brought their own understandings—particularly about labor, childhood, and youth—to Jamaica. Needless to say, for African children and youths, the trauma of the separation from family occurred long before their arrival to Jamaica. The horror of their enslavement was only heightened when they were landed, sold, and inserted into the unfamiliar context of Jamaican slavery.[36] Unfortunately, the history of childhood and child labor in precolonial Africa remains undeveloped in the scholarly literature. There is no doubt, however, that the use of child labor was prevalent. For this reason, enslaved African children brought to the island also had their own notions of child labor (and even childhood).

A recognition that African men, women, and children came to Jamaica with their own expectations about slavery explains many of the seeming contradictions in the "day-to-day character of slave life." As Sidney Mintz makes clear, Caribbean masters' ideas about the ways the enslaved should conduct themselves could never be fully imposed. There was a "space" between the expected code of behavior and the actual behavior of the enslaved. There was a space between the "real and the ideal."[37] Historians have done a good job of outlining the expectations of those who owned slaves. However, there has been much less work exploring the expectations of the enslaved. From the African point of view, there was also a "space" between the behavior of masters and that of the enslaved. They too had their own ideas about social obligations, servitude, and slavery. Moreover, within the Jamaican slave system, there were also various points of opposition at play, and how captives behaved depended on what it was that they specifically opposed: slavery in principle; their own personal enslavement; the conditions under which they were made to slave; or the racialized form of Jamaican slavery.

A meaningful understanding of how Africans maneuvered the Jamaican slave system must consider how African sensibilities and perceptions operated in the Jamaican context. Such a consideration might better explain, for example, why "a very likely wench of the Mandingo Countrey [sic]" hoped to bear a child for her owner. The woman in question had apparently been trying to get pregnant by her master for some time, but her efforts were in vain. As a result, she approached John Thistlewood (the nephew of Thomas Thistlewood) and tried to persuade him "to lay with her." Her hope was to get pregnant by John Thistlewood and mislead her owner into believing that the child was his. For this woman, who fathered the child was of less concern to her than ensuring that the child was of the appropriate racial mixture. Once the child appeared to be mulatto, questions about paternity were less likely to be raised. From all indications, it appears that this woman had no sentimental reasons for bearing her master's child but believed it to be to her advantage to do so. Other than her description as being "Mandingo," there is little personal information about this woman in the historical record, though she reportedly spoke "good English," which suggests that she was in Jamaica long enough to learn the language reasonably well.[38]

Captives labeled "Mandingo" generally came from Islam-dominated parts of the upper Guinea coast. In Islamic regions in Africa, there were very precise rules grounded in religious beliefs, about who could be enslaved and how the enslaved were to be treated. Although these rules were often corrupted and even ignored, they were the religious ideal. Africans brought to Jamaica from Islamic regions, then, had very specific expectations about the social obligations that were to guide master-slave relationships. One such social obligation was geared toward enslaved women in particular. Islam generally encouraged the manumission of enslaved women who were concubines. In addition, if an enslaved woman bore the child of a free man, the child was considered free regardless of the mother's slave status. That said, slave owners did not always acknowledge their offspring. As a result, concubines and their children were sometimes denied their freedom.[39] Nonetheless, it is tempting to suggest that when the "wench of the Mandingo Country" made the sexual proposition to John Thistlewood, she may very well have been working with African assumptions about gender relations between masters and their slaves. At the very least, she was no doubt hoping that the conditions of her enslavement would be ameliorated if her owner believed that she had his child.

Similarly, African notions of master-slave relations may have also informed the behavior of an enslaved man renamed Roger. In February 1756, John Cope Senior, who was Roger's legal owner, died. Roger was approximately twenty-four years of age and a trained mason. When Roger learned that Cope was dead, he went "to the Negroe house privately and shot himself," so that he could "Accompany [his master] into the Otherworld and there wait upon him." From an African point of view, Roger's suicide was by no means out of the ordinary. In fact, at times such behavior was considered both appropriate and acceptable. In West Africa, the enslaved were often killed so that they could attend to their masters in the afterlife. There is even some evidence to suggest that it was considered an "honor" to accompany a king into the next world, and individuals sometimes disputed among themselves for the right to participate in this privilege.[40]

In fact, as historian John Iliffe makes clear, the need to maintain personal honor inspired much of African behavior. It was the "chief ideological motivation" prior to the arrival of world religions and remained an important motivation even after this point. Honor, defined as a "right to respect," existed in all strata of African society—even among the enslaved. Furthermore, the enslaved tried to assert their claim to honor in two dimensions: in their relationship with their owner; and within the enslaved community. These assertions for "a right to respect" met with varying degrees of success or sometimes complete failure.[41] Nonetheless, what is significant is that the desire of enslaved Africans to preserve their personal honor resulted in a range of actions that could fall anywhere along a spectrum that spanned outright rebellion against their enslavement to voluntary suicide at a master's death.

The extent to which such "voluntary suicides" took place varied throughout West Africa. Although there is no certainty about from where in Africa Roger was transported, most of the captives purchased by Cope were from the Bight of Biafra. According to historian Robin Law, in the Biafran port town Old Calabar, humans were often killed at the funerals of important people. Moreover, these "funeral killings," which resulted in the deaths of primarily wives and slaves, were commonplace in several other parts of West Africa.[42] Perhaps for Roger, then, despite the fact that he was in Jamaica rather than Africa, committing suicide was an act that fulfilled his social obligations as slave. Perhaps it was an act of honor.

In contrast to Roger's loyalty to his white master is the case of Kwaku, who was resentful, not of his enslavement but of his enslavement to white men. Kwaku was never sold into the Atlantic slave trade, but he was enslaved to the Danes at Christianborg Castle on the Gold Coast. He was born at the castle in approximately 1703 and spent his entire life laboring as a "Company slave." Kwaku was trained as a mason and was in the company of about one hundred to two hundred men, women, and children who held slave status at the castle. In 1739, during a conversation with a Danish factor, he made his frustration about the terms of his enslavement at the castle quite clear. The dialogue, which was documented by another Danish factor, L. F. Rømer, was recorded as follows:[43]

Danish Factor: Qvacu, why are you working? Isn't it noon?
Kwaku: Our master [the governor of the Danish trading stations] is acting very badly towards me today. He said I had not worked enough, and so, before I can stop, I must finish this job. But I know what I shall do.
Danish Factor: What will you do?
Kwaku: When I die, I will pray to God that he not send me into the world to work as a slave for whites and if my prayer is not answered I shall beat God.
Danish Factor: What then will you be when you come into the world again?
Kwaku: Frempung's slave (Frempung was a great Akim king).
Danish Factor: Why don't you pray to become Frempung himself?

Kwaku: No, that is not possible; for I know that as often as I have been in this world I have been a slave; and as often as I shall come I must be a slave.

This dialogue makes clear that Kwaku not only accepted his slave status but also was incapable of imagining his life as anything but a slave. In his mind, the best life he could wish for would be one in which he was enslaved to a member of the African elite. The worst was to be enslaved to whites, because, based on his own experiences, whites made unfair masters.

"The negroes who caught them"

Ironically, the Jamaican plantocracy relied on the cooperation and knowledge of enslaved Africans to help sustain the machinations of the Jamaican slave system. "Seasoned" Africans, who had been resident on the island for some time, often played a pivotal role in mediating relations between newly arrived Africans and Jamaican whites. They helped to bridge the social and cultural disjuncture between the two. This chasm was a deep one. But by the late eighteenth century, Jamaica had become a matured slave society, and the plantocracy remedied the situation by soliciting the cooperation of trusted "seasoned" Africans. Such individuals were used by whites when making selections and purchasing recently arrived Africans. They also were used to communicate with the newly arrived. They even played an important role in the surveillance and policing of the slave population.

Henry Coor (who was employed as a millwright in Westmoreland, Jamaica, for fifteen years, until 1774) reported an instance in which he used an African to assist him in the purchase of "six boys and two girls." According to Coor, these children were originally from the Gold Coast. For that reason, he took an African who could communicate with the children but had also "been in the country for so long" that he could speak English very well. Coor hoped that making use of the African's language skills would help him to make an informed decision as he chose captives from a recently arrived ship. Coor had the African ask the newly arrived children, whom he hoped to purchase, whether they had already contracted yaws—a disease that was prevalent among the enslaved. They answered in the affirmative and would therefore be immune, but unfortunately for Coor, his efforts were in vain. About two months later, all the children broke out with the disease.[44]

Jamaican whites also relied on the knowledge of seasoned Africans to distinguish between the various African ethnic groups of the newly arrived. Take the case of the overseer of the Hector's River Estate, which was located on the eastern end of the island in Manchioneal. The overseer placed a notice alerting the public that "a Negro man of the Nago country" had been found. According to the notice, the escapee "pretend[ed]" not to understand English, but when "negroes of his own country . . . were put to interrogate him," he informed them that his name was George and that his master had died soon after he was bought. This situation is in contrast to the circumstances that Hugh Morrison faced when he found a "stout new negro" who was "quite naked" on the plantation Iter Boreale in St. George. Morrison was unable to identify the escapee's ethnicity because "no negro [could] be found that understands him."[45]

Captive Africans, not unlike the locally born, were also an important part of the arsenal used by the Jamaican plantocracy to keep the enslaved population under control. They played a crucial role in both the surveillance and the capture of other members of the enslaved community. In 1779, a notice was posted reporting that two men from "the Mongola Country" who could not speak English were found at Bath. The notice also stated that the Africans would be returned to their owner in exchange for the cost of the advertisement and "a small gratuity" for "the negroes who caught them." African involvement is also clear based on the experience of Coobah, the persistent runaway, discussed above. Several of the times she escaped she was captured by Africans. In one particular instance, she was captured by an adolescent "Coromante or Shanti" named Jimmy and Damsel, who was described as an eighteen-year-old "Chamboy."[46] They found her quite coincidentally on their return from fetching water and brought her home.

All three were owned by Thistlewood. It is tempting to suggest that interethnic conflict aided the planters' cause as they used Africans in their surveillance of the enslaved. Yet Thistlewood, who routinely sent out his African-born captives in search of runaways, seemed to have little concern about intraethnic loyalties. Lincoln, described as an Igbo, was also, for example, sent to look for Coobah, who was likewise identified as Igbo.[47] Of course, as discussed in chapter 3, these labels are imprecise and problematic; they do not necessarily reflect with any accuracy the ethnicity of captives. In this particular case, however, it does tell us that Thistlewood at least perceived that Lincoln and Coobah were of the same ethnic group.

The ways Africans responded to their enslavement were complex, contradictory, and inconsistent. The very Jimmy mentioned above, who returned Coobah after she escaped, was by no means a model member of the enslaved community. He was brought to Jamaica at the age of "10 or 11" in 1765. After a mere five years on the island, however, he had established a reputation for his "impudence, laziness, carelessness, lying & c." He was also quite likely an alcoholic, as he was often punished for getting drunk. From his owner's point of view, Jimmy was willfully troublesome. When sent out to run errands, he repeatedly returned late, sometimes drunk, and with the tasks incomplete or poorly done. He also seemed to taunt his owner with some of his actions. When he was about twenty years old, he was suspected of riding his master's horse, without permission, on one of his late-night escapades. Despite such seemingly reckless behavior, Jimmy often returned of his own accord knowing he would be punished for his actions. It is difficult to assess Jimmy's mind-set, based on his actions alone. Fortunately, he has left a hint in the historical record that offers some insight. In 1771, when he was about sixteen years old, Jimmy was punished for "throwing the fire about the cookroom" and for "being otherways very impudent." His open antagonism seemed to stem from a moment of absolute frustration, which was voiced when he reportedly shouted to Thistlewood that "if this be living he did not care whether he lived or died."[48]

It seems other Africans shared Jimmy's sentiment. According to William Fitzmaurice, who lived in Jamaica for fifteen years up until 1786 and was employed as an overseer for most of that time, newly arrived Africans often told him that "they preferred dying to living." And of course, some Africans acted on their frustration. In the testimony of Dr. Harrison, a medical doctor who tended to the enslaved in Jamaica from 1755 to 1765, he admitted to witnessing an enslaved African commit suicide by jumping off a bridge. This particular African "had been a man of consequence in his own country" and refused to work because "he would be a Slave to no man." Punishments by the overseer were a futile effort, and so it was decided to move the African to another plantation. While the uncompromising African was being moved, his hands were tied behind his back. This did not, however, deter him from jumping "headlong into the water" as they crossed a bridge that was en route. Death was his preferred option. In fact, much of the qualitative evidence suggests that Africans, particularly the recently arrived, were more likely to commit suicide than the Jamaican born. Fitzmaurice reported, for example, that in a single year, a dozen of his recently purchased Africans committed suicide by "dirt eating."[49]

The means Africans chose to commit suicide were quite varied. The above-mentioned Mark Cook, who was initially employed in the "planting business" and later worked as a clerk and schoolmaster in Jamaica, reportedly knew of two instances in which an enslaved man and woman each committed suicide by hanging themselves. He also knew of another instance in which an enslaved man "shot himself." Cook, who resided in Jamaica between 1774 and 1790, reported that all of these suicides were committed by enslaved persons who were African born. There are also contemporary reports of Africans cutting their own throats and poisoning themselves. In Jamaica, there was even ethnic stereotyping about African suicides. The "Ebo Negro" was perceived as particularly prone to commit suicide, captives from the Gold Coast were believed to "always cut their throats," and those of the "most inland country" were seen as most likely to hang themselves.[50]

Contemporary observers often reported that Africans believed they would be returned to their ancestral homelands after death. Vincent Brown has recently suggested that this may explain why Africans were "sanguine about suicide." Whites often used "spiritual terror" to deter Africans from committing suicide. It was not uncommon to dismember African bodies, to put bodies up on display, or even to put the heads of Africans who committed suicide on poles so that they could be viewed by the enslaved population. As Brown sees it, by beheading and dismembering the enslaved, Europeans attempted to "seize and manipulate African visions of the afterlife in an effort to govern the worldly actions of the living." Yet even Brown admits that there is little evidence to support the notion that the physical mutilation of African bodies was an effective deterrent for African suicide or that Africans believed that the mutilation of their bodies after death prevented them from returning to their homeland. In fact, there may even be some evidence to the contrary, as in some parts of West Africa, the enslaved were often beheaded so that they could continue to serve their masters in the spiritual world. Nonetheless, only a minority of Africans chose suicide as their route back to Africa. "Old Sambo" of Egypt Estate in Westmoreland, for example, opted to befriend certain white men who "promised to carry him to his country."[51]

Based on his experience in Jamaica, Coor believed that it was the "cruel treatment of whipping, hard-working, and starving" that led many Africans to the extreme act of suicide. After being "whipt," the enslaved would be sent to work in the fields without food or drink, except for water and "what little their ship-mates or countrymen might be pleased to give them."[52] Coor reportedly knew of many cases of cruelty to the enslaved. By his own account, he "often" sat on juries in cases that had been brought against overseers for such cruelty. One such example was the case brought against the overseer of the William's Field Estate. The overseer reportedly punished one of the enslaved under his charge so cruelly that the man ran away and was "that night missing in his family." The next morning, he was found hanging on a tree on the roadside near the overseer's house. Given that the Jamaican judicial system was organized to support the social and economic interests of the white planter class, it is not surprising that the overseer was acquitted of any crime. According to Coor, this incident was by no means exceptional; he offered many accounts of cruelty that resulted in the enslaved committing suicide—including the case of fourteen captives who "ran away into the woods" and "cut their throats together."[53]

Conclusion

The captive men, women, and children brought to Jamaica in the late eighteenth century used their own peculiar histories to interpret their new Jamaican reality. Although Orlando Patterson's study on slavery suggests that the enslaved were unable to "inform their understanding of social reality with the inherited meanings of their natural forebears," this chapter argues otherwise. Africans referenced their pre-Jamaica experiences to interpret their new context. Or to use Lovejoy and Trotman's term, they came to the island with certain "expectations." Scholarly discussions about the responses of the enslaved have generally been couched in terms of "resistance" and "accommodation." Yet as Mintz points out, "only a tiny fraction of daily life consisted of open resistance . . . most of life . . . [was] spent living; and most of it was lived in daily, even perfunctory, association with the holders of power." To make sense of African responses to slavery in Jamaica in all its forms, one must first determine the intention of each individual.[54] But this can only be accomplished with an awareness of how they understood their circumstances.

What were the African sensibilities at play? Certainly, the vast majority of Africans were familiar with the concept of slavery, albeit in a form very different from the racialized system into which they were inserted. Very few Africans took issue with the institution of slavery itself. The maroons of Jamaica are perhaps one of the more outstanding examples of this. The

maroons were, after all, freedom fighters, slave catchers, and slave owners, although the author of one recent study on maroons is skeptical about
the "allegation that Maroons abducted and enslaved large numbers *of their
own kind*."[55] Yet the very phrase "of their own kind" reveals an ideological
imposition. Did the maroons think of all the enslaved on the island as being "of their own kind"? It is doubtful given the regional, ethnic, and even
linguistic diversity among the enslaved. Such seeming contradictions are
rampant in the history of slavery, but they are resolved by a historical treatment that sees Africans as "wholly human," as individuals with a past and
with historical experiences that shaped their behavior. African responses to
life under slavery in Jamaica were in reaction to multiple points of opposition. For some, it might be a rejection of slavery in its Jamaican form. For
others, it was their own personal enslavement with which they took issue.
There was no doubt another group who rejected what they saw as the unfair
terms of their enslavement. Only through an appreciation of such nuances
can scholarly interpretations get closer to more accurately representing the
complexities of the African experience under slavery.

Epilogue

On March 25, 1807, the act to abolish the slave trade received Royal Assent, thereby establishing a law that made slave trading illegal throughout the British Empire. After May 1 of that year, ships could no longer legally leave Britain for the purpose of slave trading, and any ship that left on or before that date had until March 1, 1808, to reach the West Indies and sell the captive Africans they brought as "cargo." In other words, captive men, women, and children could be legally transported to and sold in Jamaica (as elsewhere in the British Empire) for almost one year after the act was passed. This permitted another known seventy-seven slave ships to arrive at the island and sentenced another 22,000 captives to a life of enslavement in Jamaica. The last of these slave ships to legally sell captives on the island was the *George*. Its captain, Hance Hamilton, purchased 261 men, women, and children at Loango and the Congo River. When the *George* arrived at Kingston on February 17, 1808, only 235 of the enslaved were still alive. They were incorporated into an enslaved population, comprising both African and Jamaican born, that was well in excess of 350,000 enslaved persons.[1] These were the last known captive Africans to put a social and cultural stamp on Jamaican slave society.

The arrival of the *George* marked the end of an era for Jamaican planters. Throughout the duration of the British slave trade, they purchased more forced African migrants than any other colony supplied by British ships (37.2 percent), and they did so in significantly greater numbers. Barbados was second to Jamaica in captive purchases, and this island purchased less than half that of Jamaica.[2] No longer did the Jamaican plantocracy have ready access to what must have seemed like an inexhaustible supply of enslaved labor. The maritime connection that had guaranteed them captive men, women, and children from the other side of the Atlantic was lost. Yet although British Caribbean planters did not have to face the reality of abolition until 1807, they were well aware that abolitionist sentiments were being expressed and legal blows being made against the British slave trade long before this. In 1772 in England, for example, there was the ruling of Lord Chief Justice Mansfield that determined that Charles Stewart could not legally send James Somerset, who was enslaved to Stewart, from England to be sold in Jamaica. Although the Mansfield decision did not emancipate all the enslaved in England (as is popularly believed), the sentiment coded in this ruling echoed loudly in the colonies, as for the duration of the case Stewart had been backed by the "wealth and influence of the West Indian lobby." In the 1780s, Caribbean planters were also to get word that slavery in the northern states of the United States had been abolished. This included states such as Pennsylvania and Massachusetts, which had strong maritime links with the Caribbean. The year 1787 brought the birth of the Society for the Abolition of the Slave Trade. Although the abolitionist movement had its roots in the 1760s, Caribbean planters no doubt recognized that the formal organization of abolitionists in this manner could be their economic death knell.[3]

But such formal attempts at "emancipation from above" in Britain were accompanied by efforts of "emancipation from below" in the Caribbean.[4] The enslaved often sought to emancipate themselves. The most spectacular of cases, without any doubt, was the Haitian Revolution. In 1791, slaveholders throughout the Caribbean began to feel its impact. In Jamaica, planters stood to benefit economically from this thirteen-year slave rebellion, as the birth of Haiti necessarily meant the death of the very prosperous sugar-producing Saint Domingue. It also meant that the number of men, women, and children being sent to Jamaica during this period underwent a significant spike. But Jamaica's economic prosperity, brought on by Saint Domingue's fall and Haiti's rise, was coupled with an assault against the social order as Jamaican planters knew it. Then more than ever, every person invested in slavery throughout the Americas became aware of his or her tenuous position. Haiti was the bold evidence that the enslaved could successfully wage war against their captors and win.

Regardless of how abolition was won, the end of the British slave trade forever changed the landscape of Jamaica. Planters had to rethink labor organization and make more deliberate efforts at encouraging the development of a self-reproducing enslaved population. They also began to explore bringing people from other parts of the world to meet their labor needs. As early as 1805, British officials were contemplating the merits of bringing in people from India and China, as they believed it would "very much diminish the price of labor." By their estimations, the costs would be low, as these people had "simple" diets and were unlikely to join forces with "African negroes" in insurrections or disturbances. By 1834, they were much further along in bringing this idea to fruition in their efforts to remedy the continuing problem of labor. The result was the migration of 450,000 people from India and China who arrived between 1834 and 1918 in the British Caribbean to work as indentured laborers. Another 90,000 indentured laborers came from Madeira (41,000), Africa (40,000), and Europe and other areas (9,000). Some of them came under coercive circumstances. Others were misled and misinformed about the terms of their labor contracts. The Africans who migrated were "liberated Africans," or more aptly put, they were "slave trade refugees." They comprised persons taken from ships illegally involved in slave-trading activities or were part of the labor emigration system that operated from Sierra Leone and Saint Helena.[5]

In total, Jamaica received about 11,000 liberated Africans and another 43,000 indentured laborers, the vast majority of whom were from India. It received the third-largest number of indentured laborers in the British Caribbean. That said, the number of indentured laborers entering Jamaica was significantly smaller than that for colonies such as British Guiana (301,000) and Trinidad (158,000). In both of these places, sugar production expanded and matured relatively late and consequently developed a heavy reliance on enslaved African labor much later than Jamaica. Combined, both colonies took in only about 130,000 enslaved men, women, and children throughout the duration of the British slave trade. This was roughly 10 percent of all the captives transported to Jamaica.[6] For those reasons, British Guiana and Trinidad, unlike Jamaica, relied quite heavily on the use of indentured labor to sustain their plantation economies after abolition.

Of course, for the enslaved, the end of forced African migration to British colonies had an entirely different meaning and brought other concerns to the forefront. Like the Haitian Revolution, it was another strike against the legality of their enslavement and hinted at the possibility of a life in which they had the legal right to be free. Legal freedom for all the enslaved, however, would take another three decades. It was not until 1838 that all the enslaved of Jamaica, and elsewhere in the British Empire, were emancipated.

The 1807 Abolition Act meant that for the next thirty years, during which slavery continued, there would be no more captive Africans to provide social and cultural reinforcements from the other side of the Atlantic. Hence, those Africans transported in the final decades of the Atlantic slave trade, and under study in this book, were an important cohort. They represented the last of the African influences brought by captives taken to Jamaica. In later decades (essentially, after all the enslaved were emancipated in the 1830s), liberated Africans exposed another generation of Jamaicans to African cultural patterns—but their influences were on a legally freed population.

Unfortunately, the tale of Atlantic slavery does not end with British abolition and emancipation. The British slave trade was merely one of many trans-Atlantic slave trades. For the duration of their involvement, the British were key players in the business of buying and selling African men, women, and children. That said, the complete dismantling of Atlantic slave trade systems and slavery was a long process. In the Americas, the era of legalized slavery ended with Brazil. As the last holdout for the Atlantic slave economy in the Western hemisphere, Brazil received captive Africans who were forcibly transported until the mid-nineteenth century, and slavery remained legal there until 1888—an entire five decades after the enslaved of Jamaica had their first taste of freedom.

Ironically, despite its long and protracted nature, abolition of the various Atlantic slave trades led to very different consequences in Africa. Involvement in the Atlantic slave trade was the dominant economic enterprise in many Atlantic African societies. Its end meant that some of these economies needed to be reoriented to produce and export "legitimate commerce" such as palm oil, peanuts, and gum. Unfortunately, the production of these "legitimate" goods generally required much labor, and these labor demands were met by an increased use of enslaved labor. In addition, there was also an increased demand for enslaved labor to produce food for urban centers involved in Atlantic trading activities. Hence, long after emancipation laws had made their way throughout all of the Americas, the problem of slavery continued to plague the African continent, and slavery remained a legal institution well into the twentieth century.[7]

Appendix

Thirteen Documents Relating to the Voyage
of the Slave Ship *African Queen* (July 1792–May 1793)

These transcribed documents were written to Bristol merchant James Rogers, the owner of the *African Queen*. The punctuation is generally consistent with the original letters. The spellings are true to the original. Illegible words are indicated by [. . .]. The names of slave ships are italicized for clarity and to provide context to the content of each document. All letters are located in the James Rogers Collection (C107/1–15, 59), housed at the National Archives (Kew Gardens) of the United Kingdom.

1) Hamet Forsyth to James Rogers, July 9th, 1792, C107/13

Context: The captain of the *African Queen*, Samuel Stribling, has died while the ship is in Africa. The letter is from Hamet Forsyth, who has taken command of the vessel.

Old Calabar 9 July 1792
M[r]. James Rogers
Sir,
this my Second and p[er] Ship *Fame* informing you of her arrival [. . .] 28 June last and receiving her Cargo on Board [. . .] *African Queen* agreeable to Invoice, likewise your letters, have been Oblidged [*sic*] to stop Trade five weeks not having a proper assortment of Cloth & then having purchaced [*sic*] 290 and on trust 160 Slaves, oweing [*sic*] to the great Mortality dayly [*sic*] in this river being the sickly time for the year, was fearfull [*sic*] of having too many Slaves on Board, and provisions for them are very high, at same time giveing [*sic*] up all hopes of the [ship] *Fames* Arrival, f[rom] the Acc[ount] of short passages made f[rom] Liverpool, here, the day before her arrival began to rig the *A[frican] Queen* and should have sailed in three weeks—now meting [*sic*] with a little longer detention but am in great hopes will not exceed six weeks—their [*sic*] is now in this river three Liverpool ships—*Perceverance, Kitty, & George,* and each expect[ing] Tenders dayley [*sic*] and are in great opposition against each others. Likewise 2 French Ships near the same but flatter myself the ship *A[frican] Queen* will meet her part much sooner than some of the above mentioned the Copper's are now on Slaves in this river f[rom] 180 to 200. I am very Sorry to inform you of the loss of forty one Negroes besides Cap[tain] Stribling and Nine [white] Men although the Greatest Care and attention has been paid them during their Sickness—at foot have the Acc[ount] of Names—have put on Board the Ship *Fran* Twenty Pun[cheons] Palm Oil 409 pounds Ivovory [*sic*] marks AQ [. . .] to 53 being Teeth & Scravelias[1] [*sic*, scrivellos], Men Slave 58 & 1 Man Boy, 128 Women, 11 Girls & 3 Infants being her Compliment [*sic*] and I have put a sufficient Quantity of all kind of provisions on board for a three months passage & [at the] same time am sorry [I] could not procure more Male slaves, being so scarce oweing [*sic*] to marching them through the Cuntry [*sic*] for the Camaroo where they receive a

greater price for them. Inclosed you have a receipt f[rom] Cap[tain] Jenkins of his Cargoe [*sic*], which [I] hope will meet good sales.

I remain your Ever Dutiful Serv[ant]
H. Forsyth.

[Deceased]
Cap[tain] Stribling
W[illiam] Stephens
Jnᵒ McKinley
Tho[mas] Harvey   *Sick*
David Aires   Mr. Loyd [*sic*]
Martin Gibson   Frank Guy
Henery [*sic*] Watts   Mr. Lang
Tho[mas] Rankin   Jaˢ Wright
William Ames   John Dixon
James Coaks   Tho[mas] Magness

2) William Blake to James Rogers, 11th November 1792, C107/5

Context: Captain Hamet Forsyth is dead. Command of the *African Queen* has been passed on to John Long. The letter is from Captain William Blake, who was also employed by James Rogers and trading at Old Calabar.

Old Callabar, 11th November 1792
Sir,
This my 5 pr ship *African Queen* am sorry the ship has buried to [*sic*] Commanders & the 3rd not fit to Command the ship we here have been obliged to Upoint [*sic*] Mr. [John] Long to the Command and have bound him to act agreeable with the Doctor & Officers for the good of the Voyage had not the *Rodney* been here or some other ship this ship must have Totally lost all—the slaves that are on board are some good & some bad the number are 295 300—Am sorry my tender is not arrived shall be obliged to [. . .] my own ship in course of 3 weeks to get Ready if no arivel [*sic*].
Inclose & Remain your Humble Serv[ant]
William Blake

3) John Shilstone to James Rogers, January 8th 1793, C107/13

Context: The *African Queen* has anchored at Dominica. The letter is from John Shilstone, captain of the ship *Marquis of Worcester*.

Dominica January 8th 1793
Mr. James Rogers
Sir,
your [*sic*] Ship *African Queen* John Long the present Master Arived [*sic*] here Last Thursday the 3rd Inst from Old Callabar he wish'd to get some Refreshment for his Slaves I apply'd to the [merchant] house of Frans & Robt Smith who Readyly [*sic*] Gave all the Assistance in they could sending Directly into the Country for plaintains [*sic*] Oranges & he said he had plenty of all Other provisions On board had been seven weeks from Old Callabar bury'd the Doctor on the passage as he Did not write himself I desired him On Saturday evening (when I went On board with people to Get him under weigh [*sic*]) to let me know what Slaves he had brought of [*sic*] the Coast and how many Bury'd that I might send you word he told me he Brought three Hundred off the Coast had Bury'd forty women twenty Eight men, eight girls and two Boys. I hope you will soon have an Account of her from Jamaica.
I am Sir your Ob[edient] Serv[ant], Jn. Shilstone

4) Francis & Robert Smyth to James Rogers, January 10^h 1793, C107/13

Context: Letter is from the Dominican merchant house of Francis & Robert Smyth, which supplied the *African Queen* with provisions for the captives.

D/que [*sic*] 10th Jan^{ry} 1793
James Rogers Esqr
Sir,
We have had this pleasure repeatedly of late & are still without suply [*sic*] even to the receipt of the Coffee by [ships] *Neptune* or *Lady Aguita*—When time will permit you we beg leave to request a few lines in reply—a few days past touched in here on her way to Jamaica your Ship the *Affrican* [*sic*] *Queen*, at present John Long master from Old Callibar [*sic*] seven weeks out, we supply'd Captain Long with every thing which he stood in need of & Captain Shilstone of the *Marquis of Worcester* rendered every service in his power—we are sorry to be obliged to say the loss on board the *Queen*, in whites & Blacks are very considerable we believe the former not less than 30 or 32 & of the latter about 78—the particulars of the latter, Captain Shilstone has given you, as we took the liberty to regard his going on board & giving such advice to the present Captain, formerly third Mate as he deemed necessary on that subject & to whose letter we beg leave to refer you—We have had no Affrican [*sic*] sales made here for some months past & our opinion is that small parcels from the Windward Coast would command pleasing Sales.

Inclosed with this we transmit the disbursements laid out for the *Affrican* [*sic*] *Queen* Mr. Long master p[er] £50. .5. .8½ currency to your debit in Account. Produce is beginning to lower in price & we think by & by it will come to some kind of a moderate standard—with great regard & due respect
We remain Sir
Your mo[st] ob[edient] s[ervants].
Fran^s & Robt Smyth

5) John Perry to James Rogers, January 21st, 1793, C107/13

Context: The *African Queen* has arrived at Jamaica. The letter is from the merchant John Perry, who reports on the condition of the captives.

James Rogers Esq.
Montego Bay 21st Jany 1793
D[ear] Sir,
Your ship *African Queen* arrived at Martha Brae in great distress a week ago—the Master no doubt will write you concerning his great loss in Sailors & Slaves.

Mr. Cunningham declined to sell her because he daily expected the *Pearl* with 500 Slaves—Mr. Grant was next applied to, He declined for want of advice & Mr. Wedderburn was next waited upon by Capt. Long who told him he could have nothing to do with his Cargo—In this Situation and the Negroes dying daily, I could not but feel for the Interest of a Gentleman whom I had known so many Years & I volunteer'd my Services the 18th Inst—I went to Mr. Cunningham & told him that rather than your property should remain in such a situation & as I understood the *Wasp* had actually sold in Grenada I would join him in taking up the Cargo bad as it was reported to be—he readily agreed to this—we then asked Capt Long whether a long or a short day would be most Advantageous for you and it was decided that as the greatest part of the Cargo are very meagre—a long day & good Feeding in the Interim would be most Serviceable [*sic*] we therefore fix'd for Wednesday 30th Inst in this Harbour. Capt. Hewan of the *Brooks* who told me that the *Wasp* had certainly sold at Grenada had also told Mr. Cunningham there could be no doubt the *Pearl* had also sold to Windward, but on the 20th at Night the *Wasp* arriv^d here & brought an Account of the *Pearl* being at Barbadoes her Situation and the Captains [*sic*] further Intentions you no doubt will hear of from thence.

Capt. [Robert] Jones [of the ship *Wasp*] told me that as his Cargo was now in very good order and would not be better he wished to sell in as few days as possible I therefore fix'd the 28th Inst. Which will not prejudice our sale as we have found by experience in this Town—I have procur'd from the Country a number of provisions for the Negroes when the ship shall come in which she cannot do just now as a great swell at Martha Brae prevents her coming out from thence. After the Sale you will hear more particularly from Mr. Cunningham & myself jointly.

We asked the Captain [of *African Queen*] how many Slaves he had on board the 18th Inst. He answer'd he could not tell exactly, but that he brought 330 from the Coast, & had buried 98—of course we should conclude he had 232 left, but the Land Surveyor who measur'd the Slaves reports only 214.

I shall soon have the pleasure to address you again, mean while [*sic*] remain D[ear] Sir
Y[our] mo[st] Obed Serv[ant]
John Perry.

6) John Cunningham to James Rogers, January 21st 1793, C107/13

Context: This letter is from the Jamaican merchant John Cunningham, who writes that he will work with merchant John Perry to sell the enslaved on the *African Queen*.

Messrs James Rogers & Coy
Jamaica Montego Bay, 21st Jany 1793
Gentl[man]
A few days ago your ship the *African Queen* under the Command of the 3rd Mate Mr. Long arrived at Martha Brae with about 220 slaves—As I expected the *Pearl* it was not my intention to have sold the Cargo but the other Guinea Factors Mr. Grant, Mr. Wedderburn & others would not take her up by the Mortality Bill she has lost upwards of 100 Slaves and those remaining are the very worst that were ever imported (to my knowledge) into this island being thus situated I requested of Mr. Perry a Gentleman well known in Bristol to Join me in the disposal of the Cargo which he on my Account assented.

Last night the ship *Wasp* belonging to Mr. Jones arrived with 201 slaves she touched at Barbadoes where she left the *Pearl* having lost her Master and the Cargo of slaves very sickley [*sic*]. The Master of the *Wasp* says that the *Pearl* had buried 260—these are unfortunate events and your losses must be immense. I sincerely wish you better luck and remain Gentle[man], Your most h[umble] Serv[ant], Jn Cunningham.

7) John Cunningham to James Rogers, February 4th 1793, C107/59

Context: Merchant John Cunningham reporting on the sale of the captives on board the *African Queen*.

Jamaica M° Bay 4 February 1793
Messrs James Rogers & Co^y
Gentl[man]
Inclosed is a Copy of which I wrote the 21st Ultimo—The ship came to this port & the Sale opened the 30th at £84—with many good purchasers Sorry am I to relate only few could be picked at that rate—Mr. Perry & self agreed to lower on purpose to get off as many as possible the first days sale—we keep [*sic*] the sale up as much as was in our power untill [*sic*] the fifth day when we had an offer of £40 p[er] head taking 70—which I was pleased to get—12 sick & very meagre slaves were sold for about £140—the number of slaves sold was 202 the gross amount will be within £200 of eleven thousands [Jamaican] currency—The ship is now preparing to take a light freight of Wood and I have desire [*sic*] the Master to use all diligence in getting it off and leaving this with all speed.

The Bills for the Cargo will be 18, 24 & 30 months. This is the usual time here at present indeed we were obliged to give very long time so as to induce the purchasers to take them of [*sic*] our hands.
I am Gentl[man],
Your most Ob[edient] Serv[ant],
Jn Cunningham.

8) John Perry to James Rogers, February 5th 1793, C107/59

Context: Merchant John Perry reporting on the sale of the captives on board the *African Queen*.

James Rogers Esqr (Triplicate)
Montego Bay, 5th February 1793
Dear Sir,
Mr. Cunningham being gone to Trelawny I embrace this opportunity to advise you that in four days we closed the sale of your very bad Cargo of Negroes p[er] *African Queen* as p[er] enclosed abstract—bad as it is it is near £7 p[er] head more than we estimated them at the day before the sale began, but we stretched the price considerably by giving 2 and 3 years Credit.

The Ship will sail in about a week by whom [I] shall write you again and more particularly, [in the] interim [I] remain very respectfully.
Dear Sir
Your most Ob[edient] Serv[ant]
John Perry

9) Record of Sale for Captives on the African Queen, March 10th 1793, C107/59

Sales of Two hundred and two slaves Imported in the ship *African Queen* John Long Master from Calabar on the Coast of Africa, sold here by John Cunningham & John Perry on Account of James Rogers of Bristol.

[Table on pages 131–33]

Errors Excepted. Jamaica Montego Bay 10th March 1793
Jn. Cunningham, John Perry

Note: During this period, financial calculations were made in pounds, shillings, and pennies: 20 shillings (s) = £1; 12 pennies (d) = 1 shilling. The sales and prices listed above were in Jamaican currency. Based on calculations below, £1.4 Jamaican = £1 Sterling. Olsen, *Daily Life*, 189.

Date	To whom sold	Men			Women			Total	Amount
		Men	Boys	Boys	Women	Girls	Girls		£.s.d
Jany 30	Robert Morris	3 @ £84	—	—	3 @ £70	—	—	6	462
	Alexr Stepn Findlater	2 @ 84	—	2 @ £53	1 @ 84	—	3 @ £55	8	523
	Joseph M. Harris	1 @ 84	—	1 @ 80	1 @ 84	—	—	3	248
	Alexr Nicoll	2 @ 84	—	1 @ 80	—	—	—	3	248
	ditto	—	—	—	—	—	1 @ 70	1	70
	Obid Boyce	1 @ 84	—	2 @ 80	—	—	2 @ 60 & 65	5	369
	ditto	2 @ 65	—	—	—	—	—	2	130
	John Mc Farlane	1 @ 84	—	—	2 @ 84	—	1 @ 60	4	312
	ditto	—	—	—	1 @ 50	—	—	—	50
	Duncan Anderson	—	—	2 @ 80	—	—	1 @ 80	3	240
	ditto	—	—	1 @ 70	—	—	—	1	70
Jany 30	John Perry	3 @ 84	—	—	—	—	—	3	252
	Thomas Roberts	1 @ 84	—	—	2 @ 84	—	—	3	252
	ditto	—	—	—	1 @ 70	—	1 @ 60	2	130
	David McCulloch	—	1 @ £82	1 @ 80	1 @ 84	—	—	3	246
	ditto	—	—	—	1 @ 60	—	1 @ 45	2	105
	George Kimber	1 @ 84	2 @ 82	—	—	—	1 @ 53	4	301
	William Taylor	3 @ 84	—	—	—	—	—	3	252
	ditto	2 @ 70	—	—	—	—	—	2	140
	ditto	1 @ 60	—	—	—	—	—	1	60
	Andrew McLean	1 @ 70	—	—	3 @ 84	—	1 @ 60	5	382
	Elizabeth Stermett	1 @ 70	—	1 @ 70	—	—	—	2	140

continued

Date	To whom sold	Men		Boys	Women		Girls	Total	Amount £.s.d
		Men	Boys		Women	Girls			
Jany 30	Green Pond Estate	4 @ 68	—	3 @ 60	3 @ 66	—	—	10	650
	William Simpson	—	—	1 @ 65	—	—	—	1	65
	John Roberts	—	—	2 @ 53	—	—	3 @ 55	5	271
	Stephen Laurence	—	—	1 @ 55	—	—	2 @ 55	3	165
	George Cathrens	—	—	1 @ 50	—	—	—	1	50
Jany 31st	Alexr B. Hay	2 @ 60	—	1 @ 55	—	—	—	3	175
	Charles Hill	—	—	1 @ 55	—	—	—	1	55
	Elizabeth Allen	—	—	1 @ 53	—	—	1 @ 53	2	106
	John Pinder	6 @ 55	—	3 @ 46	6 @ 55	—	3 @ 46	18	936
	John Stinnett	3 @ 55	—	—	3 @ 55	—	—	6	330
	James Leonard	—	—	—	1 @ 60	—	—	1	60
	John & Wm Gilzean	—	—	1	1	—	—	2	108
Feby 2	N. Gray, G. Gray, T.	23	—	5	37	—	5	70	2,800
	Leigh & C Younger	3	—	—	7	1	1	12	143.14.11
	Sold at Vendue by Jn Anderson	—	—	—	—	—	—		
	Total	65	4	31	74	1	27	202	10,896.14.11

continued

Charges [Costs Incurred by the Sale of Captives]

	[Costs Incurred during Sale]			[Total in £.s.d]
	[£]	[s]	[d]	
[Total Income from Captives Sold]				10,896.14.11
To our Commission on £10,896.14.11				
To deduct sale duty on 44 males [. . .] not allowed by the purchasers. £88.00.00				
To say 5p. Cent Commission on this Sum. . . £10,808.14.11	540	8	9	
To Sale duty on 44 males as above being refuse and not p'ble [sic] by purchasers	88	—	—	
To Import duty on 100 Males @13/4. . . . [£.s.d] 66.13.4	101	—	—	
To Import duty on 103 females @ 6/8. . . . [£.s.d] 34.6.8	8	8	4	
To paid Robert Walker for a room to sell the slaves in	8	8	—	
To paid James Farmin for printing hand Bills and Advert'g Sale	2	10	—	
To paid David McHardie for advert'g at Martha Brae		10	—	
To paid the Searcher for measuring Slaves	2	15	—	
To paid Doct'r Haddon for attending the Ship	9	16	1	
[Total Charges]	753	8	1	753.8.1
N[et] Proceeds carried to Current				10,143.6.10

10) James Rogers Esquire in Account Current with John Cunningham & John Perry, C107/59

	[Jamaican currency]		
	[£]	[s]	[d]

1793 March 10th To Amount of *African Queens* [sic] disbursements	380	3	2
To Our Commission on £10,143.6.10 for returns @ 5 p. cent	507	3	4
To John Cunninghams Bills on [. . .] Hugh Ingram @ 18 months sight. 1105.14.5	4,628	0	2
To Ditto on Ditto at 24 months 1100			
To Ditto on Ditto at 30 ditto 1100			
. . . . Stg 3305.14.5			
To John Perrys [sic] Bills on William Seyer at 18 months sight.			
. . . . 1100	4,628	0	2
To ditto on ditto at 24 months 1105.14.5			
To ditto on ditto at 30 ditto. 1100			
. . . . Stg 3,305.14.5			
	10,143	6	10
By N[et] Proceeds of 202 Slaves imported in the Ship *African Queen* as p[er] Amount Sales	10,143	6	10

Errors Excepted. Jamaica, Montego Bay, 10th March 1793
Jn. Cunningham, John Perry

Note: For information on currencies, see note on Letter 9.

11) Anonymous author to James Rogers, 1793, C107/59

202 slaves imported in the *African Queen* sold for £10,143 Jamaica Currency equal to £7,245 Sterg.

The coast comm[ission]. of £4 in £108 is £268.6.8 Sterg.[2]

Of which Cap[n] [Samuel] Stribling having purchased 60 slaves is entitled to £79.14.00

& Mr. [Hamet] Forsyth having purchased remainder to £188.12.8

August 9—Mr. Forsyth in lieu of the above £65.9. being the N[et] average of 2 slaves, which he was entitled to as mate had he lived to the West Indies.

Fame's Sales £3,424.6.4—the Comm[ission] of [£]4 p[er]. [£]104 on which is £134.5.8.[3]

African Queen's p. £10,143 Curr[y] equal to £7,245 Ster[g] Comm[ission] [£]4 in [£]108 is [£]268.6.8

Note: For information on currencies, see note on Letter 9.

12) John Cunningham & John Perry to James Rogers, March 10th 1793, C107/59[4]

Montego Bay, 10th March 1793
James Rogers Esqr.
Dr Sir,
We now hand you Account Sales, ships disbursements, and account Currents of all our transactions on acc[ount] of the *African Queens* [sic] Cargo of slaves with Six Setts Bills of Exchange—Viz.
John Perry on W[illiam] Seyer

At 18 months sight	£1100	
D[itto]—24 m[onths]	£1105.14.5	
D[itto]—30 m[onths]	£1100	
	£3305.14.5	£3305.14.5

John Cunningham on Robt & Hugh Ingram

At	18 months sight	1105.14.5	
D[itto]	24 ditto	1100	
D[itto]	30 ditto	1000	
		3305.14.5	£3305.14.5
			£6611. 8.10

Amount in all say six thousand six hundred and eleven pounds 8/10 Sterling.

We also think it our duty to communicate to you some part of Mr. Long's Conduct while here, at least such part as we consider reprehensible. Herewith are the particulars of four separate Accounts—the amount is charged in the ships [sic] disbursements, but in your settling with him a considerable part will be a charge against him more we fear than all his allowance will come to. In Mr. Angus Account no. 4 you will see a Credit of £33—for 12 B[arrels] provisions sold by Long to Angus. The day we completed the sale of slaves Mr. Long was desired to send to the Counting House an account of what provisions were on Board that we should sell the surplus, after reserving a sufficient quantity for ships [sic] use. Accordingly next day he gave a memo[randum] of having what he termed more than sufficient 27 Bushels beans, 3 [. . .] bread and two B[arrels] herrings, some beans and loose Bread was delivered to the Gentlemen who purchased the last 70 slaves the remainder we ordered to the Vendue store—Ten or Twelve days after that we learned that Long had (unknown to us) Sold to Angus at an under value several Barrels of provisions. We went on Board & asked him if he had sold any provisions he told us that he had only sold 2 Barrels at 50 p. whereas he had sold 12 Barrels Beef and pork & 2 Barrels herrings & had taken up a good deal of the amount. A few days after that 3 B[arrels] flour & 7 B[arrels] Pease was sent on shore for sale this must appear strange when you see a charge £26.16.4 in Ships [sic] Account for a stoppage of seamans allowance and from the n[et] Proceeds as p[er] account herewith you may guess the state in which bread flour & pease were landed. Yesterday he landed 3 [. . .] more of Bread and 2 B[arrels] pork saying that he did not know they were on Board, having inquired of the Mate he informed that they were on the Deck for a week & if he (the Mate) had not borrowed a boat they never would have been sent on shore. The proceeds of the Bread, flour and pease will be sent to you by the first opportunity. In short you will soon see that the man is an Idiot—& that your property has been sacrificed to his weakness. We consider ourselves very fortunate to have procured so valuable a man as Mr. Herd to go Chief Mate, as Saunders is but a Boy.

On Board of the ship is a Negro boy of about 16 he was put on Board on the Coast as a Pawn & we thought it advisable not to sell him. There is a little freight on Board the shippers are greatly disappointed there is no more, as Capt[n] Long undertook his ship should carry four times as much.

From what you have been before advised respecting the slaves we hope you will be satisfied with the sales we did our best. The Gentlemen who purchased the remains of the Cargo, we are sorry to remark cannot boast of their bargain. they have Buried 8 or 10 and sold only about 25.

We wish you better luck with the ship another time. It appears that nothing has gone right since the Death of Captn Stribling & Mr. Forsyth.
We remain very respectfully,
Dear Sir, Your very H[umble] Serv[ants]
Jn Cunningham
John Perry

13) 2 Letters to James Rogers, C107/59[5]

—12 March [1793]
With much ado we got your ship away yesterday—it was almost a coercive work being obliged to send the pilot off ourselves to get her under weigh [*sic*] nolens volens.

—Mssrs Saryenh Chambers & Co.
Bristol 2 May 1793
Sirs,
I have this day received the three Inclosed Bills on account of Ja[s] Rogers's ship *African Queen* for £3305.14.5 on Robt & Hugh Ingram which please get accepted, or if refused, let those be noted & protested in order to be sent out to Jamaica for father [*sic*] Security; the same such on account of this ship is drawn on a person in Bristol.
I am Sirs Your Most Ob[edient] Serv[ant]
I.A.

Table A.1. Captives Transported to Jamaica, 1751–1775

	Jamaica		
	Embarked in Africa	Disembarked in Jamaica	Entered the Jamaican slave-labor system
1751–1755	58,900	48,700	39,700
1756–1760	43,200	36,100	29,200
1761–1765	56,000	46,700	37,700
1766–1770	48,500	34,600	27,900
1771–1775	80,800	66,100	53,400
Total	287,400	232,200	187,900

Source: http://slavevoyages.org/tast/assessment/estimates.faces?yearFrom=1751&yearTo=17
75&disembarkation=301 (accessed March 2009).

Note: These numbers account for captives brought to Jamaica on any European ship. Approximately 98 percent of them were transported on British slave ships. For calculation purposes, numbers were rounded to the nearest hundred. Estimates on the number of captives who actually entered the Jamaican slave-labor system factor in that 5 percent of the captives who disembarked in Jamaica were dead before they could be sold and that a percentage of those calculated to have survived were re-exported to other islands (see chapter 1). Between 1751 and 1775, approximately 15 percent of captives were transported to other islands. Between 1776 and 1808, those who were transported accounted for about 18 percent. Calculations are based on the Herbert Klein and Roderick McDonald studies cited in chapter 1, note 10. For an innovative study that discusses the demography among enslaved populations in the Caribbean (including their re-exportation), see Eltis and Lachance, "Demographic Decline."

Table A.2. Captives Transported to Jamaica, 1776–1808

	Jamaica		
	Embarked in Africa	Disembarked in Jamaica	Entered the Jamaican slave-labor system
1776–1780	45,100	40,000	31,100
1781–1785	59,100	53,200	41,400
1786–1790	49,100	44,000	34,300
1791–1795	102,700	93,600	72,900
1796–1800	78,400	71,100	55,400
1801–1805	44,200	39,300	30,600
1806–1808	33,300	29,600	23,100
Total	411,900	370,800	288,800

Source: http://slavevoyages.org/tast/assessment/estimates.faces?yearFrom=1776&yearTo=18
08&disembarkation=301 (accessed March 2009).

Note: See note for table A.1.

Table A.3. Percentage of Captive Men, Women, and Children Transported on British Ships, 1751–1808

	British Slave Ships		
	Men	Women	Children
1751–1775	44%	24%	32% Boys (18%) Girls (14%)
1776–1800	52%	30%	18% Boys (10%) Girls (8%)
1801–1808	56%	27%	17% Boys (9%) Girls (8%)

Source: http://slavevoyages.org/tast/database/search.faces?yearFrom=1751&yearTo=1775&natinimp=7; http://slavevoyages.org/tast/database/search.faces?yearFrom=1776&yearTo=1800&natinimp=7; http://slavevoyages.org/tast/database/search.faces?yearFrom=1801&yearTo=1808&natinimp=7 (accessed April 2009).

Note: Not all records had data on children, so the sample size for each period varied. The 1750–1775 data on children were derived from the records of 2.1 percent of all known voyages for the period (72 voyages); the 1776–1800 data on children were derived from the records of 22.4 percent of all known voyages for the period (588 voyages); and the 1800–1808 data on children were derived from the records of 0.9 percent of all known voyages for the period (9 voyages).

Table A.4. Areas of Provenance for Captives Shipped to Jamaica in the Eighteenth Century

Areas of Provenance	1726–1750	1751–1775	1776–1800
Bight of Biafra	28.7%	30.4%	41.8%
Gold Coast	28.0%	31.9%	24.6%
West Central Africa	21.3%	9.4%	18.1%
Bight of Benin	6.5%	10.3%	6.5%
Sierra Leone	3.4%	15.0%	7.2%
Senegambia	3.2%	2.0%	1.0%
Other	9.0%	0.8%	0.8%

Source: http://slavevoyages.org/tast/database/search.faces?yearFrom=1726&yearTo=1800&mjslptimp=35100 (accessed May 2009).

Note: The category "West Central Africa" is problematic, as it does not reflect geographic nuances of the region south of Cape Lopez (in modern-day Gabon). However, the *Trans-Atlantic Slave Trade Database* (*TSTD*) includes the statistical data for slaving areas south of Cape Lopez under this category. There are a number of challenges in accurately disaggregating the statistics, and so for simplicity the term will be used here. Also, the *TSTD* provides statistics for "Sierra Leone" and the "Windward Coast." The latter term is also a problematic one. It was a nautical term used by British ship captains but had little meaning to Africans from that region. In this study, any relevant statistics for Sierra Leone include those for the region that the *TSTD* refers to as the "Windward Coast."

Table A.5. Percentage of Ships at Ports of Disembarkation in Jamaica, 1751–1808

	Kingston	Montego Bay	Other	Port unspecified
1751–1775	48.4%	2.7%	1.9%	47.0%
1776–1800	62.3%	11.3%	4.4%	22.0%
1801–1808	86.6%	6.8%	1.6%	5.0%

Source: http://slavevoyages.org/tast/database/search.faces?yearFrom=1726&yearTo=1808&mjslptimp=35100 (accessed May 2009).

Notes

Introduction

1. Jamaica Point was also known as "Jamaica Town," and Sherbro Island was also spelled "Sherboro." The term *slave factory* refers to a place where a factor or agent carried out business. Factories could be land based or ship based (i.e., floating factories). For Jamaica Point, see Utting, *Story of Sierra Leone*, 49–51. For references to captives being purchased by African traders from Jamaica Point, see Martin and Spurrell, *Journal of a Slave Trader*, 23, 39, 40.

2. For *Xaymaca*, see Senior, *Encyclopedia of Jamaican Heritage*. For an 1840 map showing Jamaica Point, see map 43 at www.afriterra.org (accessed June 2009). See also map 1232 for a French map drawn in 1833. For Sherbro-Jamaica trade links, see MacCormack, "Slaves," 284.

3. See Trouillot, *Silencing the Past*.

4. Curtin, *Atlantic Slave Trade*; Higman, *Slave Populations*.

5. For a recent study that addresses some of these issues, see Eltis and Lachance, "Demographic Decline," 335–63.

6. For a recent work assessing the concept of Atlantic history, see Greene and Morgan, *Atlantic History*.

7. It is impossible to provide a complete list of scholarly contributions here. An example of the earlier works would be Herskovits, *Myth of the Negro Past*. See also Mintz and Price, *Birth of African-American Culture*. For more recent studies, see Eltis and Richardson, *Routes to Slavery*; Gomez, *Exchanging Our Country Marks*; Lovejoy, *Identity*; Morgan, "Cultural Implications"; Nishida, *Slavery and Identity*; Sweet, *Recreating Africa*; Hall, *Africans in Colonial Louisiana*; Thornton, *Africa and Africans*; Mann, "Shifting Paradigms"; Manning, *Slavery and African Life*; Law, *Ouidah*.

8. For studies addressing enslaved women in the Caribbean, see Bush, *Slave Women*; Morrissey, *Slave Women*; Beckles, *Natural Rebels*; Moitt, *Women and Slavery*. For a recent study looking at the Americas more generally, see Morgan, *Laboring Women*. For works on enslaved children, see Aird, "Forgotten Ones"; Diptee, "African Children"; Jones, "'Suffer the Little Children'"; King, *Stolen Childhood*; Schwartz, *Born in Bondage*; Vasconcellos, "And a Child."

9. For example, according to Barry Higman, "British West Indian planters showed a clear preference for males as agricultural laborers, and this was reflected in the prices paid for slaves"; Higman, *Slave Populations*, 115. See also Walvin, *Black Ivory*, 119; Williams, *Capitalism and Slavery*, 38; Morrissey, *Slave Women*, 33; Moitt, *Women and Slavery*, 38. One exception to this is Hilary Beckles's study, which focuses specifically on Barbados. See Beckles, *Natural Rebels*, 7–23.

10. For quotation, see Patterson, *Slavery and Social Death*. See, for example, Smallwood, *Saltwater Slavery*, 59–61.

11. Frazier, *Negro Family*; Elkins, *Slavery*.

12. On "social death," see Patterson, *Slavery and Social Death*, 7. For a recent work suggesting that captives were socially dead, see Smallwood, *Saltwater Slavery*, 59–61.

13. For Thistlewood's treatment of the enslaved, see chapters 5, 6, and 7 in Burnard, *Mastery, Tyranny and Desire*. For an insightful critique of scholarly discussions addressing humanity, agency, and resistance among the enslaved, see Johnson, "On Agency," 113–24.

14. Trotman, "Africanizing and Creolizing," 218–39; Lovejoy and Trotman, "Enslaved Africans."

Chapter 1. The Atlantic Crucible

1. This point, made by John Thornton, is elaborated upon in chapter 3. See Thornton, "Cannibals, Witches," 277.

2. This is discussed in fuller detail in chapter 5.

3. See http://slavevoyages.org/tast/assessment/estimates.faces?yearFrom=1701&yearTo=1808&disembarkation=301 (accessed March 2009).

4. See http://slavevoyages.org/tast/assessment/estimates.faces?yearFrom=1776&yearTo=1808 (accessed March 2009).

5. Ragatz, *Fall of the Planter Class*, 191.

6. Sheridan, "From Jamaican Slavery," 330.

7. The last ships that could legally dock in Jamaica to sell captives did so in February 1808.

8. See http://slavevoyages.org/tast/assessment/estimates.faces?yearFrom=1775&yearTo=1808&disembarkation=301 (accessed March 2009).

9. *Jamaican Votes of Assembly* (1778), 84.

10. Calculations on the percentage of captives re-exported are based on data taken from studies done by Herbert Klein (for the period 1774–88) and Roderick McDonald (for the period 1789–1808). See table 5 in Klein, "English Slave Trade," 33; table 1 in McDonald, "Measuring the British Slave Trade," 254. For a discussion of the re-exportation of captives from the Caribbean, see Eltis and Lachance, "Demographic Decline." See also Klein, "Cuban Slave Trade."

11. Burnard, *Mastery, Tyranny and Desire*, 15. Burnard is by no means the only scholar to present high mortality and low birth rates as the sole factor influencing the importation numbers of African captives. This interpretation is, in fact, rampant in the literature.

See, for example, Cecily Jones, who argues that "most enslaved populations throughout the Caribbean failed to reproduce themselves by natural increase. As a result planters were forced to rely on the importation of enslaved Africans well into the years before slavery was finally abolished in 1807"; Jones, "'Suffer the Little Children,'" 19. Similarly, Vincent Brown maintains, "High child mortality meant that the Jamaican slave population would never sustain its numbers by natural means . . . and that Jamaican planters essentially externalized the costs of raising children to villages in Africa"; Brown, *Reaper's Garden*, 55–56.

12. Craton, "Jamaican Slave Mortality," 3. Higman also sees a link between "small islands capable of only limited expansion" and the growth of the enslaved population; Higman, *Slave Populations*, 78.

13. According to Higman, the enslaved population of Barbados "leveled off" after about 1710; Higman, *Slave Populations,* 43. For the reference to Jamaica's "saturation point," see Craton, "Jamaican Slave Mortality," 5.

14. For the quotation, see Burnard, "Theater of Terror," 246. For an interesting study that reassesses the demography of the Caribbean, see Eltis and Lachance, "Demographic Decline."

15. Craton also shows an *overall* proportional decrease in the number of Africans in Jamaica during the eighteenth century. His estimations are as follows: 89.4 percent in 1712; 76.3 percent in 1722; 81.5 percent in 1732; 76.4 percent in 1742; 78.4 percent in 1752; 72.8 percent in 1762; and 64.4 percent in 1772 ("Jamaican Slave Mortality," 24). According to Craton, there was "a trend towards demographic self-sufficiency" ("Jamaican Slave Mortality," 27). Similarly, Higman maintains that the creoles on older sugar estates were "established, if not self-supporting" (*Slave Population and Economy*, 80). For the percentage of Africans, see Higman, *Slave Population and Economy,* 76. For a recent study that takes an opposing view and sets out to explain "the failure" of the enslaved in Jamaica to reproduce, see Morgan, "Slave Women and Reproduction." Yet even Morgan acknowledges that fertility rates varied significantly between plantations.

16. Higman, *Slave Population and Economy*, 61. Other historians have estimated the total enslaved population to be slightly lower. See, for example, Watts, *West Indies*, 286.

17. The re-exportation of captive Africans from Jamaica is an area that requires further analysis, as to date there is no extensive study on this subject.

18. See http://slavevoyages.org/tast/database/search.faces?yearFrom=1750&yearTo= 1755&mjslptimp=35100 (accessed March 2009).

19. For a history of the Gold Coast, see Kea, *Settlements, Trade, and Polities*. For Cape Coast Castle and slave trade relations, see Andquandah, *Castles and Forts of Ghana*.

20. For data and quotations on Apongo and John Cope, see Hall, *In Miserable Slavery*, 106. See also Burnard, *Mastery, Tyranny and Desire*, 176, 297–98.

21. See http://slavevoyages.org/tast/database/search.faces?yearFrom=1784&yearTo= 1784&mjslptimp=35100 (accessed March 2009).

22. According to Edwards, the interview with Clara was initially recorded "without any view to publication"; Bryan Edwards, *History* (1819), 80–81.

23. Bryan Edwards, *History* (1819), 80–81.

24. Hindmarsh, *John Newton*, 18. For quotation, see Hochschild, *Bury the Chains*, 311. See also Martin and Spurrell, *Journal of a Slave Trader*, x.

25. Pybus, "Bound for Botany Bay," 93, 94.

26. James Mourgue and Richard Smith, September 25, 1784, Treasury Records, T70/33, fol. 104, National Archives; Richard Miles, Cape Coast Castle, February 1, 1783, Treasury Records, T70/33, fols. 53–54, National Archives.

27. Richard Miles, Cape Coast Castle, February 1, 1783, Treasury Records, T70/33, fol. 54, National Archives.

28. See http://slavevoyages.org/tast/database/search.faces?yearFrom=1780&yearTo=1800&anycaptain=Scasbrick (accessed March 2009). See also James Williams to James Rogers, January 23, 1791, Chancery Records, C107/14, National Archives.

29. Paley, "After Somerset," 168.

30. Testimony of George Young in Minutes of the Evidence Taken before the Select Committee, House of Commons and Lords, ZHC 1/84, 206. For examples of such violations in African-British trading relations, see Law, "Legal and Illegal Enslavement."

31. Thomas Rutherford, Secretary of the Company of Merchants, August 27, 1777, Treasury Records, T70/69, fols. 126–35, National Archives.

32. Ibid., fol. 135.

33. Eltis, "Cooperation and Resistance," 4.

34. Governor John Roberts and Council, December 24, 1780, Treasury Records, T70/32, fol. 87, National Archives.

Chapter 2. "Provided they arrive in health"

1. Simon Taylor to Robert Taylor, January 21, 1805, TAYL/1, Letter Book G, Simon Taylor Letter Books, Institute of Commonwealth Studies, London.

2. For quotation, see St. Clair, *Grand Slave Emporium*, 209. With the exception of Hilary Beckles's work on Barbados, the notion that there was a preference for enslaved adult males throughout the British Caribbean generally goes uncontested. See Beckles, *Natural Rebels*, 7–23. For example, according to Barry Higman, "British West Indian planters showed a clear preference for males as agricultural laborers, and this was reflected in the prices paid for slaves." See Higman, *Slave Populations*, 115. See also Walvin, *Black Ivory*, 119; Williams, *Capitalism and Slavery*, 38; Morrissey, *Slave Women*, 33; Moitt, *Women and Slavery*, 38.

3. Curtin, *Economic Change*, 168. For a discussion on the "peculiar needs of the slave cargo," see Richardson, "Costs of Survival."

4. Samuel Richards to James Rogers, November 1, 1791, Chancery Records, C107/7, box 2, National Archives. See also Samuel Richards to James Rogers, June 21, 1788, Chancery Records, C107/9, National Archives; James Maud to James Rogers, July 30, 1786, Chancery Records, C107/8, National Archives; Council and Assembly of Grenada (1788), Board of Trade, BT 6/11 (no folio number), National Archives.

5. See Simon Taylor to Robert Taylor, January 21, 1805 (TAYL/1, Letter Book G), December 3, 1798 (TAYL/1, Letter Book B), December 29, 1803 (TAYL/1, Letter Book F),

and March 26, 1804 (TAYL/1 Letter Book F), all from Simon Taylor Letter Books, Institute of Commonwealth Studies, London; Hall, *In Miserable Slavery*, 119; Leyland & Co to Captain Charles Molyneaux, June 14, 1791, Christopher Papers, John Hope Franklin Collection, Duke University (emphasis mine).

6. James Rolland to James Rogers, July 30, 1780 (Antigua), Chancery Records, C107/8, National Archives; Henry Dundas to Committee, *British Parliamentary Debates*, April 1792, p. 291.

7. Robert Sewell to the Committee of Correspondence, March 31, 1796, Commissioners of Correspondence, Out-Letter Book of Stephen Fuller and Robert Sewell, 1795–1801, fols. 32–34, Jamaican National Archives; "Observations on the Slave Trade," Bryan Edwards to Henry Dundas, April 7, 1797, MSS W. Ind. s8, Rhodes House, Oxford.

8. See Blouet, "Bryan Edwards"; Geggus, "Jamaica."

9. Blouet, "Bryan Edwards," 49; "Observations on the Slave Trade," Bryan Edwards to Henry Dundas, April 7, 1797, MSS W. Ind. s8, Rhodes House, Oxford.

10. Commissioners of Correspondence, Out-Letter Book of Stephen Fuller and Robert Sewell, 1795–1801, fols. 32–34, Jamaican National Archives; Circular of Duke of Portland, April 23, 1798, *British Parliamentary Papers*, 1803–4 (119), p. 14, Chancery Records, C107, National Archives. Thomas Leyland and Company to Captain Caesar Lawson, July 1803, Liverpool, in Donnan, *Documents*, 651.

11. Thomas Leyland and Company to Captain Caesar Lawson, July 1803, Liverpool, in Donnan, *Documents*, 651; James Hunt to James Rogers, July 14, 1793 (quotation cited), and May 11, 1793, Chancery Records, C107/59, National Archives.

12. Henry Dundas to Committee, *British Parliamentary Debates*, April 1792, p. 290.

13. "Observations on the Slave Trade," Bryan Edwards to Henry Dundas, April 7, 1797, MSS W. Ind. s8, Rhodes House, Oxford.

14. Martin and Spurrell, *Journal of a Slave Trader*, 72 (emphasis mine).

15. See responses of Robert Heatley and Delegates of Liverpool (signed John Matthews, Arch'd Dalzell, Robert Norris) in Answers Returned by the Committee of the Company of Merchants Trading to Africa (1788), Board of Trade, BT 6/9, National Archives.

16. Thomas Miles to I. Ashley, October 31, 1793, Letter Book of Thomas Miles, Treasury Records, T70/1484, fol. 67, National Archives (emphasis mine).

17. Fox to Committee, *British Parliamentary Debates*, April 1792, 307 (emphasis mine).

18. Jamaican National Archives, *Votes of the Jamaican House of Assembly* (1788), 93; John Cunningham to James Rogers, April 20, 1792, Chancery Records, C107/6, National Archives. According to the editors of the *TSTD*, children with a height of 4 feet 4 inches were about thirteen or fourteen years of age. See the glossary of Eltis and Halbert, *Voyages* (2009), www.slavevoyages.org.

19. John Cunningham to James Rogers, April 20, 1792, Chancery Records, C107/6, National Archives.

20. Allan White, January 12 and 27, 1793, Chancery Records, C107/6, National Archives. For another example, see Robert Peake, January 13 and February 2, 1793, Chancery Records, C107/6, National Archives. All letters were to James Rogers.

21. See Grove, Harris & Papps to James Rogers, July 14, 1793, Chancery Records, C107/59, National Archives.

22. The record of sale does not explicitly state that the slaves sold as "refuse" were elderly. However, given that the slave cargo was reportedly healthy and the chief complaint was that the adult captives were too old, this seems a reasonable assumption. Thomas and William Salmon & Company to James Rogers, June 26, 1789, Chancery Records, C107/9, National Archives; Record of Sale for James Rogers, July 28, 1789, Chancery Records, C107/6, National Archives.

23. Francis Grant to James Rogers, April 10, 1789, Chancery Records, C107/9, National Archives.

24. Lytcott & Maxwell to James Rogers, March 3, 1789, Chancery Records, C107/9, National Archives.

25. Francis Grant to James Rogers, April 10, 1789, Chancery Records, C107/9, National Archives.

26. William Laroche to James Rogers, October 1, 1791, Chancery Records, C107/12, National Archives; William Laroche to James Rogers, no date (circa September 1791), Chancery Records, C107/12, National Archives.

27. He repeatedly purchased women, youths, and children—with little, if any, complaint. For examples, see Martin and Spurrell, *Journal of a Slave Trader,* pp. 18, 19, 20, 24, 26, 28, 29, 32, 37, 39, 40–44, 51–53. For "long breasted women," see pp. 32, 35. For references to the age of captives and Newton's refusal to purchase them on this account, see pp. 17, 45, 69.

28. Martin and Spurrell, *Journal of a Slave Trader,* 37.

29. Although a minority in his position, Joseph Inikori argues that planter demands played a crucial role in determining who was exported from Africa; Inikori, "Export versus Domestic Demand," 137. For an example of scholars who argue in favor of supply forces, see chapter 4 in Curtin, *Economic Change.* See also Lovejoy, "Impact." The demand-and-supply debate has also worked its way into the studies dealing with American slave systems. See, for example, Moitt, *Women and Slavery,* 24–27; Morgan, *Laboring Women,* 60. See also Eltis, Lewis, and Richardson, "Slave Prices." For examples of historians who look at shipping costs, trans-Atlantic war, and other factors, see Behrendt, "Annual Volume and Regional Distribution"; Eltis and Engerman, "Fluctuations."

30. Hair, "Antera Duke," 362.

31. For examples of sickly adults being sold for less than children, see "Sale of 72 Negroes (Including a Child) Imported from Africa in the Schooner Flora," February 21, 1791, Chancery Records, C107/5, National Archives; "Record of Sale for 342 Slaves," July 3, 1793, Chancery Records, C107/59, National Archives. For the quotation, see Isaac Hobhouse & Co. to William Barry, cited in Richardson, "Costs of Survival," 170.

32. Martin and Spurrell, *Journal of a Slave Trader,* 67 (emphases throughout paragraph are mine). See comments of Reverend John Newton, Robert Heatley, and the "Delegates of Liverpool" (signed John Matthews, Arch'd Dalzell, Robert Norris) in Answers Returned by the Committee of the Company of Merchants Trading to Africa (1788), Board of Trade, BT 6/9 (no folio number), National Archives.

33. Alex Macleod to James Rogers, July 27, 1791, Chancery Records, C107/5, National Archives.

34. Munro MacFarlane to James Rogers, September 4, 1792, Chancery Records, C107/5, National Archives; William Jenkins to James Rogers, September 4, 1792, Chancery Records, C107/5, National Archives.

35. See "An Act to Regulate the Carrying of Slaves" in Donnan, *Documents*, 582–89. See also Behrendt, "Annual Volume and Regional Distribution"; Eltis and Engerman, "Fluctuations."

36. John Kennedy to James Rogers, March 22, 1792, Chancery Records, C107/6, National Archives. See also William Jenkins to James Rogers, September 4, 1792, Chancery Records, C107/5, National Archives.

37. Leyland & Co. to Captain Charles Molyneaux, June 14, 1791, Christopher Papers, John Hope Franklin Collection, Duke University. For the reference to George Merrick, see Pope-Hennessy, *Sins of the Fathers*, 109. Also see letters written to James Rogers relating to the voyage of the slave ship *Pearl*: William Blake, August 28 and October 9, 1790; I. P. Degreaves, October 10, 1790; Samuel Stribling, March 12 and April 24, 1791; William Blake, April 2, 1791; Alexander Lindo, May 11, 1791. For all letters, see Chancery Records, C107/12, National Archives.

38. William Dinely to James Rogers, March 3 and July 18, 1791, Chancery Records, C107/5, National Archives. For an example of a ship without a surgeon, see letter from John Kennedy of the slave ship *Ruby*. John Kennedy to James Rogers, April 3, 1792, Chancery Records, C107/6, National Archives.

39. John Goodrich to James Rogers, February 4, 1790, Chancery Records, C107/5, National Archives.

40. William Blake to James Rogers, August 28, 1790, Chancery Records, C107/12, National Archives; I. P. Degreaves to James Rogers, October 10, 1790, Chancery Records, C107/12, National Archives. For other examples, see William Dinely to James Rogers, September 1791, Chancery Records, C107/5, National Archives; Robert Peake to James Rogers, undated, Chancery Records, C107/6, National Archives.

41. Emphasis mine. William Blake to James Rogers, October 1790, Chancery Records, C107/12, National Archives. For other examples, see William Dinely to James Rogers, September 1791, Chancery Records, C107/5, National Archives; Robert Peake to James Rogers, undated, Chancery Records, C107/6, National Archives.

42. Behrendt, "Markets," 181. For references to problems of food supply, see Return from the Commissioners of Trade & Plantations, August 10, 1777, and July 11, 1780, T70/32; and January 30, 1780, T70/33, Treasury Records, National Archives.

43. John Roberts, Governor of Cape Coast Castle, July 11, 1780, Treasury Records, T70/32, National Archives. Individuals stationed as "governors" on the Gold Coast were employed by the Company of Merchants to facilitate the British slave trade with African traders. See Metcalf, "Microcosm," 378; Hair, "Antera Duke," 363.

44. Jerome Bernard Weuves, Governor of Cape Coast Castle, January 30, 1782, Treasury Records, T70/33, fol. 22, National Archives.

45. Letter from Governor and Council, November 30, 1787, Treasury Records, T70/33, fol. 110, National Archives. See also Richard Miles, Governor of Cape Coast Castle, Au-

gust 10, 1777, Treasury Records, T70/32, fol. 30, National Archives. For an example of a ship without enough food, see George Baillee & Company to James Rogers (St. Vincent), November 6, 1788, Chancery Records, C107/7, Box 2, National Archives.

46. Eltis, "Cooperation and Resistance," 6; Martin and Spurrell, *Journal of a Slave Trader*, 22 (quotation).

47. William Blake to James Rogers, January 11, 1791, Chancery Records, C107/12, National Archives. For a recent study on shipboard revolts, see Taylor, *If We Must Die*.

48. For children and shipboard revolts, see Martin and Spurrell, *Journal of a Slave Trader*, 71, 77 (quotation). For another example, see Burnard, *Mastery, Tyranny and Desire*, 6.

49. For a discussion on the complexities of "assortment bargaining," see Curtin, *Economic Change*, 249–53. See also Abbé Proyart, "History of Loango, Kakongo, and Other Kingdoms in Africa," in Donnan, *Documents*, 549–52. For quotation, see Governor John Roberts and Council, October 8, 1780, Treasury Records, T70/32, fol. 81, National Archives. See also John Roberts, July 11, 1780, Treasury Records, T70/34, National Archives.

50. Thomas Walker to James Rogers & Company, September 20, 1790, Chancery Records, C107/14, National Archives; John Roberts, July 11, 1780, Treasury Records, T70/34, National Archives. See also letter from the slave trader John Smith advising his employer of the "goods in demand": John Smith to James Rogers, May 24, 1791, Chancery Records, C107/12, National Archives. See also, for example, James Jones to Lord Hawkesbury, July 26, 1788, in Donnan, *Documents*, 589–92.

51. Leyland & Co. to Captain Charles Molyneaux, June 14, 1791, Christopher Papers, John Hope Franklin Collection, Duke University.

52. Captain Forsyth to James Rogers, July 9, 1792, Chancery Records, C107/13, National Archives.

53. Grove, Harris & Papps, March 10, 1793, Chancery Records, C107/59, National Archives. Apparently, slaves from Old Calabar were equally unpopular in other islands. For Grenada, see William Laroche, October 1, 1791, Chancery Records, C107/12, National Archives; James Baillee, April 4, 1792, Chancery Records, C107/7, box 2, National Archives. For St. Vincent, see George Baillee, November 6, 1788, Chancery Records, C107/7, box 2, National Archives. For Dominica, see Francis and Robert Smyth, February 2, 1788, Chancery Records, C107/8, National Archives. All correspondence written to James Rogers.

54. Grove, Harris & Papps, March 10, 1793, Chancery Records, C107/59, National Archives; Francis Grant, October 10, 1789, Chancery Records, C107/9, National Archives. In an earlier letter (August 4), Grant made clear that his first preference was for Gold Coast captives. In this subsequent letter, he reported a change of heart and informed Rogers that his plan was changed and that he was now "induce[d] . . . to prefer an Eboe Cargo to a Gold Coast one." Merchant James Fowler also reported that the "eboes [sic] from Bonny" were preferred; James Fowler, September 8, 1790, Chancery Records, C107/5, National Archives. All correspondence written to James Rogers.

55. See Francis and Robert Smyth to James Rogers, February 2, 1788, Chancery Records, C107/8, National Archives.

56. Lovejoy and Richardson, "'This Horrid Hole,'" 368–70; Lovejoy and Richardson, "Trust, Pawnship," 339.

57. Francis Grant to James Rogers & Co., December 30, 1788, Chancery Records, C107/7, box 2, National Archives; Simon Taylor to Robert Taylor, December 29, 1803, TAYL/1, Letter Book F, Simon Taylor Letter Books, Institute of Commonwealth Studies, London.

58. Francis Grant to James Rogers, December 30, 1788, and November 6, 1791, Chancery Records, C107/10, National Archives; Thomas Pappy to James Rogers, January 12, 1789, Chancery Records, C107/9, National Archives.

59. *Royal Gazette*, January 5–12, 1793; Simon Taylor to Robert Taylor, March 26, 1804, and December 29, 1803, TAYL/1 Letter Book F, Simon Taylor Letter Books, Institute of Commonwealth Studies, London. "Mocos" was the term used to refer to enslaved persons who were Ibibio in ethnic origin; see John Adams, *Sketches Taken*, 40.

60. See, for example, Lytcott & Maxwell (Barbados) to James Rogers, March 3, 1789, Chancery Records, C107/8, National Archives; James Baillie (Grenada) to James Rogers, April 4, 1792, Chancery Records, C107/7, box 2, National Archives; Robert Peake to James Rogers, January 13, 1793, Chancery Records, C107/6, National Archives.

61. Francis Grant to James Rogers, July 12, 1791, Chancery Records, C107/5, and March 15, 1791, Chancery Records, C107/8, National Archives; Alex McLeod to James Rogers, July 15, 1791, Chancery Records, C107/5, National Archives.

62. Thomas Pappy to James Rogers, January 12, 1789, Chancery Records, C107/9, National Archives; Return Relating to the General State of the Trade in Africa, 1777, Treasury Records, T70/177, 4–6, National Archives. The concern about "fake" Gold Coast captives is apparent in the words of merchant Francis Grant: "a small Gold Coast Cargo I should have had no objection to [selling] if well chosen & *real* Gold Coast Negroes!" (emphasis mine). Francis Grant to James Rogers, March 15, 1791, Chancery Records, C107/8, National Archives.

63. Captain Dear cited in St. Clair, *Grand Slave Emporium*, 210.

Chapter 3. "We took man, woman, and child"

1. See Minutes of the Evidence Taken before the Select Committee, House of Commons and Lords, ZHC 1/84, 123–24.

2. Some of the arguments made in this chapter were raised in my earlier study (Diptee, "African Children"), which focused on enslaved children.

3. Excerpt from Thomas Clarkson, "Essay on the Efficiency of the TRADE," in Donnan, *Documents*, 572. See Miller, *Way of Death*, 380; Alexander Falconbridge, *Account of the Slave Trade*, 14.

4. The Examination of Captain Hall in Answers Returned by the Committee of the Company of Merchants Trading to Africa (1788), February 22, 1788, Board of Trade, BT 6/9, fol. 60, National Archives; Alexander Falconbridge, *Account of the Slave Trade*; testimony of Henry Ellison in Minutes of the Evidence Taken before the Select Committee, House of Commons and Lords, ZHC 1/84, 362. For other examples of captives being

killed, see Answers Returned by the Committee of the Company of Merchants Trading to Africa (1788), Board of Trade, BT 6/9, fols. 84, 478, National Archives.

5. The Examination of Jerome Bernard Weuves, March 25, 1788, fols. 470–80. For another example, see The Examination of Robert Norris in Answers Returned by the Committee of the Company of Merchants Trading to Africa (1788), July 27, 1788, Board of Trade, BT 6/9, fols. 477, 115–20, National Archives. See also Forde, *Efik Traders of Old Calabar.*

6. James Jones to Lord Hawkesbury, July 26, 1788, in Donnan, *Documents*, 590.

7. Nwokeji, "African Conceptions of Gender," 51, 56, 61.

8. See Allan White & Co. to James Rogers & Co., January 27, 1793, Chancery Records, C107/6, National Archives; testimony of Isaac Parker in Minutes of the Evidence Taken before the Select Committee, House of Commons and Lords, ZHC, 1/84, 125.

9. For an analysis of the demographic impact of the slave trade, see Thornton, "Slave Trade"; Thornton, "Sexual Demography," 39–48. For the reference to famine caused by drought, see Miller, *Way of Death*, 158–59.

10. See http://slavevoyages.org/tast/assessment/estimates.faces?yearFrom=1780&yearTo=1805&embarkation=7 (accessed May 2009).

11. See http://slavevoyages.org/tast/database/search.faces?yearFrom=1770&yearTo=1810&mjbyptimp=60700 (accessed May 2009).

12. See table 5.1 (Angolan Population Structure, 1777–1778) in Miller, *Way of Death*, 160. For a discussion on enslaved females in Africa, see Klein, "Women in Slavery."

13. Mungo Park, *Travels in the Interior*, 261. See also Dirks, "Social Responses."

14. See Falola and Lovejoy, "Pawnship in Historical Perspective," 1–26. See also Lovejoy and Richardson, "Trust, Pawnship"; Account of a Voyage to the Coast of Africa by James Arnold, March 24, 1789, Board of Trade, BT 6/11 (no folio number), National Archives. For an example of a pawn being shipped to Jamaica, see Mr. Cunningham and John Perry to James Rogers, March 10, 1793, Chancery Records, C107/59, National Archives. See also Lovejoy and Richardson, "Business of Slaving," 82–84.

15. Law, *Ouidah*, 57, 128–29.

16. Account of a Voyage to the Coast of Africa by James Arnold, March 24, 1789, Board of Trade, BT 6/11 (no folio number), National Archives; testimony of Thomas Trotter and Clement Noble in Minutes of the Evidence Taken before the Select Committee, House of Commons and Lords, ZHC, 1/84, 83, 109, 114.

17. Testimony of William Dove and Thomas Trotter in Minutes of the Evidence Taken before the Select Committee, House of Commons and Lords, ZHC, 1/84, 83, 101.

18. Testimony of William Dove in Minutes of the Evidence Taken before the Select Committee, House of Commons and Lords, ZHC, 1/84, 101–2. See also testimony of Henry Ellison in Minutes of the Evidence Taken before the Select Committee, House of Commons and Lords, ZHC 1/84, 362.

19. See http://slavevoyages.org/tast/database/search.faces?yearFrom=1751&yearTo=1780&mjbyptimp=60200.60300&natinimp=7 (accessed May 2009).

20. Testimony of James Morley in Minutes of the Evidence Taken before the Select Committee, House of Commons and Lords, ZHC, 1/84, 153; The Evidence of Mr. William James, a Master in the Royal Navy, March 24, 1789, Board of Trade, BT 6/11 (no folio

number), National Archives; testimony of Isaac Parker and Clement Noble in Minutes of the Evidence Taken before the Select Committee, House of Commons and Lords, ZHC, 1/84, 125, 114–15.

21. Account of a Voyage to the Coast of Africa by James Arnold, March 24, 1789, Board of Trade, BT 6/11 (no folio number), National Archives. For another example, see Patterson, *Northern Gabon Coast*, 86.

22. It is uncertain what became of the infant in England. At the time of his testimony, Young had no knowledge about the infant's whereabouts; testimony of George Young in Minutes of the Evidence Taken before the Select Committee, House of Commons and Lords, ZHC 1/84, 206.

23. Testimony of Thomas Trotter in Minutes of the Evidence Taken before the Select Committee, House of Commons and Lords, ZHC, 1/84, 82; The Examination of Jerome Bernard Weuves in Answers Returned by the Committee of the Company of Merchants Trading to Africa (1788), March 25, 1788, Board of Trade, BT 6/9, fol. 476, National Archives.

24. Account of a Voyage to the Coast of Africa by James Arnold, March 21 and 24, 1789, Board of Trade, BT 6/11 (no folio number), National Archives. For another example, see Alexander Falconbridge, *Account of the Slave Trade*, 14.

25. See http://slavevoyages.org/tast/database/search.faces?yearFrom=1776&yearTo=1808&natinimp=7&mjbyptimp=60600 (accessed May 2009).

26. Lovejoy and Richardson, "Trust, Pawnship," 337; Lovejoy and Richardson, "'This Horrid Hole,'" 363–65.

27. Nwokeji, "Atlantic Slave Trade." This is consistent with contemporary observations as well. See, for example, John Adams, *Sketches Taken*, 38. See also Kolapo, "Igbo and Their Neighbours"; Northrup, "Igbo and Myth Igbo"; Chambers, "Significance of Igbo." See also chapter 6 in Hall, *Slavery and African Ethnicities*; chapter 2 in Nwokeji, "Biafran Frontier."

28. Lovejoy and Richardson, "'This Horrid Hole,'" 363–92.

29. Thomas Clarkson, *Essay on the Slavery and Commerce of the Human Species,* quoted in Lovejoy and Richardson, "'This Horrid Hole,'" 380. Bristol merchant James Jones also reported that "purchases" at Bonny were made "much quicker there than at any other place"; James Jones to Lord Hawkesbury, July 26, 1788, in Donnan, *Documents,* 589.

30. John Goodrich to James Rogers, June 20, 1791, Chancery Records, C107/5, National Archives; James Jones to Lord Hawkesbury, July 26, 1788, in Donnan, *Documents,* 589–92 (quotation on 590).

31. See http://slavevoyages.org/tast/database/search.faces?yearFrom=1700&yearTo=1808&natinimp=7&mjbyptimp=60400 (accessed May 2009); Hall, *Slavery and African Ethnicities*, 110. See also Perbi, *History of Indigenous Slavery.*

32. See http://slavevoyages.org/tast/database/search.faces?yearFrom=1700&yearTo=1808&mjbyptimp=60400 (accessed May 2009).

33. Thornton, "Coromantees," 161–64 (quotation on 162).

34. Lovejoy, *Transformations in Slavery*, 8.

35. Thornton, *Warfare in Atlantic Africa*, 57, 73.

36. Lovejoy, *Transformations in Slavery*, 8. For a discussion of warfare and Asante expansion in the Gold Coast region, see chapter 3 in Thornton, *Warfare in Atlantic Africa*; Shumway, "Between the Castle," chapter 1, note 17.

37. For a fuller discussion, see chapter 3 in Shumway, "Between the Castle."

38. The Examination of Richard Miles, March 20, 1788, Board of Trade, BT 6/9, fols. 440–41, National Archives; The Examination of Robert Norris, Board of Trade, BT 6/9, July 27, 1788, Board of Trade, BT 6/9, fol. 113, National Archives. Both in Answers Returned by the Committee of the Company of Merchants Trading to Africa (1788).

39. Jerome Bernard Weuves, in Answers Returned by the Committee of the Company of Merchants Trading to Africa (1788), Board of Trade, BT 6/9 (no folio number), National Archives. See also the response of Richard Miles (no folio number); Warner-Lewis, *Central Africa in the Caribbean*, 34.

40. David Mill, Governor of Cape Coast Castle, October 19, 1776, and December 4, 1773, Treasury Records, T70/32, National Archives.

41. See http://slavevoyages.org/tast/database/search.faces?yearFrom=1700&yearTo=1808&mjbyptimp=60700&natinimp=7 (accessed May 2009).

42. See http://slavevoyages.org/tast/database/search.faces?yearFrom=1750&yearTo=1808&mjbyptimp=60700&natinimp=7 (accessed May 2009).

43. See http://slavevoyages.org/tast/assessment/estimates.faces?yearFrom=1750&yearTo=1808&flag=3&embarkation=7 (accessed May 2009); Miller, "Central Africans," 57. French trading activities were affected by the French Revolution of 1789, the Haitian Revolution in 1791, and the abolition of slavery by the French National Assembly in 1794. See Hall, *Slavery and African Ethnicities*, 152.

44. Miller, "Numbers, Origins, and Destinations," 388, 409–10; Martin, *External Trade*, 92; Miller, *Way of Death*, 109.

45. Although captives sold at ports north and south of the Congo River tended to have the same point of origin, the commercial networks that supplied the captives to the south of the Congo were distinct from those of the north. Miller, "Numbers, Origins, and Destinations," 383–85.

46. See chapter 4 in Miller, *Way of Death*, 105–39.

47. Thornton, "African Soldiers," 60–61; Miller, "Central Africans," 55–56.

48. Accounts and Papers, xxix, Evidence of James Fraser to the Select Committee on the Slave Trade, 1790, cited in Martin, *External Trade*, 123; Hall, *Slavery and African Ethnicities*, 153. The study on runaways was completed by Douglas Chambers. Hall summarizes his conclusions in her work; see Hall, *Slavery and African Ethnicities*, 47.

49. Hall, *Slavery and African Ethnicities*, 157; Miller, "Central Africans," 22; Martin, *External Trade*, 123.

50. Miller, *Way of Death*, 225.

51. Vansina, foreword to Heywood, *Central Africans*, xi–xiii. See also Miller, "Central Africans," 55–56. Hall concludes that Kongo speakers dominate in the Caribbean; Hall, *Slavery and African Ethnicities*, 152.

52. Account of a Voyage to the Coast of Africa by James Arnold, March 24, 1789, Board of Trade, BT 6/11 (no folio number), National Archives.

53. Lovejoy and Richardson, "Trust, Pawnship," 339. See introduction in Forde, *Efik Traders of Old Calabar*; Testimony of James Penny and William James from the Report of the Committee of the Privy Council (1789), in Donnan, *Documents*, 597–98.

54. Miller, *Way of Death*, 120. See also Martin, "Trade of Loango," 211–14.

55. The Examination of Jerome Bernard Weuves, March 25, 1788, fol. 478; The Examination of Richard Miles, March 20, 1788, Board of Trade, BT 6/9, fol. 443, National Archives. Both are in Answers Returned by the Committee of the Company of Merchants Trading to Africa (1788).

56. Account of a Voyage to the Coast of Africa by James Arnold, March 24, 1789, Board of Trade, BT 6/11 (no folio number), National Archives.

57. The Examination of Jerome Bernard Weuves, March 25, 1788, Board of Trade, BT 6/9, fol. 478, National Archives; The Examination of Richard Miles, March 20, 1788, Board of Trade, BT 6/9, fols. 442–43, National Archives. Both are in Answers Returned by the Committee of the Company of Merchants Trading to Africa (1788). For the restraints used on women and children, see Patterson, *Northern Gabon Coast*, 86. For the Senegambian region, see Mungo Park, *Travels in the Interior*, 300.

58. The Examination of Jerome Bernard Weuves, March 25, 1788, Board of Trade, BT 6/9, fols. 479–80, National Archives; The Examination of Richard Miles, March 20, 1788, Board of Trade, BT 6/9, fols. 440–41, National Archives. Both are in Answers Returned by the Committee of the Company of Merchants Trading to Africa (1788).

59. Miller, *Way of Death*, 224; see also chapter 7. For the Park quotation, see "Travels of Mungo Park," in Donnan, *Documents*, 634.

60. Excerpt from Thomas Clarkson, "Essay on the Efficiency of the TRADE," in Donnan, *Documents*, 571; Mungo Park, *Travels in the Interior*, 300.

61. Excerpt from Alexander Falconbridge's *Account of the Slave Trade on the Coast of Africa* (1788), in Dow, *Slave Ships and Slaving*, 137–40.

62. Mungo Park, *Travels in the Interior*, 284–86.

63. See, for example, one such case in the Senegambian region in Mungo Park, *Travels in the Interior*, 300.

64. Law, *Ouidah*; Martin, *External Trade*; Miller, *Way of Death*; Testimony of James Penny and William James from the Report of the Committee of the Privy Council (1789), in Donnan, *Documents*, 597–98.

65. Martin, "Trade of Loango," 216. See also Martin, *External Trade*, 97–101. For a contemporary description, see "The Trade of Loango," in Donnan, *Documents*, 549–52. See also Metcalf, "Gold, Assortments," 27; Return Relating to the General State of the Trade in Africa (1777), Treasury Records, T70/177, 5, National Archives; St. Clair, *Grand Slave Emporium*, 212.

66. Martin, *External Trade*, 103.

67. Thornton, "Cannibals, Witches," 273–94.

68. John Atkins, *A Voyage to Guinea*, cited in Law, "Legal and Illegal Enslavement," 516; Bay, "Protection, Political Exile," 50. See also Law, *Ouidah*, 151. John Barnes and Mungo Park quoted in Piersen, "White Cannibals, Black Martyrs," 148.

69. Law, "Legal and Illegal Enslavement," 518. See Diouf, *Fighting the Slave Trade*.

Chapter 4. The Atlantic Crossing

1. Alpers, "Other Middle Passage," 21.

2. The Examination of Jerome Bernard Weuves, March 25, 1788, Board of Trade, BT 6/9, fols. 479–80, National Archives. Both are in Answers Returned by the Committee of the Company of Merchants Trading to Africa (1788).

3. Edward Alpers makes the argument that the middle passage was more than merely a voyage across a body of water. In his words, it "encompasses a much more complex set of forced migrations"; Alpers, "Other Middle Passage," 21. In their recent studies—both excellent works—Marcus Rediker and Emma Christopher see the slave ship as the place where captives were "produced" and the site for "making slaves" (Rediker, *Slave Ship*, 9; Christopher, *Slave Ship Sailors*, 167).

4. Rediker discusses the multifaceted purpose of the slave ship; see Rediker, *Slave Ship*, 9. For material culture and the middle passage, see Handler, "Middle Passage," 1–26.

5. Hamet Forsyth to James Rogers, July 9, 1792, Chancery Records, C107/13, National Archives. Transcriptions of the letters related to the *African Queen* can be found in the appendix. See also Richardson, *Bristol, Africa*, 203.

6. William Blake to James Rogers, November 11, 1792, Chancery Records, C107/5, National Archives; John Perry to James Rogers, January 21, 1793, Chancery Records, C107/13, National Archives. There are contradictory reports about the number of captives who left Africa, but I have opted to use the number that best supports the number of captives actually sold in Jamaica (after factoring the number of reported deaths during the voyage). See "Sale of Two Hundred and Two Slaves Imported in the Ship *African Queen*," March 10, 1793, Chancery Records, C107/59, National Archives. For details on the varying reports on the number of captives, see Richardson, *Bristol, Africa*, 203. See also John Cunningham to James Rogers, January 21, 1793, Chancery Records, C107/13, National Archives.

7. The hottest months of year are from November to May. See Kiple and Higgins, "Mortality Caused by Dehydration," 424.

8. Kiple and Higgins, "Mortality Caused by Dehydration," 425; Francis and Robert Smyth to James Rogers, January 10, 1793, Chancery Records, C107/13, National Archives. For a discussion of crew mortality on slave ships, see Steckel and Jensen, "New Evidence."

9. See Christopher, *Slave Ship Sailors*, 163–94; Sheridan, "Guinea Surgeons," 603–4.

10. Kiple and Higgins, "Mortality Caused by Dehydration," 424–28, 431; Christopher, *Slave Ship Sailors*, 169.

11. John Shilstone to James Rogers, January 8, 1793; Francis and Robert Smyth to James Rogers, January 10, 1793; John Perry to James Rogers, January 21, 1793. For all letters, see Chancery Records, C107/13, National Archives.

12. The sale of the captives was reported in Jamaican currency, which amounted to £10,896.14s.10d. This converts to approximately £7,782 sterling. Also, the number given for the mortality of captives includes the reported death of the 41 captives on the African coast and the 128 who died after the ship set sail. The number of deaths on the African

coast is very likely to have been much higher: the 41 deaths were reported in July, but the ship did not leave until November. For these points, see "Sale of Two Hundred and Two Slaves Imported in the Ship *African Queen*," March 10, 1793, Chancery Records, C107/59, National Archives. See also Richardson, *Bristol, Africa*, 203; John Cunningham and John Perry to James Rogers, March 10, 1793, Chancery Records, C107/59, National Archives.

13. Governor and Council of Cape Coast Castle, March 31, 1784. See also Richard Rogers to James Rogers, October 29, 1787, Chancery Records, C107/12, National Archives; http://slavevoyages.org/tast/database/search.faces?yearFrom=1760&yearTo=1790&natinimp=7&anycaptain=Richard+Rogers&shipname=Pearl (accessed May 2009); Behrendt, "Markets."

14. See http://slavevoyages.org/tast/database/search.faces?yearFrom=1760&yearTo=1772&shipname=Dobson&natinimp=7 (accessed May 2009); Hair, "Antera Duke," 361. The captives on the *Dobson* were sold in Barbados.

15. Mungo Park, *Travels in the Interior*, 83; St. Clair, *Grand Slave Emporium*, 78; Dow, *Slave Ships and Slaving*, 140; The Examination of Robert Norris in Answers Returned by the Committee of the Company of Merchants Trading to Africa (1788), February 27, 1788, Board of Trade, BT 6/9, fol. 120, National Archives. See also Account of a Voyage to the Coast of Africa by James Arnold, Board of Trade, BT 6/11 (no folio number), National Archives.

16. David Mills, Governor of Cape Coast Castle, September 19, 1774, Treasury Records, T70/32, National Archives.

17. For data on the ship *Sally*, see Oldham, "Insurance Litigation," 304. Oldham's reference to the ship *Sally* is with respect to "Tatham vs. Hodgson." The *TSTD* lists the vessel as having disembarked in Grenada. Other records, however, make clear that the ship *intended* to disembark in Grenada but actually did so in Barbados; see Oldham, "Insurance Litigation." See also Hogg, *African Slave Trade*, 58.

18. Klein, "English Slave Trade," 44–45. See also Haines and Shlomowitz, "Explaining the Mortality Decline."

19. The literature on mortality rates during the middle passage is extensive. See Klein and Engerman, "Long-Term Trends"; Cohn, "Deaths of Slaves"; Sheridan, "Guinea Surgeons"; Steckel and Jensen, "New Evidence."

20. For fuller elaboration on social death, see chapter 2 in Patterson, *Slavery and Social Death* (quotations from pp. 7, 38). For examples of studies that accept Patterson's notion of social death, see Burnard, *Mastery, Tyranny and Desire*, 195; Christopher, *Slave Ship Sailors*, 166–67; Smallwood, *Saltwater Slavery*, 59–61. For sharp critiques of Patterson's work, see Mintz, "More on the Peculiar Institution"; Finkelman, review of *Slavery and Social Death*; Franklin, review of *Slavery and Social Death*.

21. Taylor, *If We Must Die*. See also Uya, "Slave Revolts." For an example of multiple revolts on a single voyage, see the case cited in Oldham, "Insurance Litigation," 209.

22. Account of a Voyage to the Coast of Africa by James Arnold, March 24, 1789, Board of Trade, BT 6/11 (no folio number), National Archives.

23. Approximately 440 captives were purchased in Africa, and 60 died before this incident. Of the remaining 380, slightly over one-third were "jettisoned." See Oldham, "Insurance Litigation"; Webster, "*Zong*."

24. See chapter 2 in Christopher, *Slave Ship Sailors*; chapter 2 in Bolster, *Black Jacks*.

25. For the point on victimhood, I would like to thank Professor Michael Wayne from the University of Toronto for sharing this insight. For evidence on fictive kin, see Sells, *Remarks on the Condition*, 28–29.

26. Rediker, *Slave Ship*, 67. For specific examples in the primary sources, see Alexander Falconbridge, *Account of the Slave Trade*, 19; James Morley, Minutes of the Evidence Taken before the Select Committee, House of Commons and Lords, ZHC, 1/84, 158; Account of a Voyage to the Coast of Africa by James Arnold, March 24, 1789, Board of Trade, BT 6/11 (no folio number), National Archives; Thomas Trotter, Minutes of the Evidence Taken before the Select Committee, House of Commons and Lords, ZHC, 1/84, 84. See also Mannix, *Black Cargoes*, 104.

27. Some of these issues addressing children were raised in my earlier published article (Diptee, "African Children"). The game played by boys was also called "bush fighting." For the game and for children taking messages for adults, see Thomas Trotter, Minutes of the Evidence Taken before the Select Committee, House of Commons and Lords, ZHC, 1/84, 82, 98. For the boy who was pinched, see Account of a Voyage to the Coast of Africa by James Arnold, March 27, 1789, Board of Trade, BT 6/11 (no folio number), National Archives.

28. See chapters 2, 3, and 5 in Burg, *Boys at Sea*.

29. Account of a Voyage to the Coast of Africa by James Arnold, March 24, 1789, Board of Trade, BT 6/11 (no folio number), National Archives; see also Alexander Falconbridge, *Account of the Slave Trade*, 24. For a discussion of the slave trade and gendered experiences during the middle passage, see Bush, "'Daughters of injur'd Africk.'"

30. These less-desirable captives were co-purchased by J. Galloway and U. Gillespie, who were quite likely speculators intending to resell at a later date. For correspondence on the *Jupiter*'s voyage, see letters from Captain John Goodrich to James Rogers dated December 30, 1792; January 11, 1793; January 24, 1793; March 5, 1793; April 9, 1793; and June 15, 1793. For these letters, see Chancery Records, C107/59, National Archives.

31. See chapter 2 for an elaboration of the circumstances surrounding the death of the more than three hundred captives who died on the African coast. For a description of conditions on slave ships, see Haines and Shlomowitz, "Explaining the Mortality Decline," 263. For correspondence relating to the *Pearl*, see letters to James Rogers from William Blake dated August 28, 1790; October 9, 1790; December 19, 1790; January 11, 1791; and April 2, 1791. See also the letters to James Rogers from I. P. Degreaves, October 10, 1790; from Richard Martin, December 14, 1790; from Samuel Stribling, March 12 and April 9 and 24, 1791; and from Alexander Lindo, April 10 and May 11, 1791. The letter from Alexander Lindo dated April 10, 1791, can be found in Chancery Records, C107/10, National Archives. For all the other letters, see Chancery Records, C107/12, National Archives.

32. For a description of the health of captives during the voyage, see Sheridan, "Guinea Surgeons," 602. For mortality rates once the ship arrived in Jamaica (5 percent), see chapter 1. Quotations about sharks are excerpted from Rediker, *Slave Ship*, 39.

33. See also Lambert, *House of Commons Sessional Papers*, 259.

34. Advertisement by Smith Lee & Company in the *Royal Gazette*, April 28–May 5,

1781; advertisement by Rainford, Blundell & Rainford in the *Royal Gazette*, December 5–15, 1781.

35. Advertisement by Mures & Dunlop in the *Royal Gazette*, June 23–30, 1781.

36. James Morley, Minutes of the Evidence Taken before the Select Committee, House of Commons and Lords, ZHC, 1/84, 159.

37. For the description of sale by scramble, see Alexander Falconbridge, *Account of the Slave Trade*, 35; testimony of Thomas Trotter and Clement Noble in Minutes of the Evidence Taken before the Select Committee, House of Commons and Lords, ZHC, 1/84, 87, 119. The sale of captives by "scramble" on board ships was made illegal by the Consolidated Slave Law of 1784; see Pope-Hennessy, *Sins of the Fathers*, 111. For a sale by scramble on land in 1789, see the report of Thomas Clappeson in Lambert, *House of Commons Sessional Papers*, 212.

38. For favored customers being given first choice of captives and the manipulated conditions of sale, see Hall, *In Miserable Slavery*, 175–78. For an example of two females being returned because one had a "swelled arm" and the other had only one eye, see John Taylor to Simon Taylor, January 6, 1790, TAYL/14, Letterbook A, Institute of Commonwealth Studies, London. For speculators and "bulk" sales, see Lambert, *House of Commons Sessional Papers*, 257. For the mulatto woman purchasing the ill captive, see Alexander Falconbridge, *Account of the Slave Trade*, 32.

39. This incident took place in St. Vincent. See Account of a Voyage to the Coast of Africa by James Arnold, March 24, 1789, Board of Trade, BT 6/11 (no folio), National Archives.

40. Maria Nugent, *Lady Nugent's Journal*, 220.

Chapter 5. African Expectations, Jamaican Realities

1. For a discussion of the range of experiences faced by biracial persons during slavery, see Sio, "Marginality." For the creole from Hispaniola, see *Royal Gazette*, December 30–January 6, 1781. For the Spanish-speaking runaways, see *Royal Gazette*, September 29–October 6, 1781. For the cases of Morris and Phurah, see *Royal Gazette*, March 3–10, 1781. For the impact of the American revolution on Jamaica, see Brathwaite, *Development of Creole Society*, xiii.

2. Bryan Edwards, *History* (1819), 82–83, 87–88. Such ethnic stereotyping is rampant in the contemporary literature. For other examples, see Edward Long, *History of Jamaica*, 403–4; Piersen, "White Cannibals, Black Martyrs."

3. This is by no means an extensive list, but works that make strong links between Africa and captives in the Americas include Gomez, *Exchanging Our Country Marks*; Sweet, *Recreating Africa*; Nishida, *Slavery and Identity*; Lovejoy, "African Diaspora"; Thornton, *Africa and Africans*. For a study on slavery in Africa, see Lovejoy, *Transformations in Slavery*. For the quotations and a discussion about the "expectations" of the enslaved, see Lovejoy and Trotman, "Enslaved Africans," 67, 69.

4. Higman, *Characteristic Traits*, 9. For portraits of Africans, see lithographs in Rugendas, *Viagem pitoresca*.

5. For historical studies on scarification, see Lovejoy, "Scarification"; Ojo, "Beyond Diversity." For anthropological studies, see Bohannan, "Beauty and Scarification"; Gengenbach, "Boundaries of Beauty"; Jeffreys, "Winged Solar Disk" (see p. 97 for European misconceptions). For a description of the scars of the Breeche, see John Adams, *Sketches Taken*, 41–42.

6. For the reference to the African with marks on his right breast, see *Royal Gazette*, June 23–30, 1781. For Cuffee from the "Sucks Country," "Jack of the Eboe Country," and "Jack of the Chamba Country," see *Royal Gazette*, October 13–20, January 6–13, and April 28–May 5, 1781, respectively. For Maria, see *Royal Gazette*, January 27–February 3, 1781. For Fortune and Mary, see *Jamaica Mercury & Kingston Weekly Advertiser*, September 11–18 and July 12–19, 1779, respectively.

7. Bryan Edwards, *History* (1819), 127, 152.

8. Orlando Patterson's concept of "Social Death" is discussed in chapter 4. See chapters 1 and 2 of Patterson, *Slavery and Social Death*.

9. In my analysis of runaway advertisements, none of the descriptions for Jamaican-born enslaved made reference to scarification. Only when describing African runaways were marks caused by scarification reported. Although I found no records of ritual scarification among the Jamaican born, one runaway advertisement did report the escape of "a creole of Antigua" whose "upper front teeth to the left [were] filed"; *Royal Gazette*, January 12–19, 1791. Teeth filing was an African practice.

10. For a description of branding, see Bryan Edwards, *History* (1819), 83–84; James Morley, Minutes of the Evidence Taken before the Select Committee, House of Commons and Lords, ZHC 1/84, 163. For the reference to Philip, see *Jamaica Mercury & Kingston Weekly Advertiser*, October 16–23, 1779. For all other references, see *Royal Gazette*, April 14–21, 1781; December 30, 1780–January 6, 1781; and June 23–30, 1781. For another reference to the branding of children, see Bryan Edwards, *History* (1819), 89.

11. For Tom Dickson and Jamaica, see *Royal Gazette*, July 21–28, 1781, and January 27–February 3, 1781, respectively. For the reference to Lincoln, see Burnard, *Mastery, Tyranny and Desire*, 198.

12. *Royal Gazette*, January 20–27, 1781.

13. For Cato, see *Jamaica Mercury & Kingston Weekly Advertiser*, August 28–September 4, 1779. For the woman from the Congo region, see *Royal Gazette*, June 23–30, 1781.

14. Piersen, "White Cannibals, Black Martyrs"; Thornton, "Cannibals, Witches." For the Aro Chukwu, see Davidson, *African Slave Trade*, 212.

15. See Thornton, "Cannibals, Witches," 277. For the reference to Sang, see Bryan Edwards, *History* (1819), 127. For Thomas King, see Piersen, "White Cannibals, Black Martyrs," 149. For the quotation, see Olaudah Equiano, *Equiano's Travels*, 25, 31.

16. During a storm, the four crew members on the *Mignonette* abandoned the yacht and spent twenty-four days in a boat before being rescued. After they were rescued, three of the crew members were prosecuted for killing and eating Richard Parker—the fourth crew member. For a detailed analysis, see Simpson, *Cannibalism* (for specific references above, see pp. 5, 122, 140). For another study on cannibalism, see Hanson, *Custom of the Sea*.

17. For quotations, see Armstrong, "Slavery, Insurance, and Sacrifice," 179. See also Simpson, *Cannibalism*, 123.

18. There was also the case of the *Tiger* in 1766, in which a "negro youth," quite probably enslaved, was killed and his body smoked; see Simpson, *Cannibalism*, 125. See also Redding, *History of Shipwrecks*, 161–62. In 1727, the slave ship *Luxborough Galley* delivered 286 captives to Jamaica. Through some unfortunate circumstances, the ship caught fire. There were 22 survivors who escaped by boat. The proposal was made to throw the "Two black boys" overboard "to lighten the boat," but it was decided against. However, one of the boys (and another individual) died of natural causes and was eaten. Thereafter, all of the other dead were eaten. By the time the boat landed in Newfoundland, there were only 6 survivors. Armstrong (p. 178 in "Slavery, Insurance, and Sacrifice") writes that 600 captives were sold in Jamaica. The *TSTD* (accessed June 2009), however, makes clear that only 286 captives were delivered to the island.

19. Simpson, *Cannibalism*, 124; Thompson, "No Chance in Nature," 33–35. See Armstrong, "Slavery, Insurance, and Sacrifice," 178.

20. For sale by scramble, see Bryan Edwards, *History* (1819), 150. For Boatswain, see *Royal Gazette*, October 13–20, 1781.

21. For the "full weight" of slavery, see Thornton, "Cannibals, Witches," 277. For the quotation, see Testimony of Mark Cook, March 5, 1791, in Lambert, *House of Commons Sessional Papers*, 196.

22. These stories of enslavement in Africa were documented by Bryan Edwards. Any mention of age seems to be at the time of interview, not at the time of capture. Edwards did not give any indication of how long the captives were on the island. According to Edwards, these were initially recorded "without any view to publication"; Bryan Edwards, *History* (1819), 126–27.

23. Bryan Edwards, *History* (1819), 124–26.

24. Hugh Crow, *Memoirs*, 199. For the same claim, see John Adams, *Sketches Taken*, 41–42. For the reference to captives from the Gold Coast, see Bryan Edwards, *History* (1819), 74–75.

25. Ivor Wilks, "Abu Bakr al-Saddiq of Timbuktu," in Curtin, *Africa Remembered*, 152–53.

26. Curtin, *Africa Remembered*, 162–63 (emphasis mine).

27. Ibid., 162. Abu Bakr al-Saddiq was part of an existing Muslim community in Jamaica. See Addoun and Lovejoy, "Muhammad Kaba Saghanughu." For a study on Islam and slavery in Africa, see Hunwick, "Islamic Law and Polemics," 42–63.

28. For the reference to Killikelly, see *Royal Gazette*, February 28–March 3, 1781. For the reference to Amba, see *Royal Gazette*, April 14–21, 1781. For Alexander Rose's advertisement, see *Royal Gazette*, April 28–May 5, 1781.

29. *Jamaica Mercury & Kingston Weekly Advertiser*, May 8–15, 1779.

30. Burnard and Hall give differing accounts of Coobah's life. According to Burnard, Coobah "had a child with her husband, a free black man" (Burnard, *Mastery, Tyranny and Desire*, 217). According to Hall, Coobah gave birth to a mulatto girl named Sylvia (Hall, *In Miserable Slavery*, 142, 179). There was, however, another enslaved woman

named Coobah, who was married to "a free black man" named Nagua. This Coobah was the daughter of Thistlewood's principal lover, Phibbah. Burnard also reports that Coobah's child died in 1767, but by Hall's record she died in 1768 (Hall, *In Miserable Slavery*, 140, 144; Burnard, *Mastery, Tyranny and Desire*, 217).

31. Hall, *In Miserable Slavery*, 191–92. I have also made reference to Coobah's story in my forthcoming article "'A Great Many Boys and Girls': Igbo Youth in the British Slave Trade, 1700–1808." For a study exploring the interplay of race, gender, and punishment in Jamaican slave society, see Paton, *No Bond*.

32. Hall, *In Miserable Slavery*, 192, 195.

33. Testimony of Drewry Ottley, March 2, 1791, in Lambert, *House of Commons Sessional Papers*, 172; Council and Assembly of Grenada (1788), Board of Trade, BT 6/11 (no folio number), National Archives; Higman, *Characteristic Traits*, 9.

34. For Fortune, see *Jamaica Mercury & Kingston Weekly Advertiser*, September 11–18, 1779. For Will, see *Royal Gazette*, April 21–28, 1781. For the young boy ten to twelve years of age and the girl, see *Royal Gazette*, December 8–15, 1781.

35. These ideas on enslaved children in the Caribbean are discussed more thoroughly in Diptee, "Imperial Ideas, Colonial Realities" (for the racialization of British thinking, see p. 49). For British law and the labor of children in poverty, see Gorton and Ramsland, "Prison Playground?" 51. For the transportation of children, see Wareing, "Preventive and Punitive Regulation." For the quotation on the defense of slavery, see Petley, "Slavery."

36. Diptee, "Imperial Ideas, Colonial Realities," 55.

37. Mintz, "Slave Life," 16, 18.

38. Burnard, *Mastery, Tyranny and Desire*, 28–29.

39. For a succinct discussion on slave trading in Islamic West Africa, see Lovejoy, "Islam, Slavery." For enslaved concubines, see Klein, "Women in Slavery," 86.

40. Law, "'My Head.'"

41. See the introduction and chapter 8 in Iliffe, *Honour in African History*.

42. For Roger, see Burnard, *Mastery, Tyranny and Desire*, 176. As Robin Law points out in "Human Sacrifice," the term *voluntary suicide* is a problematic one, as such suicides "involved the internalization of the expectations of society, and were voluntary only in the formal sense" (71). In other words, some individuals may have been passive as they took part in this ritual, doing so only because it was expected of them and not because they wanted to die (Law, "Human Sacrifice," 59). For notions of death and "honour," see Law, "'My Head.'" For the area of provenance of the enslaved owned by Cope, see Burnard and Morgan, "Dynamics," 219.

43. For details on Kwaku and the excerpted dialogue, see Kea, "'But I know,'" 169–70.

44. Testimony of Henry Coor, February 19, 1791, in Lambert, *House of Commons Sessional Papers*, 95. Coor's use of an African to deal with newly arrived Africans parallels Equiano's story, which (as detailed earlier in the chapter) makes reference to seasoned Africans being brought on board the slave ship to explain to the newly arrived that they were not to be eaten by whites but were to be put to labor.

45. For the Hector's River Estate, see *Royal Gazette,* June 23–30, 1781. For Morrison, see *Royal Gazette*, November 10–17, 1781.

46. See Beckles, "Social and Political Control." It was not specifically mentioned that the enslaved who caught these "Mongola Country" runaways were African born, though the slave owner involved quite likely relied on the knowledge of at least one African to determine the ethnicity of the two escapees; *Jamaica Mercury & Kingston Weekly Advertiser*, August 28–September 4, 1779. For Chamboy, see Hall, *In Miserable Slavery*, 191, 204, 210.

47. Hall, *In Miserable Slavery*, 182.

48. Ibid., 135, 203–6. Jimmy outlived his owner. In 1786–87, after Thistlewood's death, he was thirty-two years old.

49. See the testimony of Doctor Harrison (February 12, 1791) and William Fitzmaurice (March 11, 1791), in Lambert, *House of Commons Sessional Papers*, 50 and 230, respectively. For other examples, see the testimony of Baker Davison (March 25, 1791) and Drewry Ottley (March 2, 1791), in Lambert, *House of Commons Sessional Papers*, 156 and 173, respectively.

50. Testimony of Henry Coor (February 16, 1791) and Mark Cook (March 5, 1791), in Lambert, *House of Commons Sessional Papers*, 71 and 197, respectively. It is unclear what geographic region Coor is referring to in his reference to "the most inland country." For poisoning, see Piersen, "White Cannibals, Black Martyrs," 153. For Igbo, see Bryan Edwards, *History* (1819), 88.

51. Brown, *Reaper's Garden*, 132–35. See also Law, "'My Head.'" For "Old Sambo," see Burnard, *Mastery, Tyranny and Desire*, 233.

52. Testimony of Henry Coor, February 16, 1791, in Lambert, *House of Commons Sessional Papers*, 72.

53. Ibid., 71, 74.

54. Patterson, *Slavery and Social Death*, 5; Lovejoy and Trotman, "Enslaved Africans"; Mintz, "Slave Life," 13, 15–17.

55. Thompson, *Flight to Freedom*, 225 (emphasis mine).

Epilogue

1. For details on the ship *George,* see the *TSTD*. For the number of enslaved in Jamaica by the end of the slave trade, see Higman, *Slave Population and Economy*, 61. For the abolition of slavery, see Hochschild, *Bury the Chains*.

2. See http://slavevoyages.org/tast/database/search.faces?yearFrom=1514&yearTo=1866&natinimp=7 (accessed June 2009).

3. Concerns about abolition were informing purchasing decisions in the Caribbean. Reporting on a particular sale of captives, the representatives of one merchant house commented on "the miserable choice made in the purchase of those slaves, which would scarcely have sold, but for the apprehension which for some time possessed men's minds of a total abolition of the slave trade"; Thomas and William Salmon to James Rogers, July 29, 1789, Chancery Records, C107/14, National Archives. On abolition, see Walvin, *Black*

and White, 121–29, 177–87. For the Somerset case, see Paley, "After Somerset." For abolition in Pennsylvania and Massachusetts, see Geggus, "Slavery, War, and Revolution," 2.

4. Williams, *Capitalism and Slavery*, 208.

5. For the 1805 quotation, see Robert Taylor to Simon Taylor, March 6, 1805, TAYL/13,
Letter Book A, Simon Taylor Papers, Institute of Commonwealth Studies. For statistics,
see table 5 in Look Lai, *Indentured Labor, Caribbean Sugar*, 276. For an analysis of African indentured labor in Jamaica, see Schuler, *"Alas, Alas, Kongo."* For a comparative study
on African indentured labor, see Adderley, *"New Negroes from Africa"* (for the quotation
on refugees, see pp. 3–4). See also Northrup, *Indentured Labor*.

6. For indentured labor statistics, see table 5 in Look Lai, *Indentured Labor, Caribbean
Sugar*, 276. For slave trade statistics, see estimates from the *TSTD* at http://slavevoy-
ages.org/tast/assessment/estimates.faces?yearFrom=1501&yearTo=1866&disembarkatio
n=307.310.301.

7. Law, *From Slave Trade*. See chapter 8 in Lovejoy, *Transformations in Slavery*. See
also the introduction in Miers and Roberts, *End of Slavery*.

Appendix

1. Scravelias ([*sic*], scrivellos) is a reference to elephant tusks of small size. Special
thanks to Robin Law for his assistance.

2. The captain of the *African Queen* earned a "coast commission" of £4 on every £108
made from the sale of the captives (minus associated costs).

3. James Rogers was a co-owner of the slave ship *Fame*.

4. There are two copies of the letter of John Cunningham and John Perry to James
Rogers on March 10, 1793. A few of the words are different, but the content is essentially
the same. One seems to be the original and the other a rewritten copy.

5. These two letters were scribbled at the end of one of the copies of the previous letter.

Bibliography

MANUSCRIPT SOURCES

NATIONAL ARCHIVES, LONDON

Treasury Records

Papers generated by the Company of Royal Adventurers of England Trading with Africa and Successors

Inward Letterbook (1773–1806): T70/32, T70/33, T70/34, T70/39
Outward Letterbook (1764–87): T70/69
Reports of the Parliamentary Committee (1777), Return from the Commissioners of Trade and Plantations to the House of Commons Relating to the General State of the Trade to Africa: T70/177
Company Ledgers (1766–77): T70/1265
Letterbook of Thomas Miles: T70/1484

Chancery Records

Miscellaneous accounts, papers, and correspondence of James Rogers, merchant of Bristol. Chiefly concerned with ships trading to Africa, the West Indies, and North America. Various letters from ship captains (1780–1800): C107/1–C107/15, C107/59

Board of Trade Records

BT 6/9, BT 6/11

House of Commons and Lords

ZHC 1/84

INSTITUTE OF COMMONWEALTH STUDIES, LONDON

Simon Taylor Letter Books (1770–1807)

TAYL/1, Letter Books A, B, C, D, F, G, I
TAYL/7, Letter Book B

TAYL/8, Letter Books A, B, D
TAYL/13, Letter Books A, B
TAYL/14, Letter Book A
TAYL/17, Letter Book A

MERSEYSIDE MARITIME MUSEUM, LIVERPOOL

Account book of *Enterprize,* a slave trader, 1794–1795, DX/1732

RHODES HOUSE, OXFORD

"Observations on the Slave Trade" (1797): MSS W. Ind. s8.

NATIONAL LIBRARY OF SCOTLAND, EDINBURGH

Chisholme Papers
Robertson-MacDonald Papers
Airth Papers, MS 10801–969
Cunninghame Graham Papers

JAMAICAN NATIONAL ARCHIVES, SPANISH TOWN

House of Assembly Journals (1775–1778): 1B/5/1, vols. 24–25.

Commissioners of Correspondence and Their Agents

Out-Letter Book of Stephen Fuller (1784–1792): IB/5/14, #1
Out-Letter Book of Stephen Fuller and Robert Sewell (1795–1801): IB/5/14, #2

Despatches, Jamaica to England

Governor to Secretary of State (1777–1787, 1791, 1795–1796, 1799): 1B/5/18, #3

Jamaican Votes of Assembly (1778–1807): vols. 3–6, 10–11, 13

Jamaica Almanac and Register (1798 and 1806): 7/40

Braco Journal (1795–1797): 4/2 #1

Tweedie Papers (1780–1799): 4/45

JAMAICAN NEWSPAPERS

Royal Gazette, 1780–1781, 1793
Jamaica Mercury & Kingston Weekly Advertiser, 1779–1781

JOHN HOPE FRANKLIN COLLECTION, DUKE UNIVERSITY

Christopher Papers, 1791

PUBLISHED PRIMARY SOURCES

Adams, John. *Sketches Taken during Ten Voyages to Africa, between the Years 1786 and 1800.* 1825. Reprint, London: Johnson Reprint Company, 1970.

British Parliamentary Papers. Shannon: Irish University Press, 1968.

Clarkson, Thomas. *The History of the Rise, Progress, and Accomplishment of the Abolition of the African Slave Trade by the British Parliament.* London: Longman, Hurst, Rees and Orme, 1808.

Crow, Hugh. *The Memoirs of Captain Hugh Crow.* 1830. Reprint, London: Frank Cass Publishers, 1970.

Donnan, Elizabeth, ed. *Documents Illustrative of the History of the Slave Trade to America.* Vol. 2. New York: Octagon Books, 1969.

Edwards, Bryan. *The History, Civil and Commercial, of the British Colonies in the West Indies.* Vol. 2. 3 vols. London: John Stockdale, 1801.

———. *The History, Civil and Commercial, of the British Colonies in the West Indies.* Vol. 2. 1819 edition. Reprint, New York: AMS Press, 1966.

Equiano, Olaudah. *Equiano's Travels: The Interesting Narrative of the Life of Olaudah Equiano or Gustavus Vassa, the African.* London: Heinemann, 1967.

Falconbridge, Alexander. *An Account of the Slave Trade on the Coast of Africa.* London: J. Phillips, 1788.

Forde, Cyril Daryll, ed. *Efik Traders of Old Calabar: Containing the Diary of Antera Duke, an Efik Slave-Trading Chief of the Eighteenth Century.* London: Oxford University Press, 1956.

Lambert, Sheila, ed. *House of Commons Sessional Papers of the Eighteenth Century.* Vol. 82. Wilmington, Del.: Scholarly Resources, 1975.

Long, Edward. *The History of Jamaica: Reflections on Its Situation, Settlements, Inhabitants, Climate, Products, Commerce, Law, and Government.* Vol. 2. Kingston, Jamaica: Ian Randle Publishers, 2002.

Mouser, Bruce L., ed. *A Slaving Voyage to Africa and Jamaica: The Log of the Sandown, 1793–1794.* Bloomington: Indiana University Press, 2002.

Nugent, Maria. *Lady Nugent's Journal of Her Residence in Jamaica from 1801 to 1805.* Edited by Philip Wright. Kingston: Institute of Jamaica, 1966.

Park, Mungo. *Travels in the Interior Districts of Africa.* Edited by Kate Ferguson Marsters. Durham, N.C.: Duke University Press, 2000.

Sells, William. *Remarks on the Condition of the Slaves in the Island of Jamaica.* 1823. Reprint, Shannon: Irish University Press, 1972.

SECONDARY SOURCES

Adderley, Rosanne Marion. *"New Negroes from Africa": Slave Trade Abolition and Free African Settlement in the Nineteenth-Century Caribbean.* Bloomington: Indiana University Press, 2006.

Addoun, Yacine Daddi, and Paul Lovejoy. "Muhammad Kaba Saghanughu and the Muslim Community of Jamaica." In *Slavery on the Frontiers of Islam*, edited by Paul Love-joy, 199–218. Princeton, N.J.: Markus Wiener Publishers, 2004.

Aird, Sheila. "The Forgotten Ones: Enslaved Children and the Formation of a Labor Force in the British West Indies, 1673–1838." Ph.D. diss., Howard University, 2006.

Akinjogbin, I. A. *Dahomey and Its Neighbours, 1708–1818*. Cambridge: Cambridge University Press, 1967.

Alpers, Edward. "The Other Middle Passage: The African Slave Trade in the Indian Ocean." In *Many Middle Passages: Forced Migration and the Making of the Modern World*, edited by Emma Christopher, Cassandra Pybus, and Marcus Rediker, 20–38. Berkeley: University of California Press, 2007.

Andquandah, Kwesi J. *Castles and Forts of Ghana*. Atalante: Ghana Museums and Monuments Board, 1999.

Armstrong, Tim. "Slavery, Insurance, and Sacrifice in the Black Atlantic." In *Sea Changes: Historicizing the Ocean*, edited by Bernhard Klein and Gesa MacKenthun, 167–85. New York: Routledge, 2004.

Bay, Edna G. "Protection, Political Exile, and the Atlantic Slave Trade: History and Collective Memory in Dahomey." *Slavery and Abolition* 22, no. 1 (2001): 42–60.

Beckles, Hilary. *Natural Rebels: A Social History of Enslaved Black Women in Barbados*. New Brunswick, N.J.: Rutgers University Press, 1989.

———. "Social and Political Control in the Slave Society." In *General History of the Caribbean: The Slave Societies of the Caribbean*, edited by Franklin Knight, 194–221. London: Unesco Publishing, 1997.

Behrendt, Stephen D. "Annual Volume and Regional Distribution of the British Slave Trade, 1780–1807." *Journal of African History* 38, no. 2 (1997): 187–211.

———. "Markets, Transaction Cycles, and Profits: Merchant Decision Making in the British Slave Trade." *William and Mary Quarterly* 58, no. 1 (2001): 171–204.

Blouet, Olwyn. "Bryan Edwards and the Haitian Revolution." In *The Impact of the Haitian Revolution in the Atlantic World*, edited by David Geggus, 44–57. Columbia: University of South Carolina Press, 2001.

Bohannan, Paul. "Beauty and Scarification amongst the Tiv." *Man* 56, no. 126 (1956): 117–21.

Bolster, Jeffrey W. *Black Jacks: African American Seamen in the Age of Sail*. Cambridge, Mass.: Harvard University Press, 1998.

Brathwaite, Edward. *The Development of Creole Society in Jamaica, 1770–1820*. Oxford: Oxford University Press, 1971.

Brown, Vincent. *The Reaper's Garden: Death and Power in the World of Atlantic Slavery*. Cambridge, Mass.: Harvard University Press, 2008.

Burg, B. R. *Boys at Sea: Sodomy, Indecency, and Courts Martial in Nelson's Navy*. Hampshire, U.K.: Palgrave Macmillan, 2007.

Burnard, Trevor. *Mastery, Tyranny and Desire: Thomas Thistlewood and His Slaves in the Anglo-Jamaican World*. Chapel Hill: University of North Carolina Press, 2004.

———. "Theater of Terror: Domestic Violence in Thomas Thistlewood's Jamaica, 1750–1786." In *Over the Threshold: Intimate Violence in Early America*, edited by Christine Daniels and Michael V. Kennedy, 237–53. London: Routledge, 1999.

Burnard, Trevor, and Kenneth Morgan. "The Dynamics of the Slave Market and Slave Purchasing Patterns in Jamaica, 1655–1788." *William and Mary Quarterly* 58, no. 1 (2001): 205–27.

Bush, Barbara. "'Daughters of injur'd Africk': African Women and the Transatlantic Slave Trade." *Women's History Review* 17, no. 5 (2008): 673–98.

———. *Slave Women in Caribbean Society, 1650–1838*. Bloomington: Indiana University Press, 1990.

Campbell, Mavis Christine. *The Maroons of Jamaica, 1655–1796: A History of Resistance, Collaboration and Betrayal*. Trenton, N.J.: Africa World Press, 1990.

Carrington, Selwyn H. "The American Revolution and the British West Indies' Economy." *Journal of Interdisciplinary History* 17, no. 4 (1987): 823–50.

Chambers, Douglas. "The Significance of Igbo in the Bight of Biafra Slave Trade: A Rejoinder to Northrup's 'Myth Igbo.'" *Slavery and Abolition* 23, no. 1 (2002): 101–20.

Christopher, Emma. *Slave Ship Sailors and Their Captive Cargoes, 1730–1807*. Cambridge: Cambridge University Press, 2006.

Cohn, Raymond. "Deaths of Slaves in the Middle Passage." *Journal of Economic History* 45, no. 3 (1985): 685–92.

Craton, Michael. "Jamaican Slave Mortality: Fresh Light from Worthy Park, Longville and the Tharp Estates." *Journal of Caribbean History* 3 (1971): 1–27.

Curtin, Philip. *Africa Remembered: Narratives by West Africans from the Era of the Slave Trade*. Madison: University of Wisconsin Press, 1967.

———. *The Atlantic Slave Trade: A Census*. Madison: University of Wisconsin Press, 1970.

———. *Economic Change in Precolonial Africa: Senegambia in the Era of the Slave Trade*. Madison: University of Wisconsin Press, 1975.

Davidson, Basil. *The African Slave Trade: Precolonial History, 1450–1850*. Boston: Little Brown, 1961.

Diouf, Sylviane A., ed. *Fighting the Slave Trade: West African Strategies*. Athens: Ohio University Press, 2003.

Diptee, Audra A. "African Children in the British Slave Trade during the Late Eighteenth Century." *Slavery and Abolition* 27, no. 2 (2006): 183–96.

———. "Imperial Ideas, Colonial Realities: Enslaved Children in Jamaica, 1775–1834." In *Children in Colonial America*, edited by James Marten, 48–60. New York: New York University Press, 2007.

Dirks, Robert. "Social Responses during Severe Food Shortages and Famine." *Current Anthropology* 21, no. 1 (1980): 21–44.

Dow, George Francis, ed. *Slave Ships and Slaving*. 1927. Reprint, Toronto: Coles Publishing Company, 1980.

Elkins, Stanley M. *Slavery: A Problem in American Institutional and Intellectual Life*. New York: Grosset and Dunlap, 1963.

Eltis, David. "Cooperation and Resistance: African Shaping of the Transatlantic Slave Trade." Paper presented at the ICS Post Graduate Seminar, Institute of Commonwealth Studies, London, 1996.

———. *The Rise of African Slavery in the Americas*. Cambridge: Cambridge University Press, 2000.

Eltis, David, Stephen D. Behrendt, David Richardson, and Herbert S. Klein. *The Trans-Atlantic Slave Trade: A Database on CD-ROM*. New York: Cambridge University Press, 1999.

Eltis, David, and Stanley Engerman. "Fluctuations in Sex and Age Ratios in the Transatlantic Slave Trade, 1663–1864." *Economic History Review* 46, no. 2 (1993): 308–23.

Eltis, David, and Martin Halbert. *Voyages: The Trans-Atlantic Slave Trade Database*. 2009. See www.slavevoyages.org.

Eltis, David, and Paul Lachance. "The Demographic Decline of Caribbean Slave Populations: New Evidence from the Transatlantic and Intra-American Slave Trades." In *Extending the Frontiers: Essays on the New Transatlantic Slave Trade Database*, edited by David Eltis and David Richardson, 335–63. New Haven, Conn.: Yale University Press, 2008.

Eltis, David, Frank D. Lewis, and David Richardson. "Slave Prices, the African Slave Trade, and Productivity in the Caribbean, 1674–1807." *Economic History Review* 58, no. 4 (2005): 673–700.

Eltis, David, and David Richardson. *Routes to Slavery: Direction, Ethnicity, and Mortality in the Transatlantic Slave Trade*. London: Frank Cass, 1997.

Falola, Toyin, and Paul E. Lovejoy. "Pawnship in Historical Perspective." In *Pawnship in Africa: Debt Bondage in Historical Perspective*, edited by Toyin Falola and Paul E. Lovejoy, 1–26. Boulder, Colo.: Westview Press, 1994.

Finkelman, Paul. Review of *Slavery and Social Death*. *Journal of Interdisciplinary History* 15, no. 3 (1985): 508–11.

Franklin, V. P. Review of *Slavery and Social Death*. *Journal of Negro History* 68, no. 2 (1983): 212–16.

Frazier, Franklin. *The Negro Family in the United States*. 1937. Reprint, Chicago: University of Chicago Press, 1949.

Geggus, David. "Jamaica and the Saint Domingue Slave Revolt, 1791–1793." *Americas* 38 (1981): 219–33.

———. "Sex Ratio, Age and Ethnicity in the Atlantic Slave Trade: Data from French Shipping and Plantation Records." *Journal of African History* 30, no. 1 (1989): 23–44.

———. "Slavery, War, and Revolution in the Greater Caribbean, 1789–1815." In *A Turbulent Time: The French Revolution and the Greater Caribbean*, edited by David Barry Gaspar and David Patrick Geggus, 1–50. Bloomington: Indiana University Press, 1997.

Gengenbach, Heidi. "Boundaries of Beauty: Tattooed Secrets of Women's History in Magude District, Southern Mozambique." *Journal of Women's History* 14, no. 4 (2003): 106–41.

Gomez, Michael A. *Exchanging Our Country Marks: The Transformation of African Identities in the Colonial and Antebellum South*. Chapel Hill: University of North Carolina Press, 1998.

Gonsalves, Ralph E. "Our Caribbean Civilisation: Retrospect and Prospect." *Caribbean Quarterly* 44, no. 3–4 (1998): 131–50.

Gorton, Kerin, and James Ramsland. "Prison Playground? Child Convict Labour and Vocational Training in New South Wales, 1788–1840." *Journal of Educational Administration and History* 34, no. 1 (2002): 51–62.

Greene, Jack P., and Philip D. Morgan, eds. *Atlantic History: A Critical Appraisal.* Oxford: Oxford University Press, 2009.

Haines, Robin, and Ralph Shlomowitz. "Explaining the Mortality Decline in the Eighteenth Century British Slave Trade." *Economic History Review* 53, no. 2 (2000): 262–23.

Hair, P. E. H. "Antera Duke of Old Calabar—A Little More about an African Entrepreneur." *History in Africa* 17 (1990): 359–65.

Hall, Douglas. *In Miserable Slavery: Thomas Thistlewood in Jamaica, 1750–86.* 1989. Reprint, Mona, Jamaica: University of the West Indies Press, 1999.

Hall, Gwendolyn Midlo. *Africans in Colonial Louisiana: The Development of Afro-Creole Culture in the Eighteenth Century.* Baton Rouge: Louisiana State University Press, 1992.

———. *Slavery and African Ethnicities in the Americas: Restoring the Links.* Chapel Hill: University of North Carolina Press, 2005.

Handler, Jerome. "The Middle Passage and the Material Culture of Captive Africans." *Slavery and Abolition* 30, no. 1 (2009): 1–26.

Hanson, Neil. *The Custom of the Sea.* New York: John Wiley and Sons, 1999.

Herskovits, Melville J. *The Myth of the Negro Past.* Boston: Beacon Press, 1958.

Heywood, Linda M., ed. *Central Africans and Cultural Transformations in the American Diaspora.* Cambridge: Cambridge University Press, 2002.

Higman, Barry, ed. *Characteristic Traits of the Creolian and African Negroes in Jamaica.* Mona, Jamaica: Caldwell Press, 1976.

———. *Slave Population and Economy in Jamaica, 1807–1834.* Cambridge: Cambridge University Press, 1976.

———. *Slave Populations of the British Caribbean, 1807–1834.* Mona, Jamaica: University of the West Indies Press, 1995.

Hindmarsh, Bruce. *John Newton and the English Evangelical Tradition: Between the Conversions of Wesley and Wilberforce.* Oxford: Oxford University Press, 1996.

Hochschild, Adam. *Bury the Chains: The British Struggle to Abolish Slavery.* London: Macmillan, 2005.

Hogg, Peter, ed. *African Slave Trade and Its Suppression: A Classified and Annotated Bibliography of Books, Pamphlets, and Periodical Articles.* London: Routledge, 2006.

Hunwick, John. "Islamic Law and Polemics over Race and Slavery in North and West Africa." In *Slavery in the Islamic Middle East*, edited by Shaun Marmon, 43–68. Princeton, N.J.: Markus Wiener Publishers, 1999.

Iliffe, John. *Honour in African History.* Cambridge: Cambridge University Press, 2005.

Inikori, J. E. "Export versus Domestic Demand: The Determinants of Sex Ratios in the Transatlantic Slave Trade." *Research in Economic History* 14 (1992): 117–66.

Innis, Tara. "From Slavery to Freedom: Children's Health in Barbados, 1823–1838." *Slavery and Abolition* 27, no. 2 (2006): 251–60.

Jeffreys, M. D. W. "The Winged Solar Disk." *Africa* 21, no. 2 (1951): 93–111.

Johnson, Walter. "On Agency." *Journal of Social History* 37, no. 1 (2003): 112–24.

Jones, Cecily. "'Suffer the LIttle Children': Setting a Research Agenda for the Study of Enslaved Children in the Caribbean Colonial World." *Wadabagei* 9, no. 3 (2006): 7–26.

Kea, Ray. "'But I know what I shall do': Agency, Belief and the Social Imaginary in Eighteenth-Century Gold Coast Towns." In *Africa's Urban Past*, edited by David M. Anderson and Richard Rathbone, 163–88. Oxford, U.K.: Heinemann, 2000.

———. *Settlements, Trade, and Polities in the Seventeenth-Century Gold Coast.* Johns Hopkins Studies in Atlantic History and Culture. Baltimore, Md.: Johns Hopkins University Press, 1982.

King, Wilma. *Stolen Childhood: Slave Youth in Nineteenth-Century America.* Bloomington: Indiana University Press, 1995.

Kiple, Kenneth F., and Brian T. Higgins. "Mortality Caused by Dehydration during the Middle Passage." *Social Science History* 13, no. 4 (1989): 421–37.

Klein, Herbert. "The Cuban Slave Trade in a Period of Transition, 1790–1843." *Revue francaise d'histoire d'outre-mer* 62 (1975): 67–89.

———. "The English Slave Trade to Jamaica, 1782–1808." *Economic History Review* 31, no. 1 (1978): 25–45.

———. *The Middle Passage: Comparative Studies in the Atlantic Slave Trade.* Princeton, N.J.: Princeton University Press, 1978.

Klein, Herbert S., and Stanley Engerman. "Long-Term Trends in African Mortality in the Transatlantic Slave Trade." *Slavery and Abolition* 18, no. 1 (1997): 36–48.

Klein, Martin A. "Women in Slavery in the Western Sudan." In *Women and Slavery in Africa*, edited by Claire Robertson and Martin A. Klein, 67–92. Madison: University of Wisconsin Press, 1983.

Knight, Franklin W. *The Caribbean: The Genesis of a Fragmented Nationalism.* New York: Oxford University Press, 1990.

Kolapo, Femi. "The Igbo and Their Neighbours during the Era of the Atlantic Slave-Trade." *Slavery and Abolition* 25, no. 1 (2004): 114–33.

Latham, A. J. H. *Old Calabar, 1600–1891: The Impact of the International Economy upon a Traditional Society.* Oxford, U.K.: Clarendon Press, 1973.

Law, Robin. *From Slave Trade to "Legitimate" Commerce: The Commercial Transition in Nineteenth-Century West Africa.* 1995. Revised ed., Cambridge: Cambridge University Press, 2002.

———. "Human Sacrifice in Pre-Colonial West Africa." *African Affairs* 84, no. 334 (1985): 53–87.

———. "Legal and Illegal Enslavement in West Africa in the Context of the Trans-Atlantic Slave Trade." In *Ghana in Africa and the World*, edited by Toyin Falola, 513–33. Trenton, N.J.: Africa World Press, 2003.

———. "'My Head Belongs to the King': On the Political and Ritual Significance of Decapitation in Pre-Colonial Dahomey." *Journal of African History* 30 (1989): 399–415.

———. *Ouidah: The Social History of a West African Slaving Port, 1727–1892.* Athens: Ohio State University Press, 2004.

Law, Robin, and Kristin Mann. "West Africa in the Atlantic Community: The Case of the Slave Coast." *William and Mary Quarterly* 61, no. 2 (1999): 307–34.

Look Lai, Walton. *Indentured Labor, Caribbean Sugar: Chinese and Indian Migrants to the British West Indies, 1838–1918.* Baltimore, Md.: Johns Hopkins University Press, 1993.

Lovejoy, Paul E. "The African Diaspora: Revisionist Interpretations of Ethnicity, Culture and Religion under Slavery." *Studies in World History and Slavery, Abolition and Emancipation* 2, no. 1 (1997): 1–22.

———, ed. *Identity in the Shadow of Slavery: The Black Atlantic.* London: Continuum, 2000.

———. "The Impact of the Atlantic Slave Trade on Africa: A Review of the Literature." *Journal of African History* 30, no. 3 (1989): 365–94.

———. "Islam, Slavery, and Political Transformation in West Africa: Constraints on the Trans-Atlantic Slave Trade." *Outre-Mers: Revue d'histoire* 89, no. 2 (2002): 247–82.

———. "Scarification and the Loss of History in the African Diaspora." Presented at York University, 2005.

———. *Transformations in Slavery: A History of Slavery in Africa.* Cambridge: Cambridge University Press, 1983.

Lovejoy, Paul E., and David Richardson. "The Business of Slaving: Pawnship in Western Africa, c. 1600–1810." *Journal of African History* 41, no. 1 (2001): 67–89.

———. "'This Horrid Hole': Royal Authority, Commerce and Credit at Bonny, 1690–1840." *Journal of African History* 45 (2004): 363–92.

———. "Trust, Pawnship, and Atlantic History: The Institutional Foundations of the Old Calabar Slave Trade." *American Historical Review* 104, no. 2 (1999): 333–55.

Lovejoy, Paul E., and David V. Trotman. "Enslaved Africans and Their Expectations of Slave Life in the Americas: Towards a Reconsideration of Models of 'Creolisation.'" In *Questioning Creole: Creolisation Discourses in Caribbean Culture*, edited by Verene A. Shepherd and Glen A. Richards, 67–91. Kingston, Jamaica: Ian Randle Publishers, 2002.

MacCormack, Carol. "Slaves, Slave Owners, and Slave Dealers: Sherbro Coast and Hinterland." In *Women and Slavery in Africa*, edited by Claire Robertson and Martin A. Klein, 271–94. Madison: University of Wisconsin Press, 1983.

Mann, Kristin. "Shifting Paradigms in the Study of the African Diaspora and of Atlantic History and Culture." *Slavery and Abolition* 21, no. 1 (2001): 3–21.

Manning, Patrick. *Slavery and African Life: Occidental, Oriental, and African Slave Trades.* Cambridge: Cambridge University Press, 1990.

Mannix, Daniel Pratt. *Black Cargoes: A History of the Atlantic Slave Trade, 1518–1865.* New York: Viking Press, 1962.

Martin, Bernard, and Mark Spurrell, eds. *The Journal of a Slave Trader: John Newton, 1750–1754.* London: Epsworth Press, 1962.

Martin, Phyllis. *The External Trade of the Loango Coast, 1576–1870: The Effects of Changing Commercial Relations on the Vili Kingdom of Loango.* Oxford, U.K.: Clarendon Press, 1972.

———. "The Trade of Loango in the Seventeenth and Eighteenth Centuries." In *Forced Migration: The Impact of the Export Slave Trade on African Societies*, edited by J. E. Inikori, 202–20. London: Hutchinson and Company, 1982.

McDonald, Roderick A. "Measuring the British Slave Trade to Jamaica, 1789–1808." *Economic History Review* 33, no. 2 (1980): 253–58.

McGowan, Winston. "African Resistance to the Atlantic Slave Trade in West Africa." *Slavery and Abolition* 11, no. 1 (1990): 5–29.

——. "The Origins of Slave Rebellions in the Middle Passage." In *In the Shadow of the Plantation: Caribbean History and Legacy*, edited by Alvin O. Thompson, 74–99. Kingston, Jamaica: Ian Randle Publishers, 2002.

Metcalf, George. "Gold, Assortments and the Trade Ounce: Fante Merchants and the Problem of Supply and Demand in the 1770s." *Journal of African History* 28 (1987): 27–41.

——. "A Microcosm of Why Africans Sold Slaves." *Journal of African History* 28, no. 3 (1987): 377–94.

Miers, Suzanne, and Richard Roberts. *The End of Slavery in Africa*. Madison: University of Wisconsin Press, 1988.

Miller, Joseph C. "Central Africans during the Era of the Slave Trade, c. 1490–1850." In *Central Africans and Cultural Transformation in the American Diaspora*, edited by Linda M. Heywood, 29–70. Cambridge: Cambridge University Press, 2002.

——. "The Numbers, Origins, and Destinations of Slaves in the Eighteenth-Century Angolan Slave Trade." *Social Science History* 13, no. 4 (1989): 381–419.

——. *Way of Death: Merchant Capitalism and the Angolan Slave Trade, 1730–1830*. Madison: University of Wisconsin Press, 1988.

Mintz, Sidney. "More on the Peculiar Institution." *New West Indian Guide* 58, no. 3/4 (1984): 185–99.

——. "Slave Life on Caribbean Sugar Plantations: Some Unanswered Questions." In *Slave Cultures, Cultures of Slavery*, edited by Stephan Palmie, 12–22. Knoxville: University of Tennessee Press, 1995.

Mintz, Sidney W., and Richard Price. *The Birth of African-American Culture: An Anthropological Perspective*. Boston: Beacon Press, 1992.

Moitt, Bernard. *Women and Slavery in the French Antilles, 1635–1848*. Bloomington: Indiana University Press, 2001.

Monteith, Kathleen. "The Labour Regimen on Jamaican Coffee Plantations during Slavery." In *Jamaica in Slavery and Freedom: History, Heritage and Culture*, edited by Kathleen Monteith and Glen Richards, 259–73. Mona, Jamaica: University of the West Indies Press, 2002.

——. "Planting and Processing Techniques on Jamaican Coffee Plantations during Slavery." In *Working Slavery, Pricing Freedom*, edited by Verene Shepherd, 112–29. Kingston, Jamaica: Ian Randle Publishers, 2001.

Morgan, Jennifer. *Laboring Women: Reproduction and Gender in New World Slavery*. Philadelphia: University of Pennsylvania Press, 2004.

Morgan, Kenneth. "Slave Women and Reproduction in Jamaica, c. 1776–1834." *History* 91, no. 302 (2006): 231–53.

Morgan, Philip D. "The Cultural Implications of the Atlantic Slave Trade: African Regional Origins, American Destinations and New World Developments." In *Routes to Slavery: Direction, Ethnicity, and Mortality in the Transatlantic Slave Trade*, edited by David Eltis, 122–45. London: Frank Cass, 1997.

Morrissey, Marietta. *Slave Women in the New World: Gender Stratification in the Carib-bean.* Lawrence: University Press of Kansas, 1989.

Nishida, Mieko. *Slavery and Identity: Ethnicity, Gender, and Race in Salvador, Brazil, 1808–1888.* Bloomington: Indiana University Press, 2003.

Northrup, David. "Igbo and Myth Igbo: Culture and Ethnicity in the Atlantic World." *Slavery and Abolition* 23, no. 3 (2000): 1–20.

———. *Indentured Labor in the Age of Imperialism, 1834–1922.* New York: Cambridge University Press, 1995.

Nwokeji, Ugo. "African Conceptions of Gender and the Slave Traffic." *William and Mary Quarterly* 58, no. 1 (2001): 47–68.

———. "The Atlantic Slave Trade and Population Density: A Historical Demography of the Biafran Hinterland." *Canadian Journal of African Studies* 34, no. 3 (2000): 616–55.

———. "The Biafran Frontier: Trade, Slaves, and Aro Society, c 1750–1905." Ph.D. diss., University of Toronto, 1999.

Ojo, Olatunji. "Beyond Diversity: Women, Scarification, and Yoruba Identity." *History in Africa* 35 (2008): 347–74.

Okpewho, Isidore, Carol Boyce Davies, and Ali A. Mazrui, eds. *The African Diaspora: African Origins and New World Identities.* Bloomington: Indiana University Press, 1999.

Oldham, James. "Insurance Litigation Involving the *Zong* and Other British Slave Ships, 1780–1807." *Journal of Legal History* 28, no. 3 (2007): 299–318.

Olsen, Kristen. *Daily Life in 18th Century England.* Westport, Conn.: Greenwood Press, 1999.

Paley, Ruth. "After Somerset: Mansfield, Slavery and the Law in England, 1772–1830." In *Law, Crime and English Society, 1660–1830,* edited by Norma Landau, 165–84. Cambridge: Cambridge University Press, 2002.

Paton, Diana. *No Bond But the Law: Punishment, Race, and Gender in Jamaican State Formation, 1780–1870.* Durham, N.C.: Duke University Press, 2004.

Patterson, David K. *The Northern Gabon Coast to 1875.* Oxford, U.K.: Clarendon Press, 1975.

Patterson, Orlando. *Slavery and Social Death: A Comparative Study.* Cambridge, Mass.: Harvard University Press, 1982.

Perbi, Akosua. *A History of Indigenous Slavery in Ghana: From the 15th to the 19th Cen-tury.* Accra, Ghana: Sub-Saharan Publishers, 2004.

Petley, Christer. "Slavery, Emancipation and the Creole World View of Jamaican Colo-nists, 1800–1834." *Slavery and Abolition* 26, no. 1 (2005): 93–114.

Piersen, William. "White Cannibals, Black Martyrs: Fear, Depression, and Religious Faith as Causes of Suicide among New Slaves." *Journal of Negro History* 62, no. 2 (1977): 147–59.

Pope-Hennessy, James. *Sins of the Fathers: A Study of the Atlantic Slave Traders, 1441–1807.* London: Weidenfeld and Nicholson, 1967.

Pybus, Cassandra. "Bound for Botany Bay: Martin's Voyage to Australia." In *Many Mid-dle Passages: Forced Migration and the Making of the Modern World,* edited by Emma

Christopher, Cassandra Pybus, and Marcus Rediker, 92–108. Berkeley: University of California Press, 2007.

Ragatz, Lowell J. *The Fall of the Planter Class in the British Caribbean, 1763–1833: A Study in Social and Economic History*. New York: Octagon Books, 1963.

Redding, Cyrus. *A History of Shipwrecks and Disasters at Sea*. Vol. 2. 2 vols. London: Whittaker, Treacher and Company, 1833.

Rediker, Marcus. *The Slave Ship: A Human History*. New York: Penguin Group, 2007.

Richardson, David, ed. *Bristol, Africa and the Eighteenth-Century Slave Trade to America*. Vol. 4. Bristol, U.K.: Bristol Record Society, 1996.

———. "The Costs of Survival: The Treatment of Slaves in the Middle Passage and the Profitability of the Eighteenth-Century British Slave Trade." In *De la traite a l'esclavage: Actes du Colloque international sur la traite des Noires, Nantes, 1985*, edited by Serge Daget, 169–81. Nantes: Centre de Recherche sur L'Histoire du Monde Atlantique, 1988.

———. "Shipboard Revolts, African Authority and the Atlantic Slave Trade." *William and Mary Quarterly* 58, no. 1 (2001): 69–92.

———. "Slave Exports from West and West-Central Africa, 1700–1810: New Estimates of Volume and Distribution." *Journal of African History* 30 (1989): 1–22.

Rugendas, Johann Moritz. *Viagem pitoresca através do Brasil*. 1835. São Paulo: Itatiaia/USP, 1979.

Schuler, Monica. *"Alas, Alas, Kongo": A Social History of Indentured African Immigration into Jamaica, 1841–1865*. Johns Hopkins Studies in Atlantic History and Culture. Baltimore, Md.: Johns Hopkins University Press, 1980.

Schwartz, Marie Jenkins. *Born in Bondage: Growing Up Enslaved in the Antebellum South*. Cambridge, Mass.: Harvard University Press, 2000.

Senior, Olive. *Encyclopedia of Jamaican Heritage*. Kingston, Jamaica: Twin Guinep Publishers, 2004.

Sheridan, Richard. "From Jamaican Slavery to Haitian Freedom: The Case of the Black Crew of the Pilot Boat, Deep Nine." *Journal of Negro History* 67, no. 4 (1982): 328–39.

———. "The Guinea Surgeons on the Middle Passage: The Provision of Medical Services in the British Slave Trade." *International Journal of African Historical Studies* 14, no. 4 (1981): 601–25.

———. "Simon Taylor, Sugar Tycoon of Jamaica, 1740–1813." *Agricultural History* 45, no. 4 (1971): 285–96.

———. *Sugar and Slavery: An Economic History of the British West Indies, 1623–1775*. Baltimore, Md.: Johns Hopkins University Press, 1974.

———. "The Wealth of Jamaica in the Eighteenth Century." *Economic History Review* 18, no. 2 (1965): 292–311.

Shumway, Rebecca. "Between the Castle and the Golden Stool: Transformations in Fante Society in the Eighteenth Century." Ph.D. diss., Emory University, 2004.

Simpson, A. W. Brian. *Cannibalism and the Common Law: The Story of the Tragic Last Voyage of the Mignonette and the Strange Legal Proceedings to Which It Gave Rise*. Chicago: University of Chicago Press, 1984.

Sio, Arnold A. "Marginality and Free Coloured Identity in Caribbean Slave Society." *Slavery and Abolition* 8, no. 2 (1987): 166–82.

Smallwood, Stephanie. *Saltwater Slavery: A Middle Passage from Africa to American Diaspora*. Cambridge, Mass.: Harvard University Press, 2007.

St. Clair, William. *The Grand Slave Emporium: Cape Coast Castle and the British Slave Trade*. London: Profile Books, 2006.

Steckel, Richard H., and Richard A. Jensen. "New Evidence on the Causes of Slave and Crew Mortality in the Atlantic Slave Trade." *Journal of Economic History* 46, no. 1 (1986): 57–77.

Sweet, James. *Recreating Africa: Culture, Kinship, and Religion in the African-Portuguese World, 1441–1770*. Chapel Hill: University of North Carolina Press, 2003.

Taylor, Eric Robert. *If We Must Die: Shipboard Insurrections in the Era of the Atlantic Slave Trade*. Baton Rouge: Louisiana State University Press, 2006.

Teelucksingh, Jerome. "The 'Invisible Child' in British West Indian Slavery." *Slavery and Abolition* 27, no. 2 (2006): 237–50.

Thompson, Alvin O. *Flight to Freedom: African Runaways and Maroons in the Americas*. Mona, Jamaica: University of the West Indies, 2006.

Thompson, Peter. "No Chance in Nature: Cannibalism as a Solution to Maritime Famine, c. 1750–1800." In *American Bodies: Cultural Histories of the Physique*, edited by Tim Armstrong, 32–44. New York: New York University Press, 1996.

Thornton, John. *Africa and Africans in the Making of the Atlantic World, 1400–1800*. 1992. Rev. ed., Cambridge: Cambridge University Press, 1998.

———. "African Soldiers in the Haitian Revolution." *Journal of Caribbean History* 25, no. 1–2 (1991): 58–80.

———. "Cannibals, Witches, and Slave Traders in the Atlantic World." *William and Mary Quarterly* 40, no. 2 (2003): 273–94.

———. "The Coromantees: An African Cultural Group in Colonial North America and the Caribbean." *Journal of Caribbean History* 32, no. 1 (1998): 161–78.

———. "Sexual Demography: The Impact of the Slave Trade on Family Structure." In *Women and Slavery in Africa*, edited by Martin A. Klein and Claire Robertson, 39–48. Madison: University of Wisconsin Press, 1983.

———. "The Slave Trade in Eighteenth Century Angola: Effects on Demographic Structures." *Canadian Journal of African Studies* 14, no. 3 (1980): 417–27.

———. *Warfare in Atlantic Africa, 1500–1800*. London: UCL Press, 1999.

Trotman, David Vincent. "Africanizing and Creolizing the Plantation Frontier of Trinidad, 1787–1838." In *Trans-Atlantic Dimensions of Ethnicity in the African Diaspora*, ed. Paul E. Lovejoy and David Vincent Trotman, 218–39: London: Continuum, 2004.

Trouillot, Michel-Rolph. *Silencing the Past: Power and the Production of History*. Boston: Beacon Press, 1995.

Utting, Francis. *The Story of Sierra Leone*. 1931. 2nd ed. Manchester, U.K.: Ayer Company Publishers, 1971.

Uya, Okon. "Slave Revolts in the Middle Passage: A Neglected Theme." *Calabar Historical Journal* 1 (1976): 65–88.

Vasconcellos, Colleen. "And a Child Shall Lead Them? Slavery, Childhood, and African

Cultural Identity in Jamaica, 1655–1838." Ph.D. diss., Florida International University, 2004.

Walvin, James. *Black and White: The Negro and English Society, 1555–1945*. London: Allen Lane, Penguin Press, 1973.

———. *Black Ivory: Slavery in the British Empire*. Oxford: Blackwell Publishers, 2001.

Wareing, John. "Preventive and Punitive Regulation in Seventeenth Century Social Policy: Conflicts of Interest and the Failure to Make 'stealing and transporting Children, and other Persons' a Felony, 1645–73." *Social History* 27, no. 3 (2002): 287–308.

Warner-Lewis, Maureen. *Central Africa in the Caribbean: Transcending Time, Transforming Culture*. Mona, Jamaica: University of the West Indies Press, 2003.

Watts, David. *The West Indies: Patterns of Development, Culture, and Environmental Change since 1492*. Cambridge: Cambridge University Press, 1987.

Wax, Darold D. "Preferences for Slaves in Colonial America." *Journal of Negro History* 58, no. 4 (1973): 371–401.

Webster, Jane. "The *Zong* in the Context of the Eighteenth-Century Slave Trade." *Journal of Legal History* 28, no. 3 (2007): 285–98.

Williams, Eric. *Capitalism and Slavery*. 1944. Reprint, London: Andre Deutsch, 1991.

Index

Page numbers in italics refer to figures and tables.